武大通识

博雅弘毅

文明以止

成人成才

四通六识

U0949834

珞珈博雅文库
通识教材系列

识读美国

主编 祝捷
副主编 王明月 金琳 郭丽君

WUHAN UNIVERSITY PRESS
武汉大学出版社

图书在版编目(CIP)数据

识读美国/祝捷主编;王明月,金琳,郭丽君副主编.—武汉:武汉大学出版社,2022.8

珞珈博雅文库.通识教材系列

ISBN 978-7-307-23156-6

Ⅰ.识… Ⅱ.①祝… ②王… ③金… ④郭… Ⅲ.①英语—阅读教学—高等学校—教材 ②美国—历史 Ⅳ.H319.37:K

中国版本图书馆 CIP 数据核字(2022)第 120597 号

责任编辑:罗晓华　　责任校对:李孟潇　　版式设计:韩闻锦

出版发行:**武汉大学出版社**　(430072　武昌　珞珈山)

(电子邮箱:cbs22@ whu.edu.cn 网址:www.wdp.com.cn)

印刷:武汉中科兴业印务有限公司

开本:787×1092　1/16　印张:12.75　字数:271 千字　插页:1

版次:2022 年 8 月第 1 版　2022 年 8 月第 1 次印刷

ISBN 978-7-307-23156-6　定价:36.00 元

新时代外国文学与文化系列教材
编委会

总　序

小而言之，教材是“课本”，是一课之本，是教学内容和教学方法的语言载体；大而言之，教材是国家意志的体现，是高校教学成果和科研成果的重要标志。一流大学要有一流的本科教育，也要有一流的教材体系。新形势下根据国家有关要求，为进一步加强和改进学校教材建设与管理，努力构建一流教材体系，武汉大学成立了教材建设工作领导小组、教材建设工作委员会，设立了教材建设中心，为学校教材建设工作提供了有力保障。一流教材体系要注重教材内容的经典性和时代性，还要注重教材的系列化和立体化。基于这一思路，学校计划按照学科专业教育、通识教育、创业教育等类别规划建设自成系列的教材。通识教育系列教材即是学校大力推动通识教育教学工作的重要成果，其整体隶属于“珞珈博雅文库”，命名为“通识教材系列”。

在长期的办学实践和教学文化建设过程中，武汉大学形成了独具特色的融“五观”为一体的本科人才培养思想体系，即“人才培养为本，本科教育是根”的办学观；“以‘成人’教育统领成才教育”的育人观；“厚基础、跨学科、鼓励创新和冒尖”的教学观；“激发教师教与学生学双重积极性”的动力观；“以学生发展为中心”的目的观。为深化本科教育改革，打造世界一流本科教育，武汉大学于2015年开展本科教育改革大讨论并形成《武汉大学关于深化本科教育改革的若干意见》《武汉大学关于进一步加强通识教育的实施意见》等文件，对优化通识教育顶层设计、理顺通识课程管理体制、提高通识教育课程质量、加强通识教育保障机制等方面提出明确要求。

早在20世纪八九十年代，武汉大学就有学者专门研究大学通识教育。进入21世纪，武汉大学于2003年明确提出“通专结合”，将原培养方案的“公共基础课”改为“通识教育课”，作为全国通识教育改革的先行者率先开创“武大通识1.0”；2013年，经过十年的建设，形成通识课程的七大板块共千门课程，是为“武大通识2.0”；2016年，在武汉大学本科教育改革大讨论的基础上，学校建立通识教育委员会及其工作组，成立通识教育中心，重启通识教育改革，以“何以成人，何以知天”为核心理念，以《人文社科经典导引》和《自然科学经典导引》两门基础通识必修课为课程主体，同时在通识课程、通识课堂、通识管理和通识文化四大层次全面创新通识教育，从而为在校本科生逾3万的综合性大学如何实现通识教育的品质提升和卓越教学探索了一条新的路径，是为“武大通识3.0”。

当前，高校对大学生要有效“增负”，要提升大学生的学业挑战度，合理增加课程难度，拓展课程深度，扩大课程的可选择性，真正把“水课”转变成有深度、有难度、有挑战度的“金课”。那么通识课程如何脱“水”冶“金”？如何建设具有武汉大学特色的通识教育金课？这无疑要求我们必须从课程内容设计、教学方式改革、课程教材资源建设等方面着力。

一门好的通识课程应能对学生正确价值观的塑造、健全人格的养成、思维方式的拓展等发挥重要作用，而不应仅仅是传授学科知识点。我们在做课程设计的时候要认真思考“培养什么人、怎样培养人、为谁培养人”这一根本问题，从而切实推进课程思政建设。武汉大学学科门类丰富，教学资源齐全，这为我们跨学科组建教学团队，多维度进行探讨，设计更具前沿性和时代性的课程内容，提供了得天独厚的条件。

毋庸讳言，中学教育在高考指挥棒下偏向应试思维，过于看重课程考核成绩，往往忘记了“教书育人”的初心。那么，应如何改变这种现状？答案是：立德树人，脱“水”冶“金”。具体而言，通识教育要注重课程教学的过程管理，增加小班研讨、单元小测验、学习成果展示等鼓励学生投入学习的环节，而不再是单一地只看学生期末成绩。武汉大学的“两大导引”试行“8+8”的大班授课和小班研讨，经过三个学期的实践，取得了很好的成效，深受同学们欢迎。我们发现，小班研讨是一种非常有效的教学方式，能够帮助学生深度阅读、深度思考，增加学生课堂参与度，培养学生独立思考、理性判断、批判性思维和团队合作等多方面的能力。

课程教材资源建设是十分重要的。老师们精心编撰的系列教材，精心录制的在线开放课程视频，精心设计的各类题库，精心搜集整理的与课程相关的文献资料，等等，对于学生而言，都是精神大餐之中不可或缺的珍贵元素。在长期的教学实践中，老师们不断更新、完善课程教材资源，并且教会学生获取知识的能力，让学习不只停留于课堂，而是延续到课后，给学生课后的持续思考提供支撑和保障。

“武大通识3.0”运行至今，武汉大学已形成一系列保障机制，鼓励教师更多地投入到通识教育教学中来。学校对通识3.0课程设立了准入准出机制，建设期内每年组织一次课程考核工作，严格把控立项课程的建设质量；对两门基础通识课程实施助教制，每学期遴选培训研究生和青年教师担任助教，辅助大班授课、小班研讨环节的开展；对投身通识教育的教师给予最大支持，在“351人才计划”教学岗位、“教学业绩奖”等评选中专门设立通识教育教师名额，在职称晋升等方面也予以政策倾斜；对课程的课酬实行阶梯制，根据课程等级和教师考核结果发放授课课酬。

武汉大学打造多重通识教育活动，营造全校通识文化氛围。每月举行一期通识教育大讲堂，邀请海内外一流大学从事通识教育顶层设计的领袖性人物、知名教师、知名学者、杰出校友等来校为师生做专题报告；每学期组织一次通识教育研讨会，邀请全校通识课程主讲教师、主要管理人员参加，采取专家讲座与专题讨论相结合的方式，帮助提升教师的通识教育理念；不定期开展博雅沙龙、读书会、午餐会等互动式研讨活动，有针对性地选取主题，邀请专家报告并研讨交流。这些都是珍贵的教学资源，有助于我们多渠道了解通识教育前沿和通识文化真谛，不断提升通识教育的理论素养，进而持续改进通识课程。

武汉大学的校训有一个关键词：弘毅。“弘毅”语出《论语》：“士不可以不弘毅，任重而道远。”对于“立德树人”的武大教师，对于“成人成才”的武大学子，对于“博雅弘毅，文明以止”的武大通识教育，皆为“任重而道远”。可以说，我们在通识教育改革道路上所走过的每一步，都将成为“教育强国，文化复兴”强有力的步伐。

“武大通识3.0”开启以来，我们精心筹备、陆续推出“珞珈博雅文库”大型通识教育丛书，涵盖“通识文化”“通识教材”“通识课堂”和“通识管理”四大系列。其中的“通识教材系列”已经推出“两大导引”，这次又推出核心和一般通识课程教材十余种，以后还将有更多优秀通识教材面世，使在校同学和其他读者“开卷有益”：拓展视野，启迪思想，融通古今，化成天下。

周叶中

序

据史料记载，湖北省的高校外语教育最早可以追溯至百余年前的自强学堂和方言学堂(二者皆为武汉大学的前身)。光绪十九年十月(1893年11月)，湖广总督张之洞向朝廷奏陈《设立自强学堂片》，力陈创设自强学堂的必要性，并提出了以“讲究实务、融贯中西、研精器数”为办学宗旨。他认为“盖闻经国以自强为本”“自强之道，以教育人才为先”，故取“自强”二字。自强学堂自创立伊始便是两湖最高学府，并效仿西方高等教育模式，进行分门(科)教学，设方言(外语)、格致、算学和商务四个专业，每个专业招生20人，略具综合性学校之雏形。其中，只有学方言或者修外语的学生在学校上课。张之洞非常重视外语人才的培养，甚至下令让格致和商务改课方言。到19世纪末，方言专业开设英、法、德、俄、日5国外语，延聘外籍教师8人，成为语种齐全、师资强大的“外语学院”。1902年，张之洞另择校址，成立方言学堂，令自强学堂原有学生移入。从自强学堂到方言学堂，开启了近代湖北高等外语教育乃至近代湖北高等教育的篇章。

与此同时，在英国国内，英国文学尚未成为一门真正的现代学科。20世纪初，英国文学仅仅被视为一门适合女性、工人和帝国殖民者的学科，散发着业余的气息，在牛津大学和剑桥大学始终被看作半瓶子醋学科。第一次世界大战之后，英国打败德国，在民族骄傲和爱国情绪之中，还夹杂一种“精神上的饥渴”，这种渴求恰好在英国文学中得到了满足和振奋。正如伊格尔顿所言，英国文学借着战时民族主义的东风一跃登上了权力的宝座。1917年，剑桥大学成立了英文系。及至20世纪20年代，在利维斯、理查兹和燕卜逊等人的努力下，英国文学最终获得了合法性，成为一门具有科学客观性的严肃学科。

从湖北最初的外语教育到现在，从英国文学被确立为一门严肃独立的学科到现在，百余年的历史光阴倏忽而逝。与其他的学科相比，中国的外国文学研究其实是一个相当年轻的学科。如今，西方的文学批评理论一度高歌猛进并完成了体制化，业已进入了后理论时代；放眼寰球，世界格局已然发生了巨大的变化。在这样的全球化境遇中，中国的外国文学研究者应该怎样理解和研究外国文学与文化，应该有何作为？我们能否在多年紧紧跟随西方理论的动静冷热之后，将西方理论资源转化为自己的学术话语体系并在此基础上完成学术创新？

“新时代外国文学与文化系列教材”便是武汉大学外国语言文学学院同仁们近些年的教学研究和学术思考的结晶，是对上述两个问题的部分解答。本系列教材作为入选“武大通识3.0”的规划教材，具有鲜明的特点，即文学文本（text）与文化语境（context）的相互参照，文学研究与文化研究之间的重叠。举一二例加以说明。《莎士比亚戏剧与西方社会》将莎剧文本与社会语境相结合，不仅深入研究莎剧所反映的社会维度，同时探索这一社会维度如何反作用于莎剧。《英语诗歌欣赏》知人论世，在赏析诗歌的文学形式与审美特征之外，将诗歌流派与社会文化思潮勾连起来相互印证，引导读者深入浅出于文学文化之表里。《电影中的俄罗斯文学》则在欣赏经典电影的同时评述俄罗斯文学名著的主题思想、写作技巧、语言风格和时代性意义，并且探究广义上的俄罗斯民族的价值观念和性格情感。

在武汉大学外国语言文学学院和经济与管理学院之间的郁郁林荫之中，张之洞的雕像稳稳地端坐在那里，日复一日地淡然陪伴着来往穿行的师生。虽然他的“自强学堂”以及一系列的“自强”活动已经成为历史，但他的“自强”精神依然是我们宝贵的精神遗产，时常提醒我们这些外国文学与文化研究者们在与他者文化相遇时自觉保持主体意识和文化自信。

王爱菊

2019年6月于武汉大学湖滨

前　言

“识读美国”(Reading America)课程是为了响应“武大通识3.0”教改，由四位大学英语教师组队，结合多年教学经验、海外经历，为武汉大学本科生精心设计、量身打造并讲授的通识课程。自2020年2月开课以来，课程已连续授课5个学期，受到学生的普遍欢迎和喜爱。

本课程选取美国历史上发挥过重要影响的，且在当今仍具现实意义的经典文献、著名演讲、学术典籍与文学名作。课程以原文文本为中心，结合年代背景或历史事件，分为美国形成、独立战争、西进运动、美国内战、民权运动与女权运动等阶段，涉及契约精神、社会平等、边疆精神、实用主义、个人主义、环保主义、女性主义、民权、多元文化、美国梦、美国精神等多重元素，以便学生系统全面地把握美国文化内涵，充分认识美国政治、社会、文化发展的脉络和实质。

在授课过程中，任课教师将思想意识与历史背景、文学流变相结合，引导学生接触不同文本、文体，以不同的视角和解读方式阅读文本，理解、欣赏文本原文(语言文字、篇章结构等)，避免误读和曲解；融入课程思政，引导学生批判、赏析、理解美国国家及民族共核；鼓励学生拓宽视野，树立正确的世界观、人生观和价值观；培养学生的独立思考能力，提升他们的社会责任感，以增强家国情怀和自身身份意识。

本书为五个学期教学实践经验的结晶，以历史时期为单元，除了精心选取的、体现美国历史特征的典型文本以外，每个单元配有时代背景说明、针对文本设计的阅读练习，以帮助学生更准确地理解主旨及细节，并附有一至两篇延伸阅读和思考题。编写具体分工如下：祝捷负责第一至第四章；王明月负责第五、六章；金琳负责第七章；郭丽君负责第八章。

课程筹划和教学实施得到了教学团队老师的大力支持和倾情付出，还得到了潘迎春教授的热情帮助和指点，以及大学英语部领导和同事的关心和帮助。在此一并致谢！同时，感谢武汉大学为教师自主设计课程提供宝贵的教学平台；感谢武汉大学外国语言文学学院为本书的出版提供项目支持；感谢武汉大学出版社外语分社谢社长、罗编辑的细致审阅。

编　者

2022 年 6 月于珞珈山

目　录

第一章
形成中的美国

第一节　时代背景

一、早期美洲人

最早的美洲人可能是在35000年前当海平面下降的时候乘坐原始船只从现在的白令海峡到达美洲的。

大约10000年前，冰川世纪结束，海平面再次回升，通道受阻，居住在美洲的人被隔离在美洲大陆，长达数千年。

在1492年欧洲人到达美洲之前，大约5400万人居住在美洲大陆，他们分成了无数个部落，操2000多种语言，形成了多种多样的宗教、文化和生活方式。

二、欧洲人进入美洲

1492年意大利航海家克里斯托弗·哥伦布(Christopher Columbus，1451—1506)成功游说西班牙君主资助他三艘单夹板帆船进行海上探险。经过6个星期的航海，1492年10月12日，巴哈马群岛的一座岛屿进入了船员的视线，一个崭新的世界也由此进入了欧洲人的视线。哥伦布坚信他到达的是印度(Indies)，于是称当地人为“印度人”(Indians)。

新世界几千年来一直不为世人所知，欧洲探险者对眼前的一切惊叹不已：从未见过的玉米、豆类、番茄、土豆等植物，不仅让他们大开眼界，而且逐渐变革了欧洲人的饮食内容，为养活迅速增长的欧洲人口作出了巨大贡献。直至今日，世界上五分之三的庄稼原产地是美洲。与此同时，欧洲人也将一些“旧世界”的作物和动物引入了美洲：牛、猪和马。欧洲人还将衣服靴子上的微生物和细菌带到了美洲，引发了天花、黄热病和疟疾等疾病，致使大量土著印第安人死亡。

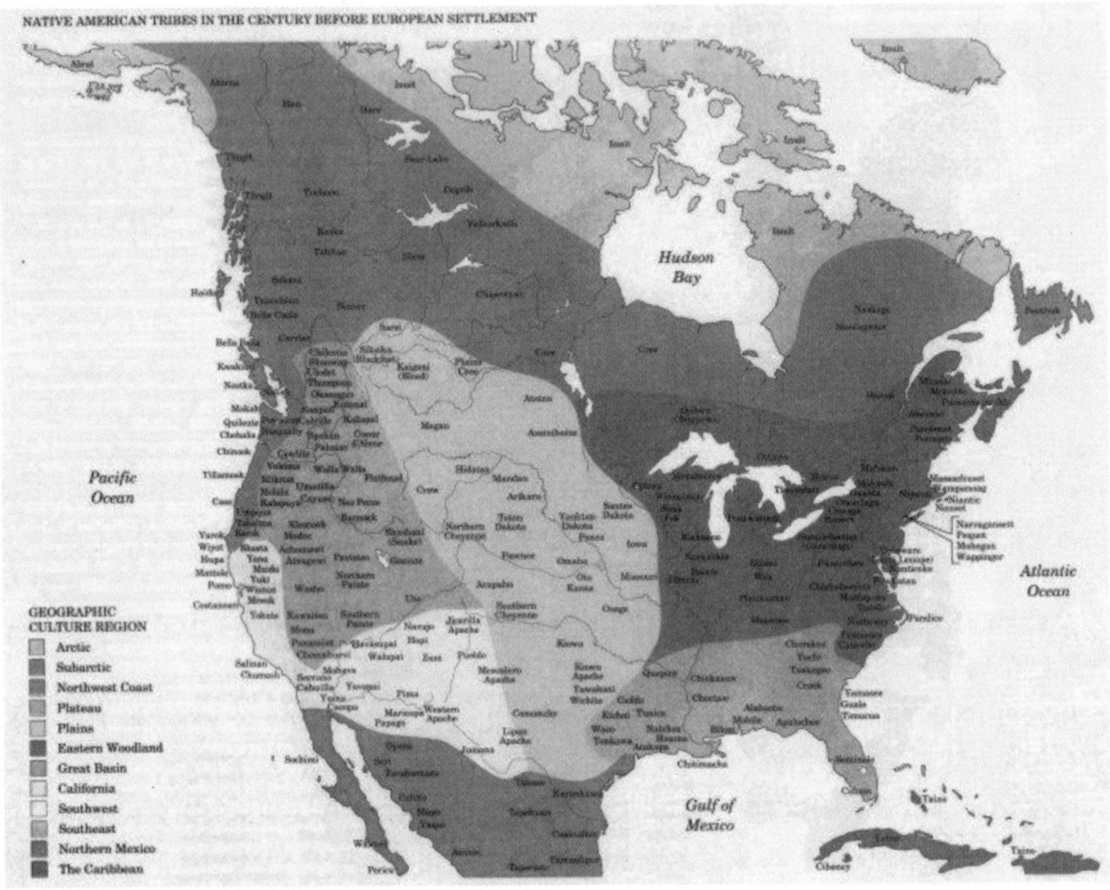

欧洲人初抵北美大陆时土著印第安人的大致分布

三、17 世纪的北美

时间进入 1600 年，17 世纪。北美仍是一片荒原，随后三支欧洲列强几乎在同时于北美的三个角分别建立了定居点：

1607 年，英国于弗吉尼亚的詹姆斯敦(Jamestown)建立定居点。

1608 年，法国于魁北克建立定居点。

1610 年，西班牙于圣达菲(Santa Fe)建立定居点。

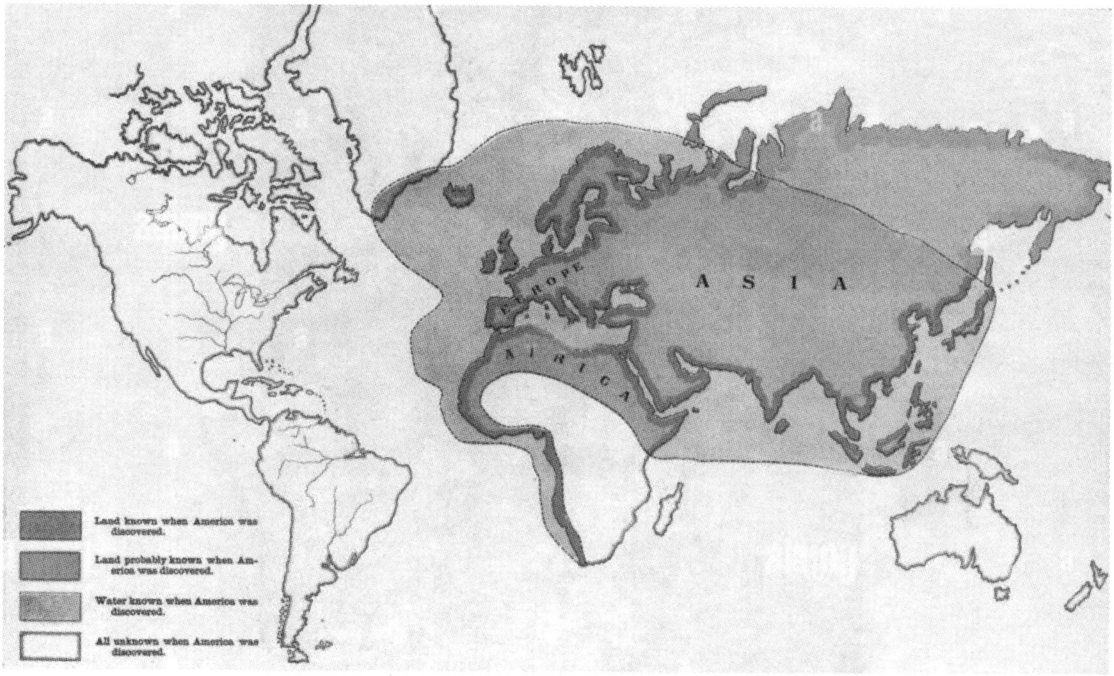

1492 年欧洲人已知的世界(阴影区域)

四、英国殖民北美

虽然英国早在 15 世纪末就已涉足北美，比哥伦布晚不了几年，但是由于国内形势动荡以及与西班牙的关系等原因，之后暂停了海上探险。直到跃跃欲试的伊丽莎白一世执政(1558—1603 在位)后，情况得到了改变。

1585 年，沃尔特·雷利爵士受伊丽莎白一世女王的鼓励组建了一支探险队到达北美，他把着陆点取名为弗吉尼亚，以此向女王致敬(因伊丽莎白一世终身未婚，被称为“童贞女王”)。

1588 年，英国舰队击败西班牙“无敌舰队”，从此英国占据了北大西洋的海上主动权，逐渐发展成统一的强国，并且结束了长期以来新教与天主教之间的争端，实现了宗教统一：新教终于成为英国的国教，英国人的民族身份意识也日渐强烈。

1604 年，英国与西班牙终于签署和平条约，英国人开始了他们在新世界建立殖民帝国的历程。

伊丽莎白一世女王(1533—1603)

五、《弗吉尼亚公司宪章》

1606 年，一家名为伦敦弗吉尼亚的股份公司得到詹姆斯一世国王下发的宪章，允许该公司在新世界建立定居点，希望能够找到黄金并开辟一条从美洲通往印度群岛的航线。《弗吉尼亚公司宪章》是美国历史上很重要的一份文件，因为它给予英国海外定居者以国内公民的同等权利，有利于此后的殖民者保持对英国的国家归属感以及保持英国的传统体制。

1607 年 5 月 24 日，受雇于伦敦弗吉尼亚公司的大约一百个英国人到达弗吉尼亚，为了纪念国王，他们把定居点取名为詹姆斯敦(Jamestown)。

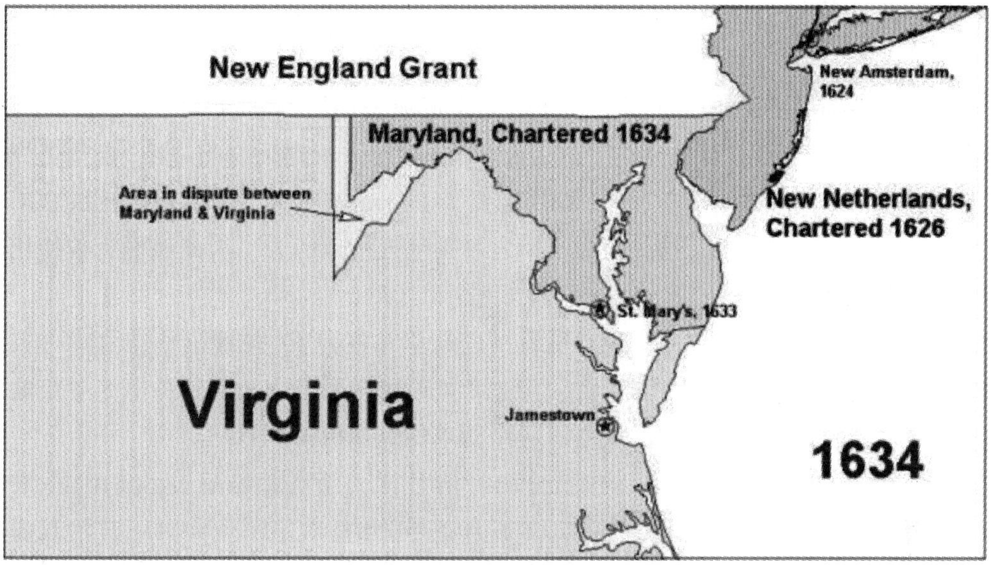

早期马里兰和弗吉尼亚

六、英国的宗教改革

1517年，德国修士马丁·路德挑战罗马教廷和教皇的权威，宣称只有《圣经》才是上帝旨意的唯一来源，由此开启了宗教改革，即“新教运动”(Protestant Reformation)。之后加尔文主义产生于日内瓦，主张上帝预定说，认为人的救赎与否皆由上帝指定。

16世纪30年代，这种教义传到英国，当时的国王亨利八世正在与罗马天主教会断绝关系，自立为教会之首。这一切激发了英国的一些宗教改革者决心彻底净化英国基督教，这些人被称为“清教徒”，其中最虔诚的清教徒被称为“独立派”或“分离派”，他们发誓要与英国教会决裂。

詹姆斯一世在位时(1603—1625)意识到，如果臣民可以否认他精神领袖的地位，那么有朝一日，他们也可以否认他的国王身份。于是他威胁要将这些独立派逐出英国。

1608年，一批独立派清教徒逃亡至荷兰。在荷兰艰苦生活了12年之后，他们为下一代的“荷兰化”感到担心，并且渴望找到一片乐土，能够作为英国人生活和信教。于是，美洲成了他们的理想目的地。

七、《五月花号公约》

1620 年，在荷兰的一批独立派清教徒与弗吉尼亚公司协商之后，乘坐“五月花号”前往美洲。经过 65 天的海上航行，船上 102 人（其中清教徒不到乘客的一半）抵达美洲。他们没有在原定的 Plymouth Rock 上岸，而是选择了 Plymouth Bay。由于 Plymouth Bay 不属于弗吉尼亚公司的管辖范围，这些人成了擅自占用他人土地的人，因此他们无权使用这片土地也无权建立政府。

出于各种担心，在上岸之前，清教徒首领们起草并签署了《五月花号公约》。《五月花号公约》虽然日后被认为是宪法的雏形，但究其本质并不是宪法，只是一份简单粗略的协议，制定了大多数人同意的规定，成立了一个简单的管理机构。

41 名成年男性在公约上签名，包括分离派清教徒、探险者和商人，其中 11 人享有“先生”头衔，仆人和两名船员没有签名。《五月花号公约》奠定了迈向真正自治政府的基础，很快男性定居者便集会共同商议法律条文，这些都是非常重要的尝试。难得的是，英国殖民者从一开始就带来并实施了公约所包含的政治理念，而且历经四百余年基本未变。

1620 年在“五月花号”上签署公约的情景（绘画：Jean Leon Gerome Ferris，1899 年）

1620—1621 年的冬季十分难熬，102 人中仅 44 人幸存，然而当次年春季五月花号驶回英国时，没有一个清教徒选择跟船返航，他们的决心可见一斑。

1621 年秋季情况开始好转，随着大丰收和皮毛业、渔业、木业等良好的经济状况，清教徒们迎来了他们在新英格兰的第一个感恩节。

17 世纪 30 年代出现了移民潮，大批清教徒为了躲避英国国内持续的经济萧条和查尔斯一世的宗教迫害逃往马萨诸塞湾殖民地(Massachusetts Bay Colony)，普利茅斯殖民地直到 1691 年的人口也只有七千人，逐渐消失融入马萨诸塞湾殖民地。

八、17 世纪的英国殖民地

自 17 世纪 30 年代至 80 年代，英国陆续在北美大陆建立了罗德岛、康涅狄格、纽黑文、东泽西、西泽西和宾夕法尼亚等多个殖民地，其中东泽西、西泽西是从荷兰人手中夺走新荷兰殖民地成立的。

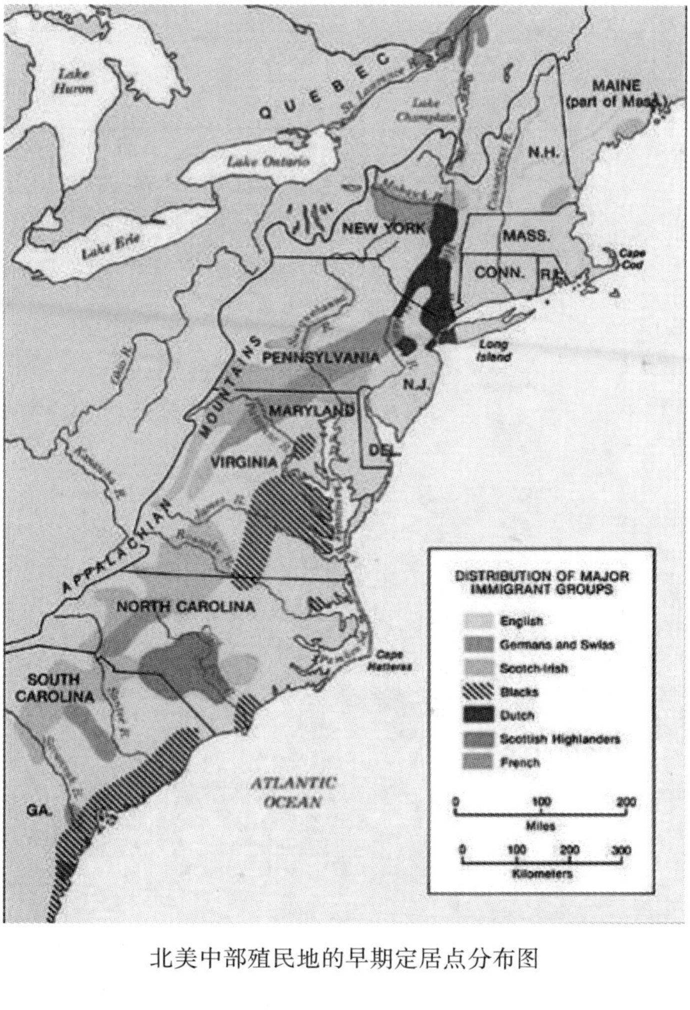

北美中部殖民地的早期定居点分布图

至 18 世纪，这些殖民地越来越焕发生机，交通通信条件持续改善，人口激增，英国依旧实行“放手”政策，殖民者们得以经营管理自治的政府、教堂和商贸活动。殖民者们终于感受到离开母国之后，他们已不是仅仅苟且活命，而是生活兴旺。

九、1700—1775 年的殖民地社会

直至 1775 年，英国在北美(包括加拿大、佛罗里达和加勒比群岛)统治了 32 个殖民地，其中人们所熟知的 13 个殖民地加入了独立战争，战争原因从当时 13 个殖民地的社会、经济和政治结构中可见一斑。

13 个殖民地人口数量统计(粗略值)

年代	总人口	黑人人口	英国人口：殖民地人口
1770	< 300000	20000	20 : 1
1775	2500000	500000	3 : 1

1775 年移民分布图

从以上图表和移民分布图我们可以看出以下几点：

(1)在短短的五年间，北美13个殖民地的人口激增，与母国英国的人口比迅速缩小，值得一提的是，殖民地人口的平均年龄只有16岁，这是一个与母国情感越来越淡薄，朝气蓬勃的新兴社会。

(2)黑人奴隶数量占比也快速增长，在某些地区甚至超过了白人数量，奠定了南方殖民地的奴隶制经济形式。

(3)在独立战争爆发前夕，这些英属殖民地已经构成多民族融合的社会结构，之后又有大量移民涌入，尤其是苏格兰-爱尔兰移民。

所有这些现象表明：在18世纪的美洲殖民地逐渐出现了一个不同于任何时期、任何地区的社会和全新的民族：美国。

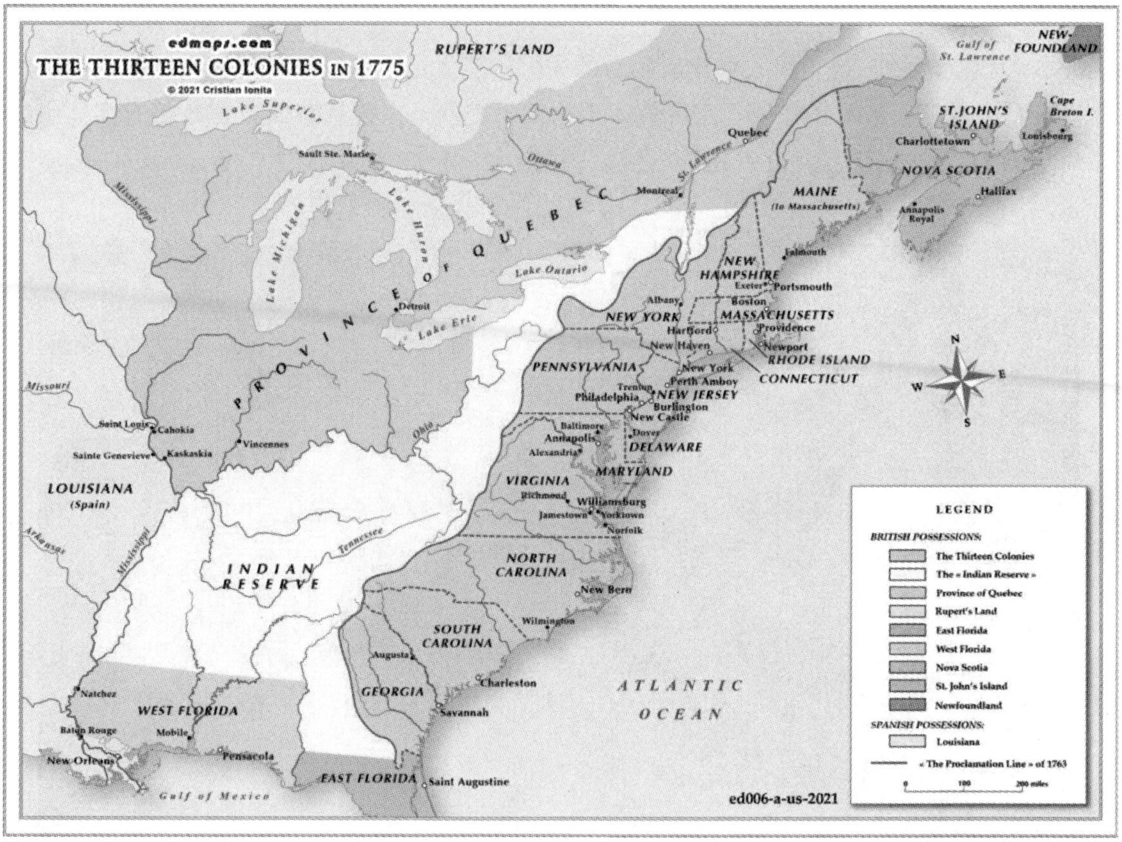

1775年的北美13州分布图

第二节　文本阅读

——《五月花号公约》

一、文本导读

《五月花号公约》的篇幅只有不到二百词，但是包含了美国初创时期的一个理念：社会应由其成员共同治理。从此，普利茅斯殖民地作为一个自治政体宣告成立。殖民地每年举行一次选举，选出当年的总督、秘书和理事。总之，《五月花号公约》在殖民地的作用相当于宪法。

《五月花号公约》是美国人创建新政府的先例，建立了一个基于自愿原则的稳定的政治制度和社会秩序，被看作开创国家价值体系的重要文献。在普利茅斯，至今仍有团体组织于每年的 12 月 22 日纪念“五月花号”登陆，并将这天定为“先父日”(Forefathers' Day)。

精心重建的普利茅斯种植园简陋村落基本保留了 400 年前的原样，现已成为旅游景点。

二、《五月花号公约》原文

Mayflower Compact[1]

IN THE NAME OF GOD, AMEN. We, whose names are underwritten, the Loyal Subjects of our dread Sovereign Lord King *James*, by the Grace of God, of *Great Britain*, *France*, and *Ireland*, King, *Defender of the Faith*, & c. Having undertaken for the Glory of God, and Advancement of the Christian Faith, and the Honour of our King and Country, a Voyage to plant the first Colony in the northern Parts of *Virginia*; Do by these Presents, solemnly and mutually, in the Presence of God and one another, covenant and combine ourselves together into a civil Body Politick, for our better Ordering and Preservation, and Furtherance of the Ends aforesaid: And by Virtue hereof do enact, constitute, and frame, such just and equal Laws, Ordinances, Acts, Constitutions, and Officers, from time to time, as shall be thought most meet and convenient for the general Good of the Colony; unto which we promise all due Submission and Obedience. **IN WITNESS** whereof we have hereunto subscribed our names at *Cape-Cod* the eleventh of November, in the Reign of our Sovereign Lord King *James*, of *England*, *France*, and *Ireland*, the eighteenth, and of *Scotland* the fifty-fourth, *Anno Domini*; 1620.

Mr. John Carver
William Bradford
Mr. Edward Winslow
Mr. William Brewster
Mr. Isaac Allerton
Capt. Myles Standish
John Alden
Mr. Samuel Fuller
Mr. Christopher Martin
Mr. William Mullins
Mr. William White
Mr. Richard Warren
John Howland
Mr. Stephen Hopkins
Edward Tilley
John Tilley
Francis Cooke
Thomas Rogers
Thomas Tinker
John Rigsdale
Edward Fuller
John Turner
Francis Eaton
James Chilton
John Crackstone
John Billington
Moses Fletcher
John Goodman
Degory Priest
Thomas Williams
Gilbert Winslow
Edmund Margeson
Peter Browne
Richard Britteridge
George Soule
Richard Clarke
Richard Gardiner
John Allerton
Thomas English
Edward Doty
Edward Leister

Note

1. 《五月花号公约》原名 *Agreement Between the Settlers of New Plymouth*，威廉·布拉德福德在《普利茅斯种植园开发史》中称之为“盟约”（combination）。直到 1793 年他注意到此公约与卢梭的《社会契约论》之间的内在联系，才开始用“公约”（compact）一词称呼这份文献。

Vocabulary

subject *n.* [正式]（君主国的）臣民，国民
sovereign *n.* [正式] 君主；国王
grace *n.* [正式]（上帝的）恩典
covenant *n.* 契约，合同
furtherance *n.* [正式] 促进，增进
aforesaid *adj.* [法律] 上述的，前述的
ordinance *n.* 法令，法规
constitution *n.* 宪法；章程，法规
colony *n.* 殖民地
Anno Domini 简称 AD，公元

Reading comprehension exercises

I. Choose the best answer to the following questions.

1. Who signed the compact?

   A) King James.

   B) All the passengers on board *Mayflower*.

   C) The Puritans who were against King James.

   D) Forty-one adult male passengers on board *Mayflower* who declared loyal to King James.

2. According to the document, King James was King of the following EXCEPT ________.

   A) England　B) Scotland　C) Ireland　D) Holland　E) France

3. Why did these Puritans decide to go to the New World?

   A) To explore the unknown world and have adventures.

   B) To find gold and fortunes.

   C) For religious purposes.

   D) To establish a country of their own.

4. What did they want to achieve by signing this compact?

A) To set up a crude government.

B) To pass unanimously the compact which served the function of constitution.

C) To agree upon some laws to ensure a better survival.

D) All of the above.

II. Comprehension questions

1. What are the main features of this document?

2. Why *Mayflower Compact* has been considered a significant document in American history?

第三节 延伸阅读

——《论君主政体和世袭》节选

一、文本导读

本文节选自《常识》第二章。《常识》(*Common Sense*)是被称为“美国革命之父”的托马斯·潘恩(Thomas Paine，1737—1809)写于1776年1月的政治小册子。潘恩思想激进，言辞犀利，极力宣扬美国脱离英国，建立自己的共和制国家。《常识》一经问世就受到广泛欢迎，多次再版，极大地推动了美国宣布独立的进程。

《常识》主要包含四个部分：

(一)论政府的起源与目的，兼议英国政体

潘恩在这部分评价了个人、社会和政府的关系。经典论断有：“社会在任何情况下都是人民的福祉”①，“而政府则来自人性的邪恶与不道德”②。他进而论述道，英国政体分为国王(King)、贵族(Lords)和平民(Commons)三个阶层，根本不是共和制。

(二)论君主制与世袭制

潘恩在这部分严厉抨击君主制和世袭制，他大量引用《圣经》，如：上帝诅咒希伯来人，因为他们本来有机会共和，却拥立了君主；因为在上帝面前人人平等，因此任何一个

① 托马斯·潘恩. 常识[M]. 计毅，译. 哈尔滨：北方文艺出版社，2017：1.

② 托马斯·潘恩. 常识[M]. 计毅，译. 哈尔滨：北方文艺出版社，2017：1.

家族自恃高人一等都是可憎的，而征服者威廉更是加剧了问题的恶化：“一个法国杂种领着一群全副武装的恶棍霸占了英国本土，违背英伦人民的意志自立为王，毫不客气地说，这种王权的起源根本就是卑劣的流氓行径，哪有半点神圣可言。”①

（三）对当前北美形势的看法

潘恩在这部分用简单的事实、朴实的道理和常识分析欧洲已经令人绝望地腐败，因此美国必须独立，才能得以发展自由港，长期享有强劲的商业，才能保证经济繁荣、人民幸福和国家安全。

著名论断有：“独立的时刻到了”!② “让一整片大陆都臣服于一个岛国，未免太荒谬了。在自然界中，卫星永远不可能大于它的行星，然而英国与美国彼此之间的依附关系却恰恰违背了这一自然规律。这两者显然应该隶属于不同的体系；英国属于欧洲，美洲大陆只属于她自己。”③“让我们收留这个四处飘零的流浪者，为人们保留一块自由之地吧!”④

（四）论现阶段北美的能力，兼谈几点杂感

潘恩在这部分盘点了美国的优势，尤其是海上实力，预测一旦发生战争，美国必胜。同时建议要让全世界知晓美国遭受到的来自英国政府的不公正待遇，由此促成了几个月之后《独立宣言》的问世。

在之后的附记中出现了被引用次数最多的一段话：“现在有无数的绝佳机会以及来自各方的支持摆在我们的面前，去建立一个世界上最高尚、最纯洁的政治体制……一个崭新的时代即将诞生。”⑤尽管有各种声音和立场，尽管贵格党人不主张动用武力，潘恩在小册子的末尾继续解释了与英国作战的必要性。

潘恩以平实却强烈的语言和鼓舞人心的意象使《常识》成功地吸引了美国大众，让许多美国人彻底相信独立不仅不可避免，而且是他们唯一的选择。随着人们对《常识》的热议，其他作者的作品也应运而生，如：约翰·亚当斯的《关于政府的思考》(*Thoughts on Government*)、詹姆士·查尔默斯(James Chalmers)的《实话》(*Plain Truth*)，以及很多费城激进作家进入公众视线，他们后来都积极参与了制宪工作。《常识》以前所未有的方式激发了美国人对自己前途未来的认真思考，彻底改变了是否脱离英国争论的结果，以及美国人对共和制意义的认识。

---

① 托马斯·潘恩. 常识[M]. 计毅，译. 哈尔滨：北方文艺出版社，2017：20.
② 托马斯·潘恩. 常识[M]. 计毅，译. 哈尔滨：北方文艺出版社，2017：36.
③ 托马斯·潘恩. 常识[M]. 计毅，译. 哈尔滨：北方文艺出版社，2017：42.
④ 托马斯·潘恩. 常识[M]. 计毅，译. 哈尔滨：北方文艺出版社，2017：56.
⑤ 托马斯·潘恩. 常识[M]. 计毅，译. 哈尔滨：北方文艺出版社，2017：89.

托马斯·潘恩(1737—1809)

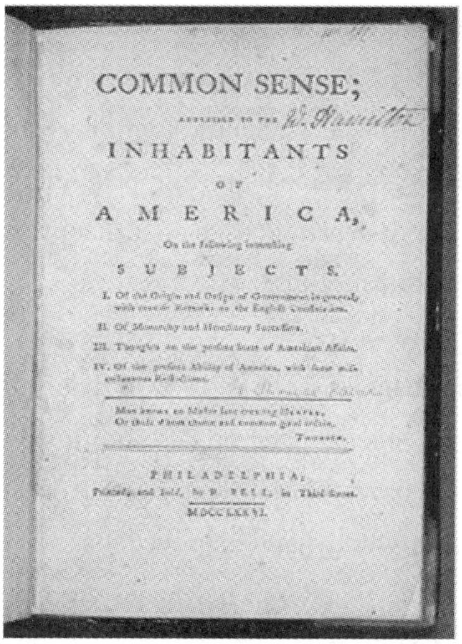

《常识》(1776)

二、原文节选

OF MONARCHY AND HEREDITARY SUCCESSION

Thomas Paine

MANKIND being originally equals in the order of creation, the equality could only be destroyed by some subsequent circumstance; the distinctions of rich, and poor, may in a great measure be accounted for, and that without having recourse to the harsh ill sounding names of oppression and avarice. Oppression is often the *consequence*, but seldom or never the *means* of riches; and though avarice will preserve a man from being necessitously poor, it generally makes him too timorous to be wealthy.

But there is another and greater distinction for which no truly natural or religious reason can be assigned, and that is, the distinction of men into KINGS and SUBJECTS. Male and female are the distinctions of nature, good and bad the distinctions of heaven; but how a race of men came into the world so exalted above the rest, and distinguished like some new species, is worth enquiring into, and whether they are the means of happiness or of misery to mankind.

In the early ages of the world, according to the scripture chronology, there were no kings; the consequence of which was there were no wars; it is the pride of kings which throw mankind into confusion. Holland without a king hath enjoyed more peace for this last century than any of the monarchical governments in Europe. Antiquity favors the same remark; for the quiet and rural lives of the first patriarchs hath a happy something in them, which vanishes away when we come to the history of Jewish loyalty.

Government by kings was first introduced into the world by the Heathens, from whom the children of Israel copied the custom. It was the most prosperous invention the Devil ever set on foot for the promotion of idolatry. The Heathens paid divine honors to their deceased kings, and the christian world hath improved on the plan by doing the same to their living ones. How impious is the title of sacred majesty applied to a worm, who in the midst of his splendor is crumbling into dust!

As the exalting one man so greatly above the rest cannot be justified on the equal rights of nature, so neither can it be defended on the authority of scripture; for the will of the Almighty, as declared by Gideon and the prophet Samuel, expressly disapproves of government by kings. All anti-monarchical parts of scripture have been very smoothly glossed over in monarchical governments, but they undoubtedly merit the attention of countries which have their governments yet to form. "*Render unto Cæsar the things which are Cæsar's*" is the scripture doctrine of courts, yet it is no support of monarchical government, for the Jews at that time were without a king, and in a state of vassalage to the Romans.

Near three thousand years passed away from the Mosaic account of the creation, till the Jews under a national delusion requested a king. Till then their form of government (except in extraordinary cases, where the Almighty interposed) was a kind of republic administered by a judge and the elders of the tribes. Kings they had none, and it was held sinful to acknowledge any being under that title but the Lord of Hosts. And when a man seriously reflects on the idolatrous homage which is paid to the persons of Kings, he need not wonder, that the Almighty ever jealous of his honor, should disapprove of a form of government which so impiously invades the prerogative of heaven.

Monarchy is ranked in scripture as one of the sins of the Jews, for which a curse in reserve is denounced against them. The history of that transaction is worth attending to.

To the evil of monarchy we have added that of hereditary succession; and as the first is a degradation and lessening of ourselves, so the second, claimed as a matter of right, is an insult and an imposition on posterity. For all men being originally equals, no *one* by *birth* could have a right to set up his own family in perpetual preference to all others for ever, and though himself might deserve *some* decent degree of honors of his contemporaries, yet his descendants might be far too unworthy to inherit them. One of the strongest *natural* proofs of the folly of hereditary right in kings, is, that nature disapproves it, otherwise she would not so frequently turn it into ridicule by giving mankind an *ass for a lion*.

Secondly, as no man at first could possess any other public honors than were bestowed upon him, so the givers of those honors could have no power to give away the right of posterity, and though they might say "We choose you for *our* head," they could not, without manifest injustice to their children, say "that your children and your children's children shall reign over *ours* for ever." Because such an unwise, unjust, unnatural compact might (perhaps) in the next succession put them under the government of a rogue or a fool. Most wise men, in their private sentiments, have ever treated hereditary right with contempt; yet it is one of those evils, which when once established is not easily removed; many submit from fear, others from superstition, and the more powerful part shares with the king the plunder of the rest.

It is not so much the absurdity as the evil of hereditary succession which concerns mankind. Did it ensure a race of good and wise men it would have the seal of divine authority, but as it opens a door to the *foolish*, the *wicked*, and the *improper*, it hath in it the nature of oppression. Men who look upon themselves born to reign, and others to obey, soon grow insolent; selected from the rest of mankind their minds are early poisoned by importance; and the world they act in differs so materially from the world at large, that they have but little opportunity of knowing its true interests, and when they succeed to the government are frequently the most ignorant and unfit of any throughout the dominions.

Another evil which attends hereditary succession is, that the throne is subject to be possessed by a minor at any age; all which time the regency, acting under the cover of a king, have every opportunity and inducement to betray their trust. The same national misfortune happens, when a king worn out with age and infirmity, enters the last stage of human weakness. In both these cases the public becomes a prey to every miscreant, who can tamper successfully with the follies either of age or infancy.

The most plausible plea, which hath ever been offered in favour of hereditary succession, is, that it preserves a nation from civil wars; and were this true, it would be weighty; whereas, it is the most barefaced falsity ever imposed upon mankind. The whole history of England disowns the fact. Thirty kings and two minors have reigned in that distracted kingdom since the conquest, in which time there have been (including the Revolution) no less than eight civil wars and nineteen rebellions. Wherefore instead of making for peace, it makes against it, and destroys the very foundation it seems to stand on.

The nearer any government approaches to a republic the less business there is for a king. It is somewhat difficult to find a proper name for the government of England. Sir William Meredith calls it a republic; but in its present state it is unworthy of the name, because the corrupt influence of the crown, by having all the places in its disposal, hath so effectually swallowed up the power, and eaten out the virtue of the house of commons (the republican part in the constitution) that the government of England is nearly as monarchical as that of France or Spain. Men fall out with names without understanding them. For it is the republican and not the monarchical part of the constitution of England which Englishmen glory in, viz. the liberty of choosing a house of commons from out of their own body—and it is easy to see that when republican virtue fails, slavery ensues. Why is the constitution of England sickly, but because monarchy hath poisoned the republic, the crown hath engrossed the commons?

In England a king hath little more to do than to make war and give away places; which in plain terms, is to impoverish the nation and set it together by the ears. A pretty business indeed for a man to be allowed eight hundred thousand sterling a year for, and worshipped into the bargain! Of more worth is one honest man to society and in the sight of God, than all the crowned ruffians that ever lived.

Comprehension questions

1. What problems/evils of monarchy and hereditary succession did Paine point out?
2. How did Paine comment on British political system?
3. How did Paine's ideas contribute to the production of *Declaration of Independence*?

——《普利茅斯种植园开发史》第四章(节选)

一、文本导读

本文选自威廉·布拉德福德(William Bradford)的《普利茅斯种植园开发史》(或译《普利茅斯拓殖记》《普利茅斯垦区史》)第四章。

威廉·布拉德福德(1590—1657)为“五月花号”清教徒领袖之一，文化修养好，会希伯来语、希腊语、拉丁语、法语、荷兰语等语言。由于威望高，自1621年殖民地首任总督约翰·卡弗去世后，威廉·布拉德福德连任30次每年选举一次的总督职位。他用平实的语言记录殖民地的生活和历史，为后世留下了珍贵的文字记录。该手稿几经辗转，终于于20世纪初以书名 *Of Plymouth Plantation*(《普利茅斯种植园开发史》)正式出版。

Of plimoth plantation

And first of ye occasion, and Indusments ther unto; the which that I may truly unfould, I must begine at ye very roote & rise of ye same. The which I shall endevor to manefest in a plaine stile; with singuler regard unto ye simple trueth in all things, at least as near as my slender Judgmente can attaine the same.

1. Chapter

It is well knowne unto ye godly, and judicious, how ever since ye first breaking out of ye lighte of ye gospell, in our Honourable Nation of England (which was ye first of nations, whom ye Lord adorned ther with, after ye grosse darknes of popery which had covered, & overspred ye Christian world) what warrs, & opposisions ever since Satan hath raised, maintained, and continued against the Saincts, from time, to time, in one sorte, or other. Some times by bloody death & cruell torments; other whiles Imprisonments, banishments, & other hard usages. As being loath his kingdom should goe downe, the trueth prevaile; and ye Churches of God reverte to their anciente puritie; and recover, their primative order, libertie & bewtie. But when he could not prevaile by these means, against the maine trueths of ye gospell; but that they began to take rooting in many places; being watered with ye blooud of ye martires, and blessed from heaven with a gracious encrease. He then begane to take him to his anciente strategemes, used of old against the first Christians. That when by ye bloody, & barbarous persecutions of ye Heathen Emperours, he could not stoppe, & subuerte the course of ye gospell; but that it speedily overspred, with a wounderfull celeritie, the then best known parts of ye world. He then begane to sow errours, heresies, and wounderfull dissentions amongst ye professours them selves (working upon their pride, & ambition, with other corrupte passions, incidente to all mortall men; yea to ye saints them selves in some measure) By which wofull effects followed; as not only bitter contentions, & hartburnings, schismes, with other horrible confusions. But Satan tooke occasion & advantage therby to foyst in a number of vile ceremoneys, with many unprofitable Cannons, & decrees which have since been as snares, to many poore, & peacable souls, even to this day. So as in ye anciente times, the persecutio

威廉·布拉德福德手写稿《普利茅斯种植园开发史》首页

二、原文节选

Chapter 4 Showing the reasons and causes of their removal.

After they had lived in this city about some 11 or 12 years, (which is the more observable being the whole time of that famous truce between that state and the Spaniards,) and sundry of them were taken away by death, and many others began to be well stricken in years, the grave Mistress Experience having taught them many things, those prudent governours with sundry of the sagest members began both deeply to apprehend their present dangers, and wisely to foresee the future, and thine of timely remedy. In the agitation of their thoughts, and much discourse of things hear about, at length they began to incline to this conclusion, of removal to some other place. Not out of any newfangledness, or other such like giddy humor, by which men are oftentimes transported to their great hurt and danger, but for sundry weighty and solid reasons; some of the chief of which I will hear briefly touch. And first, they saw and found by experience the hardness of the place and country to be such, as few in comparison would come to them, and fewer that would bide it out, and continue with them. For many that came to them, and many more that desired to be with them, could not endure that great labor and hard fare, with other inconveniences which they underwent and were contented with. But though they loved their persons, approved their cause, and honoured their sufferings, yet they left them as it were weeping, as Orpah did her mother in law Naomie, or as those Romans did Cato in Utica, who desired to be excused and borne with, though they could not all be Catoes. For many, though they desired to enjoy the ordinances of God in their purity, and the liberty of the gospel with them, yet, alas, they admitted of bondage, with danger of conscience, rather than to endure these hardships; yea, some preferred and chose the prisons in England, rather then this liberty in Holland, with these afflictions. But it was thought that if a better and easier place of living could be had, it would draw many, and take away these discouragements. Yea, their pastor would often say, that many of those who both wrote and preached now against them, if they were in a place where they might have liberty and live comfortably, they would then practise as they did.

Secondly, they saw that though the people generally bore all these difficulties very cheerfully, and with a resolute courage, being in the best and strength of their years, yet old age began to steal on many of them, (and their great and continual labours, with other crosses and sorrows, hastened it before the time,) so as it was not only probably thought, but apparently seen, that within a few years more they would be in danger to scatter, by necessities pressing them, or sink under their burdens, or both. And therefore according to the divine proverb, that a wise man seeth the plague when it cometh, and hideth himself, Pro. 22. 3., so they like skillful and beaten soldiers were fearful either to be entrapped or surrounded by their enemies, so as they should neither be able to fight nor flee; and therefore thought it better to dislodge betimes to some place of better advantage and less danger, if any such could be found. Thirdly, as necessity was a taskmaster over them, so they were forced to be such, not only to their servants, but in a sort, to their dearest chldren; the which as it did not a little wound the tender hearts of many a loving father and mother, so it produced likewise sundry sad and sorrowful effects. For many of their children, that were of best dispositions and gracious inclinations, having learned to bear the yoke in their youth, and willing to bear part of their parents' burden, were, often times, so oppressed with their heavy labors, that though their minds were free and willing, yet their bodies bowed under the weight of the same, and became decrepit in their early youth; the vigor of nature being consumed in the very bud as it were. But that which was more lamentable, and of all sorrows most heavy to be borne, was that many of their children, by these occasions, and the great licentiousness of youth in that county, and the manifold temptations of the place, were drawn away by evil examples into extravagant and dangerous courses, getting the reines off their necks, and departing from their parents. Some became soldiers, others took upon them far voyages by sea, and other some worse courses, tending to dissoluteness and the danger of their soules, to the great greif of their parents and dishonour of God. So that they saw their posterity would be in danger to degenerate and be corrupted.

Lastly, (and which was not least,) a great hope and inward zeal they had of laying some good foundation, or at least to make some way there unto, for the propagating and advancing the gospel of the kingdom of Christ in those remote parts of the world; yea, though they should be but even as stepping-stones unto others for the performing of so great a work.

These, and some other like reasons, moved them to undertake this resolution of their removal; the which they afterward prosecuted with so great difficulties, as by the sequel will appear.

The place they had thoughts on was some of those vast and unpeopled countries of America, which are fruitful and fit for habitation, being devoid of all civil inhabitants, where there are only salvage and brutish men, which range up and downe, little otherwise than the wild beasts of the same. This proposition being made public and coming to the scanning of all, it raised many variable opinions amongst men, and caused many fears and doubts amongst themselves. Some, from their reasons and hops conceived, laboured to stir up and encourage the rest to undertake and prosecute the same; others, again, out of their fears, objected against it, and sought to divert from it, alleging many things, and those neither unreasonable nor improbable; as that it was a great design, and subject to many inconceivable perils and dangers; as, besides the casualties of the seas (which none can be freed from) the length of the voyage was such, as the weak bodies of women and other persons worn out with age and traville (as many of them were) could never be able to endure. And yet if they should, the miseries of the land which they should be exposed unto, would be to hard to be borne; and likely, some or all of them together, to consume and utterly to ruinate them. For there they should be liable to famine, and nakedness, and the want, in a manner, of all things. The change of air, diet, and drinking of water, would infect their bodies with sore sickness, and grievous diseases. And also those which should escape or overcome these difficulties, should yet be in continual danger of the savage people, who are cruel, barbarous, and most treacherous, being most furious in their rage, and merciless where they overcome; not being content only to kill, and take away life, but delight to torment men in the most bloody manner that may be; flaying some alive with the shells of fishes, cutting of the members and joints of others by piecemeal, and broiling on the coals, eat the collops of their flesh in their sight whilst they live; with other cruelties horrible to be related. And surely it could not be thought but th every hearing of these things could not but move the very bowels of men to grate within them, and make the weak to quake and tremble. It was furder objected, that it would require greater sums of money to furnish such a voyage, and to fit them with necessaries, then their consumed estates would amount to; and yet they must as well look to be seconded with supplies, as presently to be transported. Also many precedents of ill success, and lamentable miseries befallen others in the like designs, were easy to be found, and not forgotten to be alleged; besides their own experience, in their former troubles and hardships in their removal into Holland, and how hard a thing it was for them to live in that strange place, though it was a neighbor country, and a civil and rich commonwealth.

It was answered, that all great and honourable actions are accompanied with great difficulties, and must be both enterprised and overcome with answerable courages. It was granted the dangers were great, but not desperate; the difficulties were many, but not invincible. For though there were many of them likely, yet they were not certain; it might be sundry of the things feared might never befall; others by provident care and the use of good means, might in a great measure be prevented; and all of them, through the help of God, by fortitude and patience, might either be borne, or overcome. True it was, that such attempts were not to be made and undertaken without good ground and reason; not rashly or lightly as many have done for curiosity or hope of gain, etc. But their condition was not ordinary; their ends were good and honorable; their calling lawful, and urgent; and therefore they might expect the blessing of God in their proceeding. Yea, though they should lose their lives in this action, yet might they have comfort in the same, and their endeavors would be honourable. They lived hear but as men in exile, and in a poor condition; and as great miseries might possibly befall them in this place, for the twelve years of truce were now out, and there was nothing but beating of drums, and preparing for war, the events whereof are always uncertain. The Spaniard might prove as cruel as the savages of America, and the famine and pestilence as sore hear as ther, and their liberty less to look out for remedy. After many other particular things answered and alleged on both sides, it was fully concluded by the major part, to put this design in execution, and to prosecute it by the best means they could.

Comprehension questions

1. What was Plymouth like when the pilgrims first arrived?
2. What is the author's attitude toward the native Americans? Is it fair?
3. How did the pilgrims manage to survive in this uninviting region?

第二章
宣 告 独 立

第一节　时 代 背 景

一、英国针对殖民地的新法令

从 17 世纪末期至 18 世纪中期，英国、法国、西班牙等欧洲列强，在欧洲不断掀起战争，尤其是英国与法国之间的七年战争（1756—1763），英国虽然确立了在欧洲的霸主地位，但由于连年战争的消耗，英国面临巨大的财政危机。

为了转嫁战争消耗和缓解财政压力，英国想到了之前一直实行“甩手”政策的北美殖民地，制定了一系列政策，加紧对北美殖民地的控制和掠夺。

1763 年，英国国王乔治三世（1738—1820）和议会决定，禁止殖民地人民向阿巴拉契亚山脉迁移，以避免与印第安人发生冲突，而殖民地人从未放弃向西迁移的愿望，从而引发强烈不满。

为了制止殖民地的走私活动，英国议会颁布了《海关改革法》（*The Custom Service Reform*），以确保殖民地只能使用英国船只，只能从英国进口一些物品，如茶叶等，也只能将烟草、蔗糖、毛皮等物产出口英国。

此外，英国国王和议会还认为，既然北美 13 个殖民地长期享受英国保护又没有什么财政贡献，现在应该交税供养英国在北美的驻军了。于是，英国议会出台了一系列税收法，以期增加收入：

1764 年通过《糖税法》(*The Sugar Act*)和《货币法》(*The Currency Act*)，对食糖、咖啡、酒、纺织品等征税以及禁止殖民地发行货币，只能使用英国货币。

1765 年出台《印花税法》(*The Stamp Act*)，要求殖民地的所有印刷品必须购买印花税，这一法案涉及殖民地的每一个人。

1767 年又颁布《汤森法案》(*The Townshend Acts*，汤森时任英国财政大臣)，向殖民地的纸张、玻璃、茶叶、油漆等进口物品征收新的进口税。

二、殖民地与英国的矛盾对抗

英国在短短四五年间连续出台的一连串榨取殖民地利益的严苛法令和税收政策，让殖民地人民的不满情绪日益高涨，矛盾冲突也逐步激化升级。

尤其是《印花税法》损害了包括北方商人和南方种植园主几乎所有人的利益，引发共愤，他们提出"没有代表权就不能征税"(no taxation without representation)。1765 年 10 月北美 13 个殖民地中的 9 个派代表在纽约召开"反印花税大会"，通过了《权利与不满宣言》(*Declaration of Rights and Grievances*)，这是这些殖民地第一次为反抗英国而联合召开会议。他们还向英国递交了请愿书，但英国置之不理。之后殖民地人民又进行了其他抗议行动，最终，《印花税法》于 1766 年被废除。

1770 年 3 月 5 日，殖民地人民与驻波士顿英军发生冲突，英军士兵打死打伤数人，这次事件被称为"波士顿大屠杀"(Boston Massacre)，更加激怒了殖民地人民，迫于压力，副总督哈钦森上尉命令英军撤退到军舰上，英国议会也废除了《汤森法案》，但茶税依然保留。

1773 年，不甘心的英国政府把北美殖民地的茶叶出口垄断权给予面临财政困境的东印度公司。同年 12 月 16 日晚上，一群激进革命人士伪装成印第安人登上停靠在波士顿港口的三艘东印度公司的茶叶运输船，将船上货箱里的茶叶扔进大海，这就是著名的"波士顿倾茶事件"(Boston Tea Party)。

波士顿倾茶事件也大大激怒了英国政府，他们决心惩罚殖民地，先后于 1774 年 5 月和 6 月通过四项"强制法令"(The Coercive Acts)，在茶叶得到赔偿之前关闭波士顿港口，停止波士顿港口的对外贸易；禁止殖民地人民群体集会；改变马萨诸塞的政体，押解一些罪犯到英国受审；英军可以随意进入殖民地老百姓家里等。这些新法令被殖民地称为"不可容忍法案"(The Intolerable Acts)。

波士顿倾茶事件，1773 年 12 月 16 日

三、北美殖民地的联合

英国政府强硬政策的一步步升级，导致殖民地人民的不满、愤怒和反抗随之一步步升级，同时也使原本各自为政的 13 个殖民地越来越团结。

1774 年 5 月，弗吉尼亚议会提议召开殖民地会议，得到积极响应。1774 年 9 月 5 日，除佐治亚缺席外，其余 12 个殖民地共派代表 55 人在费城召开第一次大陆会议（Continental Congress）。会议达成了 5 项决议，主要包括组建一个“大陆议会”，相当于政权机关组织协调抵制英国进口商品的行动，提出对英国实行“不进口、不出口、不消费”（non-importation，non-exportation，and non-consumption）；进一步向宗主国请愿以达成妥协；如果殖民地的要求得不到满足，第二年 5 月再召开第二次会议。

第一次大陆会议之后，各殖民地开始紧锣密鼓组建武装组织并训练民兵，而英军也随之加紧侦察和镇压这些武装组织。1775 年 4 月，英军听说波士顿郊区的列克星敦镇（Lexington）和康科德（Concord）藏有民兵组织的军火库，于是派出一支部队前往列克星敦镇，与殖民地民兵组织遭遇，双方交火，英军打死打伤民兵十几人，这就是“列克星敦惨案”（Lexington Massacre），美国独立战争的第一枪由此打响。之后，英军又在康科德遭到民兵组织抵抗，双方伤亡数百人。美国独立战争的序幕由此拉开。

进一步升级的武装冲突使得第二次大陆会议如期于 1775 年 5 月 10 日在费城召开，这次所有 13 个殖民地都派了代表参会，虽然佐治亚的代表秋季才到达。这次会议最主要的内容是组建大陆军(the Continental Army)，任命乔治·华盛顿担任大陆军总司令。但是会议并没有要求独立，而是再次向乔治三世请愿要求满足殖民地的诉求。

四、北美殖民地的独立

事实上，参加第二次大陆会议的代表中没有多少人是支持脱离英国全面独立的，但是之后8个月发生的一系列事件使得这些殖民地与母国英国的妥协调和越来越不可能。

作为对列克星敦和康科德事件的回应，1775年8月3日，英国国王乔治三世正式宣布殖民地的行为是“公然反叛”(open and avowed rebellion)，同年12月英国议会宣布北美殖民地不再在皇冠的保护之下，并正式终止与北美殖民地的贸易。这些决定导致1776年春，北美殖民地中人口最多的马萨诸塞和弗吉尼亚联合起来支持独立，而支持和谈不脱离英国的妥协派也发现他们的目的越来越难实现。

1776年1月，托马斯·潘恩署名“一个英国人”撰写的小册子《常识》(*Common Sense*)言辞犀利、激烈，无情地谴责批判英国的君主制，直截了当地提出人口与面积都与英国本土相当的北美殖民地脱离宗主国独立是天经地义的常识。《常识》一经出版就受到广泛欢迎，销量巨大，为统一北美殖民地各派观点，一致同意彻底与英国决裂起到了重要作用。(详见本书第一章“延伸阅读”部分)

1776年第二次大陆会议继续召开，5月10日会议号召各殖民地成立自己自由独立的政府，退出对英国国王的效忠。6月7日激进的弗吉尼亚代表理查德·亨利·李正式提出北美首个殖民地独立，完全解除与英国的所有关系。6月11日，大陆会议任命由约翰·亚

五位起草人向第二次大陆会议呈交《独立宣言》草案(油画：约翰·特朗布尔，1817年)

当斯、本杰明·富兰克林、托马斯·杰斐逊、罗伯特·利文斯顿、罗杰·舍曼组成委员会，起草《独立宣言》。委员会挑选托马斯·杰斐逊执笔起草文件，之后仅仅经过少量修改，于1776年7月4日上报大陆会议，得到一致通过。

五、独立战争

《独立宣言》发表后，英国国王和政府当然不会轻易同意北美殖民地独立，正式的战争不可避免。开始时英军占有优势，尤其在争夺如纽约、费城、波士顿这样的大城市时优势明显。但是英军的强大实力主要在其海军，随着战线逐渐向西深入北美内陆，英军不论军事实力还是后勤供给都开始力不从心，而殖民地军队在华盛顿的率领下愈战愈勇，加上法国军队的援助，终于于1781年10月19日迫使英军正式投降。

战争虽然胜利了，但是北美殖民地作为独立的国家并没有得到英国的承认，直到大约两年后，即1783年9月，英美在法国巴黎签署《巴黎和约》，英国才正式承认美国为独立主权的国家，并为了不让法国乘虚而入，而大方许诺给这个新兴国家大片疆域：东西从大西洋至密西西比河；南北从西班牙属佛罗里达边界至五大湖。

六、宪法的产生

俗话说，打江山容易守江山难。新兴的美国拥有丰厚的土地资源和丰富的自治经验，但是1783年真正赢得独立之后面临诸多问题，最主要的问题是在那之前全世界都缺乏建立共和国的经验，谁敢肯定北美这片实验田就一定能成功呢？

早在1776—1777年，大陆会议就开始授权各殖民地起草新宪法，也称为《邦联条例》(*Articles of Confederation*)，直到1781年才正式被13个州通过。但是邦联条例显然不具备足够的权威性，13个州仍像13个独立的政府，即使不停修改条例也解决不了当时存在的大量问题，出台一份权威的纲领性的文件，并以此为指导建立真正意义上的政府迫在眉睫。

自1787年13个州开始就新的宪法方案进行商讨、修改，于9月向各州提交新宪法等待通过。出于对新政府不同的理念和见解，出于保护各州自身的利益，13个州的代表们经过长时间的激烈争论甚至争吵，新宪法终于于1788年6月21日生效，因为当天新罕布什尔州成为第九个通过新宪法的州，按照规定，13个州中只要有9个州通过，新宪法就可以生效。但是很显然，对于刚刚成立的美利坚合众国来说，只有13个州全部通过，新宪法才具有真正的意义和权威性。这一天一直等到了1790年6月29日，罗得岛州终于同意妥协，作为第13个，也是最后一个州以微弱票数优势勉强通过宪法。

宪法于1788年6月刚生效不久，各州代表便开始提议各种修正方案，在詹姆斯·麦迪逊(James Madison，被认为是美国宪法之父)的努力下，国会于1789年9月25日采纳了10项修正案，即《权利法案》(*The Bill of Rights*)。

从《独立宣言》到《联邦条例》再到《美国宪法》的漫长过程，美国的宪法经历了构思、修改、争论、妥协等艰难历程，最终得以生效，体现了美国建国元勋们的治国理念，而且确保了这个年轻国家终于有了完整的政府机构。同时，《美国宪法》成为世界上最早的成文宪法，不仅是美国历史上的里程碑，也为日后其他国家制定宪法开了先河。

(《美国宪法》具体内容介绍请见本章“延伸阅读”部分。)

1787年签署《美国宪法》的场景，坐在最高处的是乔治·华盛顿。

七、第一届美国政府

在宪法通过并生效后，美国终于有了法律依据建立第一届政府，定都华盛顿特区。乔治·华盛顿将军以卓越的军事成就和德高望重的人品威望当选第一任总统，于1789年4月30日宣誓就职，他是美国历史上唯一一个以全票通过当选的总统。约翰·亚当斯(John Adams)任副总统。

华盛顿组建的内阁虽然规模不大，但实力雄厚：托马斯·杰斐逊任国务卿(Secretary of State)，亚历山大·汉密尔顿(Alexander Hamilton)任财政部长(Secretary of Treasury)，亨利·诺克斯(Henry Knox)任陆军部长(Secretary of War)，埃德蒙·伦道夫(Edmund Randolph)任司法部长。

八、建国初期的外交策略

美国独立战争的胜利和最终得到国际承认从而得以建国，离不开法国的大力援助，而且以杰斐逊和麦迪逊为代表的民主共和派十分看重与法国的结盟，主张支持法国大革命以及法国与英国的冲突。

而华盛顿总统考虑到建国初期国力尚弱，百废待兴，冷静明智地决定应尽一切可能避免战争，韬光养晦，采取中立的外交政策，远离欧洲的矛盾旋涡，集中精力做好国家基础建设。1793 年英法战争爆发不久，华盛顿毅然颁布了《中立宣言》，正式宣布了中立的外交立场，同时也警醒美国公民对各武装阵营采取不偏不倚的态度。

事实证明，这种高瞻远瞩的策略是十分正确的，法国也因此而获益。1793 年年初华盛顿结束了第一任任期，又连任一届，在 1796 年任满后坚决表示不再连任，从此开启了美国总统任期不超过两届的惯例。卸任后华盛顿解甲归田，但始终是世世代代美国人心目中的建国英雄，最受尊敬的总统。

这幅画像集中体现了美国人对乔治·华盛顿总统的爱戴。

九、汉密尔顿的经济对策

战后的美国债台高筑，面临严峻的财政危机，这个问题自然要靠财政部长汉密尔顿来解决。

汉密尔顿(1755—1804)主张建立强势的中央政府，为了复苏经济，同时增强政府信誉及民众对政府的信任，在总统华盛顿的支持下，他大胆尝试了多种对策，主要体现在三个方面：(1)连本带利按面额支付各种债务(funding at par)。(2)指导国会出台一系列征税法令，在增加财政收入的同时也刺激了制造业和民族工业。(3)于1791年通过集资的方式在费城建立了国家银行"合众国银行"，发行统一货币，并进行投资等。

汉密尔顿的种种尝试在当时非常大胆，也遭到了不少人的强烈反对，幸运的是这些措施最终成功地改善了经济形势，使年轻的共和国逐渐步入正轨。

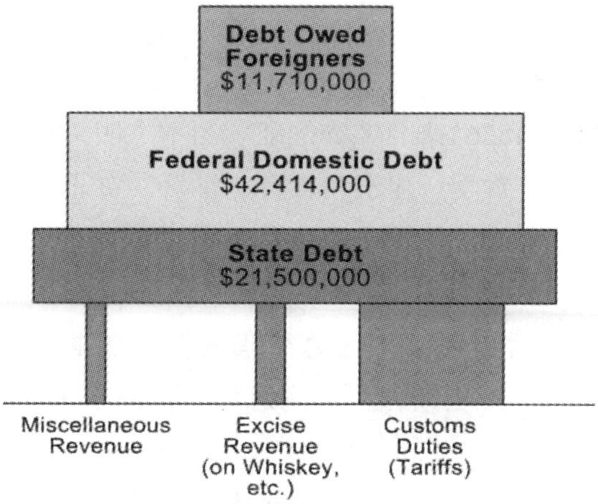

汉密尔顿的财政对策结构图

十、党派的产生

北美13个殖民地在母国英国日益收紧的高压强硬政策下，在维护各自利益的共同目标驱使下，逐渐走到了一起，联合起来一致反抗英国，最终建立了独立的新兴共和制合众国。13个殖民地成为13个州，它们之间的关系并不牢固，虽然最后全部通过宪法，对共和制表示认同，但是各个州，包括功不可没的国父们，对共和制以及对政府功能的理解一直存在很大分歧。直到汉密尔顿的经济政策出台，不同政见愈发明显，分成了两大阵营。

汉密尔顿是美国国父中最年轻的，他态度鲜明，年轻气盛，敢想敢做，主张突出政府的中央集权，政策向“精英人士”倾斜，以确保他们更好地为国家作贡献。他的立场得到了华盛顿总统和副总统亚当斯的支持，这个阵营被称为“联邦党”(Federalist Party)。

而以起草《独立宣言》的杰斐逊和美国宪法之父麦迪逊为主要代表的民主共和党(Democratic-Republican Party)阵营则极力反对汉密尔顿的国家政策，他们提倡民主原则，认为集权的中央政府削弱了各州的自主权，也损害了人民个体的利益，更容易滋生腐败。民主共和党的支持者大多为普通老百姓。

不同政见导致的不同阵营从此开启了美国的党派斗争。

第二节 文本阅读

——《独立宣言》

一、文本导读

托马斯·杰斐逊(1743—1826)来自弗吉尼亚。与本杰明·富兰克林一样，杰斐逊兴趣广泛，涉猎众多领域：法律、哲学、建筑、教育、科学、农业、机械等。他深受欧洲启蒙运动思想影响，尤其是孟德斯鸠、约翰·洛克等人有关政府的观点，这些观点在《独立宣言》中有突出体现。

美国独立后，杰斐逊先后担任第一任总统华盛顿内阁的国务卿、美国驻法国大使，1796 年以微弱劣势不敌约翰·亚当斯，当选副总统，最终于 1800 年成功当选总统，之后又连任一届。

《独立宣言》全文不到 1400 词，主要可以分为三大部分，第一部分阐述政府的理念，即：人与生俱来被赋予某些权利，若政府破坏或不能保障这些天赋的人权，人民有权推翻这个政府并建立新的政府。这部分是全文观点的精华，也是语言最精彩的部分；第二部分是篇幅最长的一部分，细数英国国王乔治三世对北美 13 个殖民地犯下的种种暴政行为，共 27 项指控。详细具体的指控向世人全方位展现了乔治三世的暴行和殖民地人民遭受的不公正待遇，使殖民地的独立理由充分，并成功获得了国际同情和帮助；第三部分是结束部分，明确提出文件的最终目的：北美 13 个殖民地宣告独立，正式组建新的国家——美利坚合众国。

《独立宣言》是美国立国的重要文献，不仅是美国历史的里程碑，更是将 18 世纪欧洲启蒙运动的哲学思想付诸实践，之后又反过来极大地影响了欧洲的革命运动，以及世界其他国家和地区，在世界各地涌现出了许多“独立宣言”。

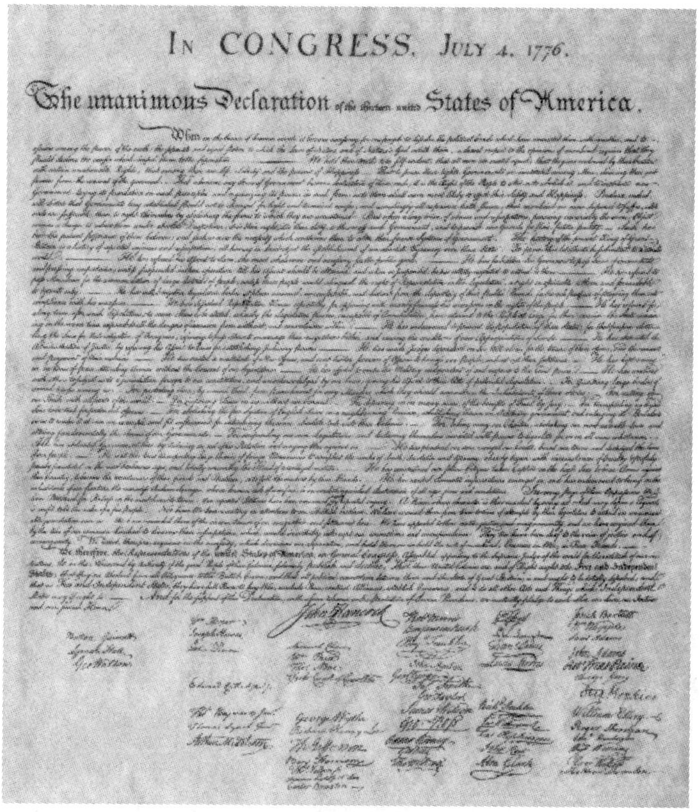
IN CONGRESS, JULY 4, 1776.

The unanimous Declaration of the thirteen united States of America.

《独立宣言》手稿图片

托马斯·杰斐逊(1743—1826)

杰斐逊写给自己的墓志铭如下："这里埋葬的是托马斯·杰斐逊，《独立宣言》的作者、弗吉尼亚宗教自由雕像碑文的作者，以及弗吉尼亚大学的创始人。"

二、《独立宣言》原文

In Congress, July 4, 1776.

The unanimous Declaration of the thirteen United States of America

1 When in the Course of human events, it becomes necessary for one people to dissolve the political bands which have connected them with another, and to assume among the powers of the earth, the separate and equal station to which the Laws of Nature and of Nature's God entitle them, a decent respect to the opinions of mankind requires that they should declare the causes which impel them to the separation.[1]

2 We hold these truths to be self-evident, that all men are created equal, that they are endowed by their Creator with certain unalienable Rights, that among these are Life, Liberty and the pursuit of Happiness. —That to secure these rights, Governments are instituted among Men, deriving their just powers from the consent of the governed, —That whenever any Form of Government becomes destructive of these ends, it is the Right of the People to alter or to abolish it, and to institute new Government, laying its foundation on such principles and organizing its powers in such form, as to them shall seem most likely to effect their Safety and Happiness. Prudence, indeed, will dictate that Governments long established should not be changed for light and transient causes; and accordingly all experience hath shewn, that mankind are more disposed to suffer, while evils are sufferable, than to right themselves by abolishing the forms to which they are accustomed. But when a long train of abuses and usurpations, pursuing invariably the same Object evinces a design to reduce them under absolute Despotism, it is their right, it is their duty, to throw off such Government, and to provide new Guards for their future security. —Such has been the patient sufferance of these Colonies; and such is now the necessity which constrains them to alter their former Systems of Government. The history of the present King of Great Britain is a history of repeated injuries and usurpations, all having in direct object the establishment of an absolute Tyranny over these States. To prove this, let Facts be submitted to a candid world.[2]

3 He has refused his Assent to Laws, the most wholesome and necessary for the public good.

4 He has forbidden his Governors to pass Laws of immediate and pressing importance, unless suspended in their operation till his Assent should be obtained; and when so suspended, he has utterly neglected to attend to them.

5 He has refused to pass other Laws for the accommodation of large districts of people, unless those people would relinquish the right of Representation in the Legislature, a right inestimable to them and formidable to tyrants only.

6 He has called together legislative bodies at places unusual, uncomfortable, and distant from the depository of their public Records, for the sole purpose of fatiguing them into compliance with his measures.

7 He has dissolved Representative Houses repeatedly, for opposing with manly firmness his invasions on the rights of the people.

8 He has refused for a long time, after such dissolutions, to cause others to be elected; whereby the Legislative powers, incapable of Annihilation, have returned to the People at large for their exercise; the State remaining in the mean time exposed to all the dangers of invasion from without, and convulsions within.

9 He has endeavoured to prevent the population of these States; for that purpose obstructing the Laws for Naturalization of Foreigners; refusing to pass others to encourage their migrations hither, and raising the conditions of new Appropriations of Lands.

10 He has obstructed the Administration of Justice, by refusing his Assent to Laws for establishing Judiciary powers.

11 He has made Judges dependent on his Will alone, for the tenure of their offices, and the amount and payment of their salaries.

12 He has erected a multitude of New Offices, and sent hither swarms of Officers to harass our people, and eat out their substance.

13 He has kept among us, in times of peace, Standing Armies without the Consent of our legislatures.

14 He has affected to render the Military independent of and superior to the Civil power.

15 He has combined with others to subject us to a jurisdiction foreign to our constitution, and unacknowledged by our laws; giving his Assent to their Acts of pretended Legislation:

16 For Quartering large bodies of armed troops among us:

17 For protecting them, by a mock Trial, from punishment for any Murders which they should commit on the Inhabitants of these States:

18 For cutting off our Trade with all parts of the world:

19 For imposing Taxes on us without our Consent:

20 For depriving us in many cases, of the benefits of Trial by Jury:

21 For transporting us beyond Seas to be tried for pretended offences

22 For abolishing the free System of English Laws in a neighbouring Province, establishing therein an Arbitrary government, and enlarging its Boundaries so as to render it at once an example and fit instrument for introducing the same absolute rule into these Colonies:

23 For taking away our Charters, abolishing our most valuable Laws, and altering fundamentally the Forms of our Governments:

24 For suspending our own Legislatures, and declaring themselves invested with power to legislate for us in all cases whatsoever.

25 He has abdicated Government here, by declaring us out of his Protection and waging War

against us.

26 He has plundered our seas, ravaged our Coasts, burnt our towns, and destroyed the lives of our people.

27 He is at this time transporting large Armies of foreign Mercenaries to complete the works of death, desolation and tyranny, already begun with circumstances of Cruelty & perfidy scarcely paralleled in the most barbarous ages, and totally unworthy the Head of a civilized nation.

28 He has constrained our fellow Citizens taken Captive on the high Seas to bear Arms against their Country, to become the executioners of their friends and Brethren, or to fall themselves by their Hands.

29 He has excited domestic insurrections amongst us, and has endeavoured to bring on the inhabitants of our frontiers, the merciless Indian Savages, whose known rule of warfare, is an undistinguished destruction of all ages, sexes and conditions.

30 In every stage of these Oppressions We have Petitioned for Redress in the most humble terms: Our repeated Petitions have been answered only by repeated injury. A Prince whose character is thus marked by every act which may define a Tyrant, is unfit to be the ruler of a free people.

31 Nor have We been wanting in attentions to our British brethren. We have warned them from time to time of attempts by their legislature to extend an unwarrantable jurisdiction over us. We have reminded them of the circumstances of our emigration and settlement here. We have appealed to their native justice and magnanimity, and we have conjured them by the ties of our common kindred to disavow these usurpations, which, would inevitably interrupt our connections and correspondence. They too have been deaf to the voice of justice and of consanguinity. We must, therefore, acquiesce in the necessity, which denounces our Separation, and hold them, as we hold the rest of mankind, Enemies in War, in Peace Friends.

32 We, therefore, the Representatives of the United States of America, in General Congress, Assembled, appealing to the Supreme Judge of the world for the rectitude of our intentions, do,

in the Name, and by Authority of the good People of these Colonies, solemnly publish and declare, That these United Colonies are, and of Right ought to be Free and Independent States; that they are Absolved from all Allegiance to the British Crown, and that all political connection between them and the State of Great Britain, is and ought to be totally dissolved; and that as Free and Independent States, they have full Power to levy War, conclude Peace, contract Alliances, establish Commerce, and to do all other Acts and Things which Independent States may of right do. And for the support of this Declaration, with a firm reliance on the protection of divine Providence, we mutually pledge to each other our Lives, our Fortunes and our sacred Honor.

Georgia
Button Gwinnett
Lyman Hall
George Walton
North Carolina
William Hooper
Joseph Hewes
John Penn
South Carolina
Edward Rutledge
Thomas Heyward, Jr.
Thomas Lynch, Jr.
Arthur Middleton
Massachusetts
John Hancock
Maryland
Samuel Chase
William Paca
Thomas Stone
Charles Carroll of Carrollton
Virginia
George Wythe
Richard Henry Lee
Thomas Jefferson
Benjamin Harrison
Thomas Nelson, Jr.
Francis Lightfoot Lee
Carter Braxton
Pennsylvania
Robert Morris
Benjamin Rush
Benjamin Franklin
John Morton
George Clymer
James Smith
George Taylor
James Wilson
George Ross
Delaware
Caesar Rodney
George Read
Thomas McKean
New York
William Floyd
Philip Livingston
Francis Lewis
Lewis Morris
New Jersey
Richard Stockton
John Witherspoon
Francis Hopkinson
John Hart
Abraham Clark
New Hampshire
Josiah Bartlett
William Whipple
Matthew Thornton
Massachusetts
Samuel Adams
John Adams
Robert Treat Paine
Elbridge Gerry
Rhode Island
Stephen Hopkins
William Ellery
Connecticut
Roger Sherman
Samuel Huntington
William Williams
Oliver Wolcott

Notes

1.《独立宣言》正文第一段只有一个句子，很长，而且包含多种结构和主从复合句，属于长难句。要想正确理解这句话，或者这段话，首先需要认清句子成分之间的语法关系。这段话的主要句子结构为 when 引导的主从复合句，在主句 it becomes necessary for... to...结构中有两个并列不定式(to dissolve 和 to assume)。在第二个不定式中出现了一个介词 to，后面跟了 which 引导的定语从句，这个 to 属于介词前置，它实际上应与定语从句中的 entitle 搭配，还原后的完整结构应为：the Laws of Nature entitle people to the separate and equal station among the powers of the earth。
2.《独立宣言》正文第二段的内容非常重要，阐述了殖民地决定独立的理论依据和政府理念，信息量大，逻辑论证一环扣一环。作者巧妙地多次运用了并列结构，例如：五个 that 引导的并列同位语从句阐明不言而喻的真理；三个并列不定式说明人民与生俱来的权利；两个 it is their... to...并列句型表明推翻暴君统治的坚定立场和决心。这些并列结构不仅简洁明了地表述了一系列复杂的观点和论证，并且铿锵有力、掷地有声，一些句子成为经典名言。

Vocabulary

unanimous *adj.* 一致通过的
dissolve *v.* 正式终止
entitle (to) *v.* 使有权利
endow *v.* 给予，赋予，捐助
unalienable *adj.* 不可剥夺的
consent *n.* 许可，允许
prudence *n.* 谨慎
transient *adj.* [正式]短暂的
be disposed to 倾向于某事物
usurpation *n.* [正式]篡夺
evince *v.* [正式]表明，表露
despotism *n.* 专制，暴政
constrain *v.* 阻止，限制
tyranny *n.* 暴政，苛政
candid *adj.* 坦诚的
legislative *adj.* 立法的
judiciary *n.* [正式]司法部门
harass *v.* 骚扰
quarter *v.* 驻扎
mock *adj.* 假装的
arbitrary *adj.* 专横的，武断的
suspend *v.* 终止
abdicate *v.* 放弃
wage (war) *v.* 发动，进行(战争或斗争)
plunder *v.* [尤指战时]掠夺，抢劫
ravage *v.* 严重毁坏，摧毁
mercenary *n.* 雇佣兵
desolate *v.* 破坏
perfidy *n.* 不忠，背信弃义
insurrection *n.* 起义
petition *v.* 请愿，请求
redress *n.* 修正，修改

brethen *n.* 同 brother
magnanimity *n.* 宽宏大量
conjure *v.* 恳请
disavow *v.* 否认
consanguinity *n.* [正式]血缘；血亲关系
acquiesce *v.* [正式]默许
denounce *v.* 谴责
rectitude *n.* 正直
absolve *v.* 使免除
allegiance *n.* 忠诚
levy (war) *v.* 宣战
conclude (peace) *v.* 缔结
Providence *n.* 天命，上苍，上帝

Reading comprehension exercises

I. Filling the blanks according to the structure of *The Declaration of Independence.*

Paragraph(s)	Main Idea
1	Preamble: explaining why the 1)________ have overthrown their ruler and chosen to take their place as a separate nation in the world.
2	• There are certain 2)________ rights that governments should never violate. • When a government 3)________ to protect those rights, the people should establish a 4)________ that is designed to protect those rights. • Governments are rarely overthrown, and should not be overthrown for 5)________ reasons.
3-29	6)________ is guilty of 27 specific abuses.
30-31	After many 7)________ attempts, the colonists have no choice but to declare 8)________ from Great Britain.
32	• The new nation will be called 9)________ and will have no further connections with Great Britain. • The new government will reserve the right to levy war, make peace, make 10)________ with foreign nations, conduct trade, and do anything else that nations do.

II. Fill in the blanks and recite the following sentences.

1. We hold these truths to be 1)________, that all men are 2)________ equal, that they are endowed by their 3)________ with certain unalienable Rights, that among these are 4)________, 5)________ and 6)________.
2. ...that as 7)________ and 8)________ States, they have full Power to 9)________ War, 10)________ Peace, contract Alliances, establish Commerce, and to do all other Acts and Things which Independent States may of right do.

III. Translate the following sentences into Chinese.

1. When in the Course of human events, it becomes necessary for one people to dissolve the political bands which have connected them with another, and to assume among the powers of the earth, the separate and equal station to which the Laws of Nature and of Nature's God entitle them, a decent respect to the opinions of mankind requires that they should declare the causes which impel them to the separation.
2. Prudence, indeed, will dictate that Governments long established should not be changed for light and transient causes; and accordingly all experience hath shewn, that mankind are more disposed to suffer, while evils are sufferable, than to right themselves by abolishing the forms to which they are accustomed.
3. He has refused for a long time, after such dissolutions, to cause others to be elected; whereby the Legislative powers, incapable of Annihilation, have returned to the People at large for their exercise; the State remaining in the mean time exposed to all the dangers of invasion from without, and convulsions within.
4. And for the support of this Declaration, with a firm reliance on the protection of divine Providence, we mutually pledge to each other our Lives, our Fortunes and our sacred Honor.

IV. Comprehension questions

1. Do you agree that the five truths mentioned in Paragraph 2 are self-evident? Give your reasons.
2. What attitudes towards women and Native Americans does the Declaration reveal?
3. Give some examples to show the influence of the Declaration on present America.

第三节 延伸阅读

——《美国宪法》节选

一、文本导读

宪法的主要功能是通过制定一套法规来决定如何在国家范围内依法行使权力。《美国宪法》反映了18世纪欧洲启蒙运动的政治思想，旨在限制政府的权力以便更好地保障人民的自由与平等。

《美国宪法》包括序言(prelude)和7条正文(article)，每条正文包含若干款(section)。

序言部分虽然只有一句话共52个单词，但阐明了国父们制定宪法的理论基础和目的，尤其最开头的三个单词“We the People”后来成为被引用频率最高的部分。

美国宪法条例目录

条(Article)	主要内容
Ⅰ	立法机构
Ⅱ	行政机构
Ⅲ	司法机构
Ⅳ	各州与人民
Ⅴ	修改宪法
Ⅵ	宪法的最高地位
Ⅶ	宪法的通过流程

7条正文中第一、二、三条为主干部分，最核心的内容为：

(1)美利坚合众国实行联邦制(federation)。

(2)政体为三权分立(separation of powers)且相互制衡(checks and balances)的共和政体。

(3)国会(Congress)为立法机构(the legislative branch)；行政权(the executive branch)归属总统；联邦最高法院(the supreme court)行使司法权(the judicial branch)。

《美国宪法》为世界上第一个成文的宪法，其问世经历了各州之间长时间的激烈争吵和博弈，最后达成妥协才得以通过，妥协的结果主要有以下三个特点：

(1)三权分立和相互制衡。政府的权力由立法、行政和司法三个部门分担，相互独立又相互牵制，以确保权力不会过于集中到某一个部门或个人。

(2)各州众议员的代表数量按人口比例分配：每3万人选举1人，参议员数量则是每州2名，与州的实际人口数量无关。经过妥协，一名黑人奴隶可以折算为五分之三个人口。

(3)总统并不是经全体选民直接投票产生，而是由各州以及哥伦比亚特区组成的选举院(Electoral College)最终选举产生。

本节延伸阅读材料选自《美国宪法》序言、第一条节选以及第二、三条。

《美国宪法》第一条第一款规定立法权属于国会，国会由参议院(Senate)和众议院(House of Representatives)组成。第二款详细说明众议员的参选资格：年满25岁，成为美国公民至少7年并为该州居民。第三款有关参议员的选举：每个州均拥有2个名额，与人口数量无关，任期 6 年；参议员必须年满 30 岁，成为美国公民至少 9 年，并成为该州居民；参议院主要负责对总统行动和任命的审核和认可，有权力提出弹劾总统。

《美国宪法》第二条规定行政权归总统。总统的参选资格为：出生时必须为美国公民，年满 35 岁，在美国居住至少 14 年。根据《美国宪法》，总统执行法律，拥有很大的权力，包括一定的立法权，以及否决国会的立法。在战时状态下，总统即为最高元帅。

《美国宪法》第三条有关司法，规定司法权属于最高法院，以及国会规定和设立的下级法院。法官由总统任命，参议院确认。法官为终身制，以便其他部门不具有司法权，也不能对法官施加影响或因法官的判断而弹劾他们。

二、《美国宪法》节选

The Constitution of the United States

We the People of the United States, in Order to form a more perfect Union, establish Justice, insure domestic Tranquility, provide for the common defence, promote the general Welfare, and secure the Blessings of Liberty to ourselves and our Posterity, do ordain and establish this Constitution for the United States of America.

Article Ⅰ.

Section 1.

All legislative Powers herein granted shall be vested in a Congress of the United States, which shall consist of a Senate and House of Representatives.

Section 2.

The House of Representatives shall be composed of Members chosen every second Year by the People of the several States, and the Electors in each State shall have the Qualifications requisite for Electors of the most numerous Branch of the State Legislature.

No Person shall be a Representative who shall not have attained to the Age of twenty five Years, and been seven Years a Citizen of the United States, and who shall not, when elected, be an Inhabitant of that State in which he shall be chosen.

Representatives and direct Taxes shall be apportioned among the several States which may be included within this Union, according to their respective Numbers, which shall be determined by adding to the whole Number of free Persons, including those bound to Service for a Term of Years, and excluding Indians not taxed, three fifths of all other Persons. The actual Enumeration shall be made within three Years after the first Meeting of the Congress of the United States, and within every subsequent Term of ten Years, in such Manner as they shall by Law direct. The Number of Representatives shall not exceed one for every thirty Thousand, but each State shall have at Least one Representative; and until such enumeration shall be made, the State of New Hampshire shall be entitled to chuse three, Massachusetts eight, Rhode-Island and Providence Plantations one, Connecticut five, New-York six, New Jersey four, Pennsylvania eight, Delaware one, Maryland six, Virginia ten, North Carolina five, South Carolina five, and Georgia three.

When vacancies happen in the Representation from any State, the Executive Authority thereof shall issue Writs of Election to fill such Vacancies.

The House of Representatives shall chuse their Speaker and other Officers; and shall have the sole Power of Impeachment.

Section 3.

The Senate of the United States shall be composed of two Senators from each State, chosen by the Legislature thereof, for six Years; and each Senator shall have one Vote.

Immediately after they shall be assembled in Consequence of the first Election, they shall be divided as equally as may be into three Classes. The Seats of the Senators of the first Class shall be vacated at the Expiration of the second Year, of the second Class at the Expiration of the fourth Year, and of the third Class at the Expiration of the sixth Year, so that one third may be chosen every second Year; and if Vacancies happen by Resignation, or otherwise, during the Recess of the Legislature of any State, the Executive thereof may make temporary Appointments until the next Meeting of the Legislature, which shall then fill such Vacancies.

No Person shall be a Senator who shall not have attained to the Age of thirty Years, and been nine Years a Citizen of the United States, and who shall not, when elected, be an Inhabitant of that State for which he shall be chosen.

The Vice President of the United States shall be President of the Senate, but shall have no Vote, unless they be equally divided.

The Senate shall chuse their other Officers, and also a President pro tempore, in the Absence of the Vice President, or when he shall exercise the Office of President of the United States.

The Senate shall have the sole Power to try all Impeachments. When sitting for that Purpose, they shall be on Oath or Affirmation. When the President of the United States is tried, the Chief Justice shall preside: And no Person shall be convicted without the Concurrence of two thirds of the Members present.

Judgment in Cases of Impeachment shall not extend further than to removal from Office, and disqualification to hold and enjoy any Office of honor, Trust or Profit under the United States: but the Party convicted shall nevertheless be liable and subject to Indictment, Trial, Judgment and Punishment, according to Law.

Article Ⅱ.

Section 1.

The executive Power shall be vested in a President of the United States of America. He shall hold his Office during the Term of four Years, and, together with the Vice President, chosen for the same Term, be elected, as follows.

Each State shall appoint, in such Manner as the Legislature thereof may direct, a Number of Electors, equal to the whole Number of Senators and Representatives to which the State may be entitled in the Congress: but no Senator or Representative, or Person holding an Office of Trust or Profit under the United States, shall be appointed an Elector.

The Electors shall meet in their respective States, and vote by Ballot for two Persons, of whom one at least shall not be an Inhabitant of the same State with themselves. And they shall make a List of all the Persons voted for, and of the Number of Votes for each; which List they shall sign and certify, and transmit sealed to the Seat of the Government of the United States, directed to the President of the Senate. The President of the Senate shall, in the Presence of the Senate and House of Representatives, open all the Certificates, and the Votes shall then be counted. The Person having the greatest Number of Votes shall be the President, if such Number be a Majority of the whole Number of Electors appointed; and if there be more than one who have such Majority, and have an equal Number of Votes, then the House of Representatives shall immediately chuse by Ballot one of them for President; and if no Person have a Majority, then from the five highest on the List the said House shall in like Manner chuse the President. But in chusing the President, the Votes shall be taken by States, the Representation from each State having one Vote; A quorum for this Purpose shall consist of a Member or Members from two thirds of the States, and a Majority of all the States shall be necessary to a Choice. In every Case, after the Choice of the President, the Person having the greatest Number of Votes of the Electors shall be the Vice President. But if there should remain two or more who have equal Votes, the Senate shall chuse from them by Ballot the Vice President.

The Congress may determine the Time of chusing the Electors, and the Day on which they shall give their Votes; which Day shall be the same throughout the United States.

No Person except a natural born Citizen, or a Citizen of the United States, at the time of the Adoption of this Constitution, shall be eligible to the Office of President; neither shall any Person be eligible to that Office who shall not have attained to the Age of thirty five Years, and been fourteen Years a Resident within the United States.

In Case of the Removal of the President from Office, or of his Death, Resignation, or Inability to discharge the Powers and Duties of the said Office, the Same shall devolve on the Vice President, and the Congress may by Law provide for the Case of Removal, Death, Resignation or Inability, both of the President and Vice President, declaring what Officer shall then act as President, and such Officer shall act accordingly, until the Disability be removed, or a President shall be elected.

The President shall, at stated Times, receive for his Services, a Compensation, which shall neither be increased nor diminished during the Period for which he shall have been elected, and he shall not receive within that Period any other Emolument from the United States, or any of them.

Before he enter on the Execution of his Office, he shall take the following Oath or Affirmation: —"I do solemnly swear (or affirm) that I will faithfully execute the Office of President of the United States, and will to the best of my Ability, preserve, protect and defend the Constitution of the United States."

Section 2.

The President shall be Commander in Chief of the Army and Navy of the United States, and of the Militia of the several States, when called into the actual Service of the United States; he may require the Opinion, in writing, of the principal Officer in each of the executive Departments, upon any Subject relating to the Duties of their respective Offices, and he shall have Power to grant Reprieves and Pardons for Offences against the United States, except in Cases of Impeachment.

He shall have Power, by and with the Advice and Consent of the Senate, to make Treaties, provided two thirds of the Senators present concur; and he shall nominate, and by and with the Advice and Consent of the Senate, shall appoint Ambassadors, other public Ministers and Consuls, Judges of the supreme Court, and all other Officers of the United States, whose Appointments are not herein otherwise provided for, and which shall be established by Law: but the Congress may by Law vest the Appointment of such inferior Officers, as they think proper, in the President alone, in the Courts of Law, or in the Heads of Departments.

The President shall have Power to fill up all Vacancies that may happen during the Recess of the Senate, by granting Commissions which shall expire at the End of their next Session.

Section 3.

He shall from time to time give to the Congress Information of the State of the Union, and recommend to their Consideration such Measures as he shall judge necessary and expedient; he may, on extraordinary Occasions, convene both Houses, or either of them, and in Case of Disagreement between them, with Respect to the Time of Adjournment, he may adjourn them to such Time as he shall think proper; he shall receive Ambassadors and other public Ministers; he shall take Care that the Laws be faithfully executed, and shall Commission all the Officers of the United States.

Section 4.

The President, Vice President and all civil Officers of the United States, shall be removed from Office on Impeachment for, and Conviction of, Treason, Bribery, or other high Crimes and Misdemeanors.

Article Ⅲ.

Section 1.

The judicial Power of the United States, shall be vested in one supreme Court, and in such inferior Courts as the Congress may from time to time ordain and establish. The Judges, both of the supreme and inferior Courts, shall hold their Offices during good Behaviour, and shall, at stated Times, receive for their Services, a Compensation, which shall not be diminished during their Continuance in Office.

Section 2.

The judicial Power shall extend to all Cases, in Law and Equity, arising under this Constitution, the Laws of the United States, and Treaties made, or which shall be made, under their Authority; —to all Cases affecting Ambassadors, other public Ministers and Consuls; —to all Cases of admiralty and maritime Jurisdiction; —to Controversies to which the United States shall be a Party; —to Controversies between two or more States; — between a State and Citizens of another State, —between Citizens of different States, —between Citizens of the same State claiming Lands under Grants of different States, and between a State, or the Citizens thereof, and foreign States, Citizens or Subjects.

In all Cases affecting Ambassadors, other public Ministers and Consuls, and those in which a State shall be Party, the supreme Court shall have original Jurisdiction. In all the other Cases before mentioned, the supreme Court shall have appellate Jurisdiction, both as to Law and Fact, with such Exceptions, and under such Regulations as the Congress shall make.

The Trial of all Crimes, except in Cases of Impeachment, shall be by Jury; and such Trial shall be held in the State where the said Crimes shall have been committed; but when not committed within any State, the Trial shall be at such Place or Places as the Congress may by Law have directed.

Section 3.

Treason against the United States, shall consist only in levying War against them, or in adhering to their Enemies, giving them Aid and Comfort. No Person shall be convicted of Treason unless on the Testimony of two Witnesses to the same overt Act, or on Confession in open Court.

The Congress shall have Power to declare the Punishment of Treason, but no Attainder of Treason shall work Corruption of Blood, or Forfeiture except during the Life of the Person attainted.

Comprehension questions

1. What purposes is this constitution supposed to achieve, according to the prelude?
2. Choose one or two sections or articles as examples to illustrate how this constitution is designed to achieve those purposes.
3. Draw a mind map to show how the legislative, executive, and judicial powers work with each other.
4. Are there any potential risks or difficulties in balancing the three powers?

第三章
西 进 运 动

第一节 时 代 背 景

一、西进进程

欧洲殖民者在北美从来没有停止过向西扩张的脚步。第一次大的西进运动于 1791—1803 年完成，使得佛蒙特、肯塔基、田纳西、俄亥俄四个州纳入美国领土，使版图扩大一倍。

随着 1820 年颁布的《土地法案》授权购地者仅用 1.25 美元现金就可以购买 80 英亩未开发的土地，吸引了大批欧洲移民前往俄亥俄，实现了每个人都是土地拥有者，每个人都平等。同时，19 世纪 20 年代，蒸汽船在俄亥俄的使用、从宾夕法尼亚州伊利运河开始向西延伸的国家公路都随着西进运动刺激人们继续开发西部深处的广袤地区。

1812 年与英国的战争结束之后，美国急欲扩大联邦规模，向西扩张的心情更加迫切，于 1816—1821 年又扩增六个州：印第安纳、密西西比、伊利诺伊、阿拉巴马、缅因和密苏里。

虽然人们抱着对实现梦想的憧憬热情高涨地向西部挺进，但是现实中严峻的西部生活却与梦想大相径庭。彼时的西部缺衣少粮、房屋简陋，人们不得不长期忍受疾病、忧郁和孤独的折磨，妇女的孤独无助感尤甚。受这种与世隔绝的环境因素影响，在西部的人们逐渐形成了闭塞、迷信、个人主义色彩浓重的特点。

西进的人们主要以皮毛交易为生。早在 19 世纪 20 年代，人们就开始在落基山脉区域

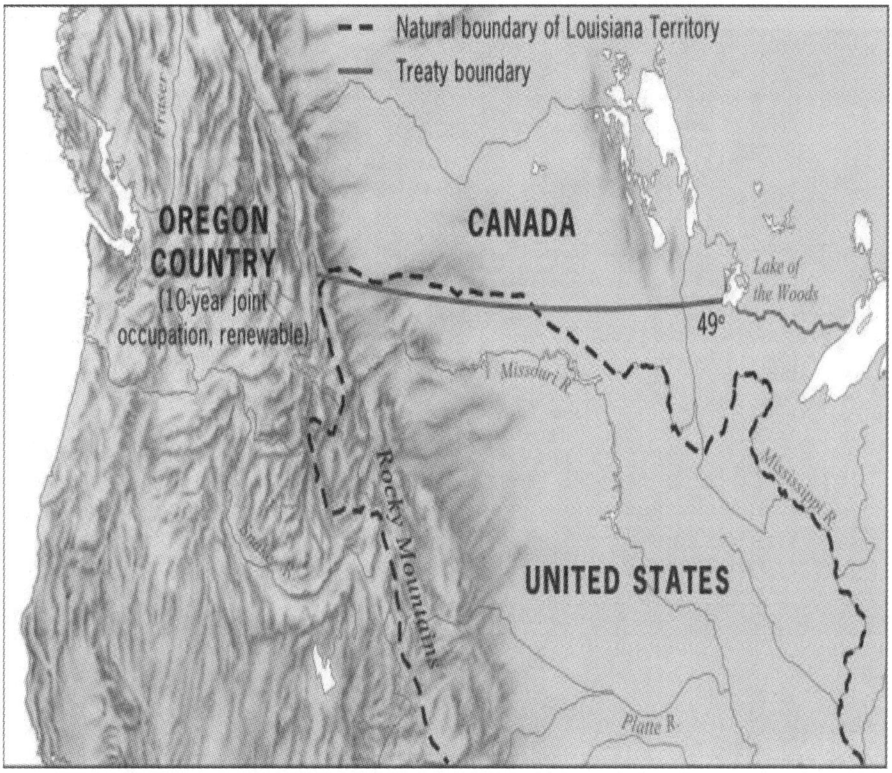

1818 年美国第五任总统门罗与英国和加拿大进行多边谈判，成功将疆土的使用权西扩至落基山脉以及俄勒冈。1846 年与英国签订又一项条约之后，将北纬 49°线延伸至太平洋海岸。

广设陷阱捕猎河狸，与东部过来的商人交换其他商品。水牛皮和水獭皮也是交易的主要货品。过度捕猎导致这些生物几近绝迹，极大地破坏了生态，这种对西部自然资源的大肆掠取被后来的历史学家称为“生态帝国主义”。

一个叫乔治·卡特林的画家注意到了这种现象，呼吁人们保护自然环境，在他的倡导下，终于于 1872 年建立了国家公园体系，黄石公园成为第一个国家公园。

随着西部扩张的进程，人口也与日俱增，19 世纪中叶前，每 25 年人口就会增长一倍，移民人口中爱尔兰人和德国人占比最多，这些移民，尤其是德国移民对美国社会的文化和教育产生了很大影响，他们还强烈反对奴隶制。

到 1860 年，美国版图已包含 33 个州，成为西方世界继俄罗斯、法国、奥地利之后的第四大人口大国，美国人也愈发拥有民族归属感。

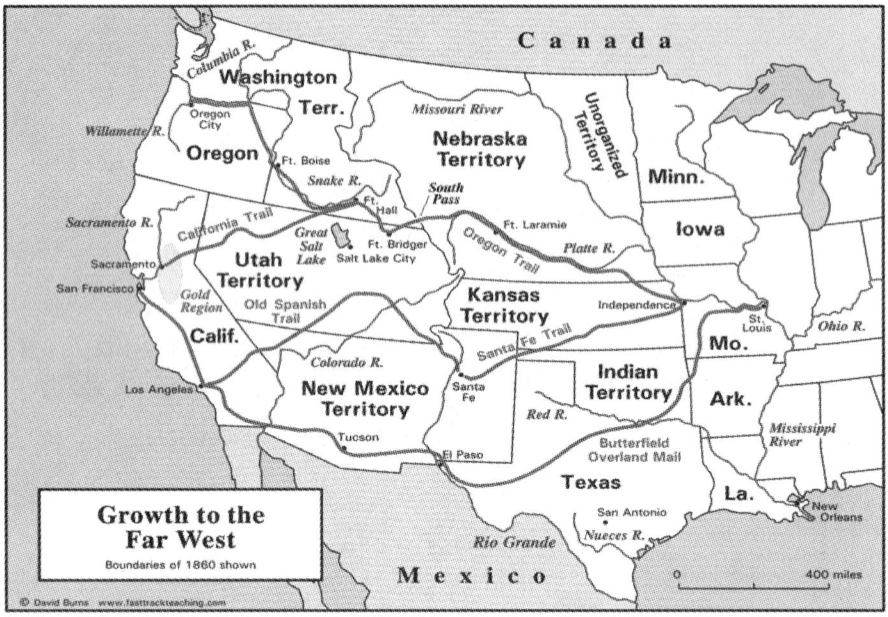

美国内战前西扩的主要路线图

美国西进运动大致进程时间表

年代	事件和结果
1791—1803	新增四个州：佛蒙特、肯塔基、田纳西、俄亥俄； 1803 年路易斯安那购地案使版图扩大一倍
1812—1818	1812 年战争：将英国驱逐出境； 美英边界协定：版图进一步大幅扩大
1816—1821	又新增六个州：印第安纳、密西西比、伊利诺伊、阿拉巴马、缅因、密苏里
1830—1846	驱逐印第安人
1846—1848	墨西哥战争，新增四个州：得克萨斯、新墨西哥、加利福尼亚、俄勒冈，版图扩至太平洋海岸
1860	版图增至 33 个州
1880	西部扩张结束

二、西进进程中的大事件

(一)路易斯安那购地案(Louisiana Purchase)

1803 年年初，杰斐逊总统派两名特使前往巴黎，意欲从法国手中以不超过一千万美元的价格买下新奥尔良以及尽可能多的土地，如果不成功，形势对美国来说就会变得严峻，不得不与英国开启和谈。就在这紧要关头，拿破仑突然转变态度，决定放弃自己的“新奥尔良帝国”梦想计划，把这片土地统统卖掉，以期增强美国未来的军事实力从而遏制英国在新大陆的势力。

经过一周时间的讨价还价，双方终于于 1803 年 4 月 30 日签订合约：美国以一千五百万美元的价格从法国买到了包括路易斯安那在内的相当于当时美国领土面积的大片西部土地，共约 83 万平方英里，约合每英亩 3 美分。本来只预期购买一个城市，没想到达成了如此划算的土地交易，路易斯安那因此被称为“天赐路易斯安那”(The Louisiana Godsend)。

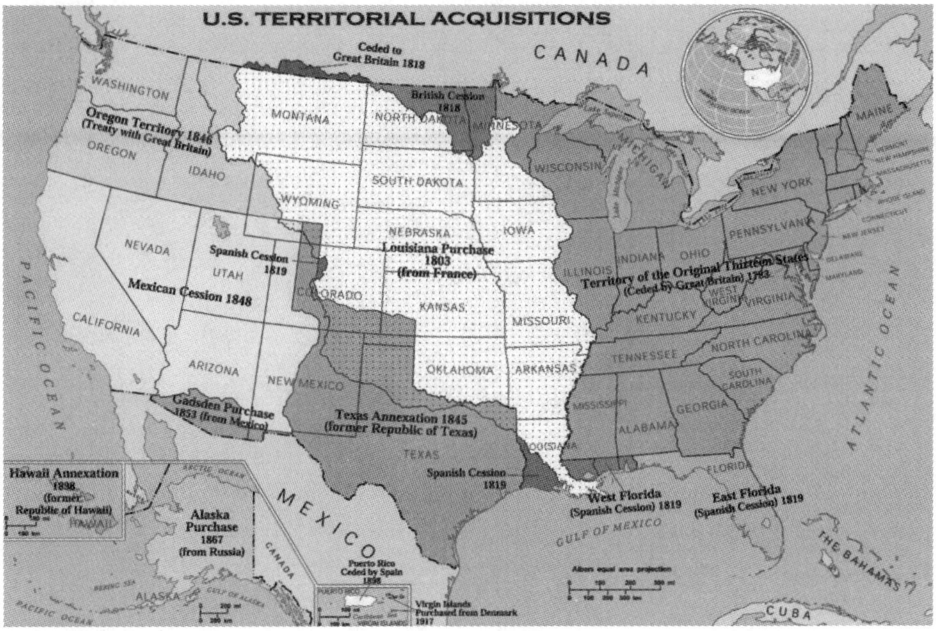

白色区域为路易斯安那购地的范围：北至加拿大，南至墨西哥湾，东至密西西比河，西至落基山脉。

路易斯安那购地案以及1812年对英战争中的胜利进一步去除了英国的势力，美国作为一个新兴国家的民族归属感随之增强，其核心内容可以理解为欲望和扩张，在扩张的进程中印第安人被看作挡路石，美国政府开始想办法清理障碍。

(二)印第安人迁移(Indian Removal)

独立战争之后美国政府就开始着手驱逐西部边界的印第安人，到19世纪初，印第安人的数量已大幅减少，仅剩的以小群落的方式生活在远离社会的西部边界地区。1812年战争之后美国政府对印第安人的态度进一步强硬。1830年国会通过《印第安人迁移法》，决定将印第安人迁移至永远不受白人侵蚀的“印第安领地”(Indian Territory，位于现俄克拉荷马州)。在接下来的10年间，印第安人被武力逼迫踏上了迁移之路，无数人在这条“血泪之路”(Trail of Tears)上丧命。

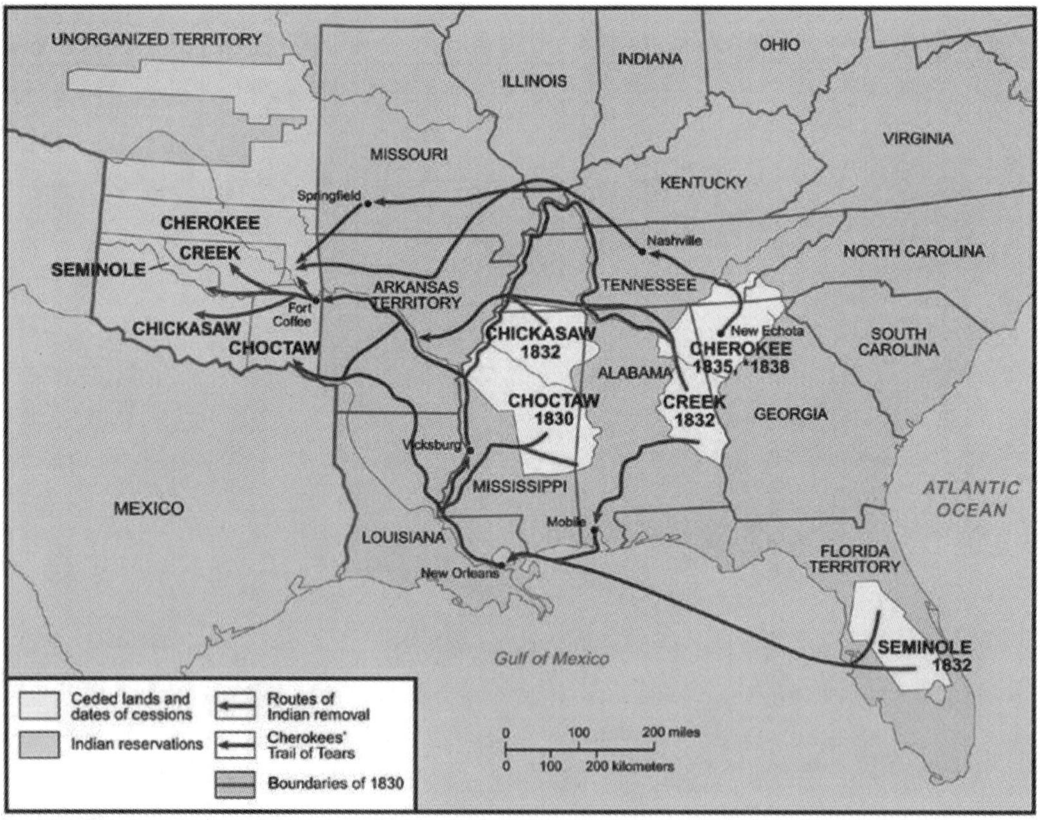

INDIAN REMOVAL

1830—1846年的印第安人迁移路线图，西南区域标注CHEROKEE、CREEK、SEMINOLE、CHICKASAW等字样范围为“印第安人保护区”。

(三)墨西哥战争

中西部持续发展之时，美国政府又将目标聚焦更西部的地区。美国人开始涉足西班牙人控制的得克萨斯，并发动起义试图让得克萨斯独立。1845 年美国将得克萨斯纳入联邦，这一举动激怒了墨西哥政府，1846—1848 年两国之间展开了墨西哥战争，以美国的大获全胜而告终，美国由此控制了得克萨斯、新墨西哥和加利福尼亚，1846 年又吞并了俄勒冈区域，美国西扩的脚步直指太平洋沿岸。

(四)交通工业化与城市的兴起发展

交通运输的革新催生了新兴的城镇，西部也经历着巨大的变化。1830 年前，几乎所有的主要城市都位于主要的河流两岸，而运河系统大大提升了诸如布法罗、底特律和芝加哥这些湖区城市的重要性，1830—1840 年，河流沿岸的居住人口比例从 75%降到了 20%。

运河系统也彻底改变了美国的交易方式。例如第一条提供美国东海岸与西部内陆快速运输工具的伊利运河将一个只有几百人的罗切斯特小村庄变成了 9000 人的繁华城镇。而城镇的发展又吸引了更多的人来到西部，从而刺激了制造业的发展，也影响了城市的政治格局。

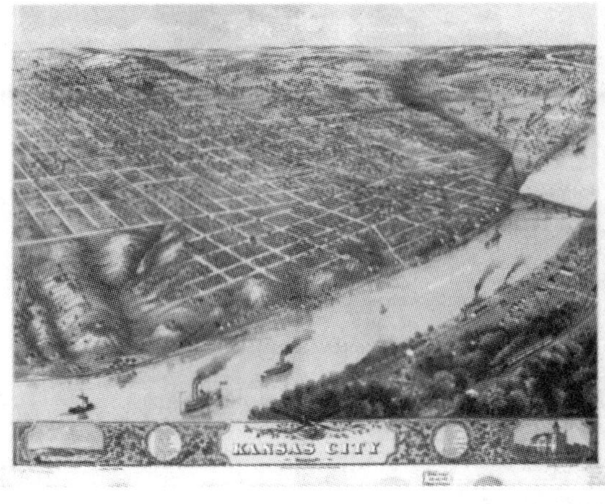

1869 年(左图)和 1908 年(右图)的汉尼拔桥(Hannibal Bridge，位于堪萨斯)。
铁路桥梁改变了堪萨斯城。

(五)加利福尼亚淘金热

1848 年，一位木匠偶然在加利福尼亚发现了金矿，从此开启了淘金狂潮的帷幕。短短几个月的时间，各路人马蜂拥而至，仅仅两年时间，淘金客的数量从 1848 年的 400 人猛增至 1850 年的 4. 4 万人。这些人鱼龙混杂，抢劫犯罪、强占他人金矿，甚至杀人都司空见惯，治安状况糟糕。正是这种自由的无政府状态，加之丰富的矿藏、加利福尼亚有利的地理位置，还有淘金人的高智商引发了淘金热的井喷，甚至震动了全世界。

金矿的发现是美国人的成就，美国在金矿开采技术和水利开发方面也有许多发明创造，开创了独特的加利福尼亚砂矿开采方式。同时也为大量新移民的涌入做好了准备。

这些新来者大多是年轻男性，他们聪明、肯干，幸运的是他们得到了足够的财富报偿，黄金开采量逐年增加，40 年里加利福尼亚的黄金产值高达 12 亿美元。

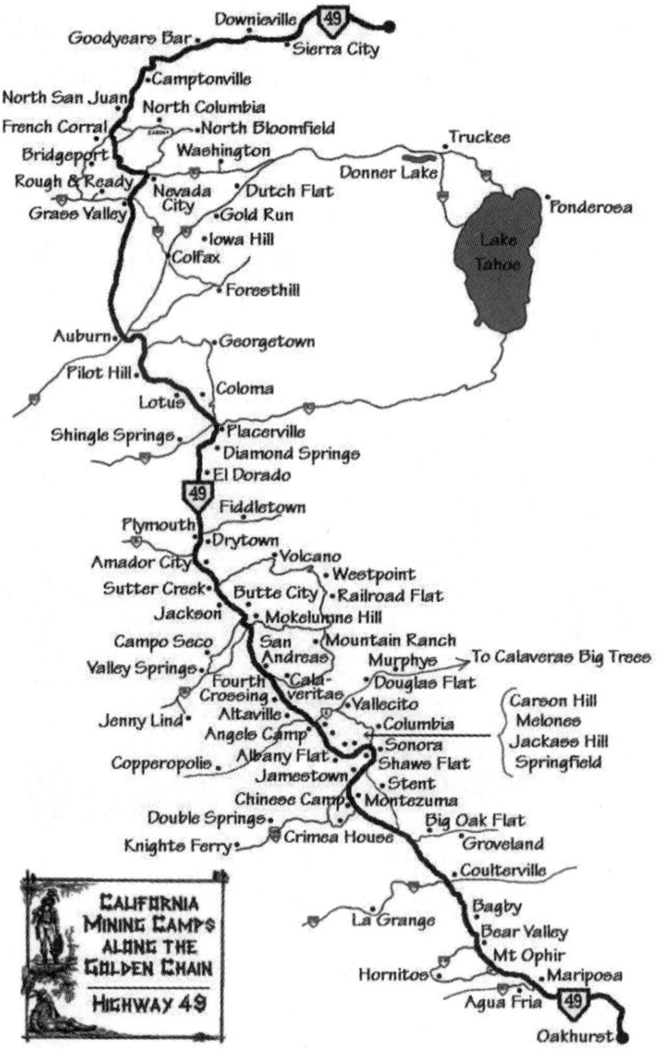

加利福尼亚各金矿的名称反映出淘金人来自世界各地。

淘金热彻底改变了加利福尼亚的一切：从操西班牙语社区变为操英语社区；从文盲人群变为高智商人群；人们的职业也在不停改变，从最初的农场工变为矿工然后又变回农耕；人口从不到1万增至120万；从与世隔绝变为极为便利地与文明社会交流。

淘金热彻底改变了加利福尼亚，使旧金山跃升为人才济济、极具吸引力的城市的同时，也使美国的国家财富暴增，强烈吸引欧洲移民，刺激航运和西部铁路运输发展，带动内华达等州的矿产发展。

三、西部牛仔

美国历史上的牛仔起源于墨西哥北部的放牛娃传统，如今，“牛仔”这个说法泛指整个西部地区，尤其是大平原和落基山脉地区。

随着操英语的商人的不断向西部深入与农畜品交易生产物资，英国文化与西班牙文化开始融合，逐渐发展变化为美国文化中独特的“牛仔”文化。

16世纪佛罗里达才有了牛和马，18世纪印第安人开始进入佛罗里达，在西班牙人留下的牧场开展畜牧活动。到了19世纪，美国政府派白人定居者不断将印第安人向西向南驱赶，佛罗里达广阔的牧场变成了白人放牧者的天下。他们生产的牛肉在南北战争期间为南方政府提供了重要的供给。

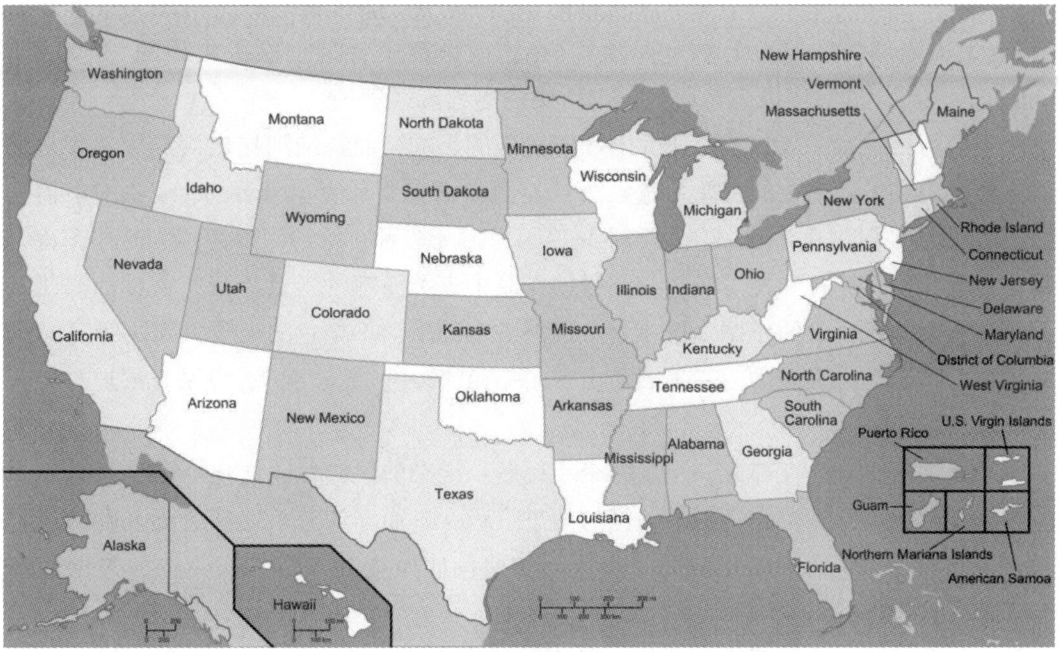

美国地图

操英语的人于1821年到达得克萨斯定居，而加利福尼亚直到墨西哥战争结束之后才有白人进入，这两个地区最后成为牛仔文化标志性的地方。随着牛肉产业的扩大，放牧的范围也随之向北向西延伸，牛仔们逐渐适应了寒冷的气候。

长期以来牛仔们基本是自给自足，直到南北战争将近结束时，牛肉包装业开始兴起，牛肉的需求量迅速增长，养牛业的利润也随之增大。但是大多数牛仔仍来自底层社会，收入水平不高，他们当中约三分之一是墨西哥后裔，五分之一是黑人。

严峻的生活生产条件使美国西部牛仔逐渐形成了独特的具有浓厚个人色彩的牛仔文化，结合了边疆特点以及英国文化崇尚的骑士精神，看重独立能力和个人主义。

第二节　文本阅读

——《论边疆在美国历史上的重要性》节选

一、文本导读

弗雷德里克·杰克逊·特纳(1861—1932)为美国历史学家，曾在威斯康星大学和哈佛大学执教多年，作品颇丰。本文节选自特纳于1893年芝加哥举办的哥伦比亚世博会上的发言稿《论边疆在美国历史上的重要性》。在这次讲话中特纳首次提出他的“边疆假说”(frontier thesis)，这一假说成为研究美国历史的里程碑式理论。

之前的历史学家一般较着重研究欧洲对美国的影响，而特纳则提出西部边疆才是塑造美国自己历史和民族属性的主要力量。法裔美国作家克莱弗克(Crevecoeur)在书中描述了“原始的”西部如何迅速将欧洲移民改造为美国边疆开拓者，特纳深以为然。此外，特纳还借用本杰明·富兰克林和托马斯·杰斐逊的作品中有关西部的观点，富兰克林和杰斐逊认为西部边疆起着安全阀的作用，把在人口拥挤的东部生活不如意的人吸引到西部。

特纳的边疆学说发表之后，美国又出现了拓殖海外的“新边疆”，以及肯尼迪总统著名的“太空边疆”。

本书摘文可以分为三部分，加了两个小标题：混杂的民族性；文化特点。

在第一部分中特纳首先概述了美国的西进进程，进而详细分析美国边疆和欧洲边疆的差异：流动性和再生性，以及美国西部边疆如何彻底改变欧洲移民为纯粹的美国边疆开拓者。

第二部分重点分析西部边疆开拓者的不同民族来源，并提出了“熔炉”(crucible)这一说法，更正人们以为西部开拓者都是英国人这一错误印象。

第三部分在前文的基础上总结了美国西部边疆的独特条件塑造了属于美国自己独有的文化特点：粗鲁强壮、精力旺盛、极端个人主义，等等。

需要指出的是，特纳主要以欣赏和赞许的眼光评价美国的西进运动，忽略了在此过程中环境遭到的大肆破坏，尤其是印第安人遭受到的毁灭性迫害。

1893 年芝加哥哥伦比亚世界博览会

二、原文节选

The Significance of the Frontier in American History

Frederick Jackson Turner

1 In a recent bulletin of the Superintendent of the Census for 1890 appear these significant words: "Up to and including 1880 the country had a frontier of settlement, but at present the unsettled area has been so broken into by isolated bodies of settlement that there can hardly be said to be a frontier line. In the discussion of its extent, its westward movement, etc., it cannot, therefore, any longer have a place in the census reports." This brief official statement marks the closing of a great historic movement. Up to our own day American history has been in

a large degree the history of the colonization of the Great West. The existence of an area of free land, its continuous recession, and the advance of American settlement westward, explain American development.

2 Behind institutions, behind constitutional forms and modifications, lie the vital forces that call these organs into life and shape them to meet changing conditions. The peculiarity of American institutions is, the fact that they have been compelled to adapt themselves to the changes of an expanding people—to the changes involved in crossing a continent, in winning a wilderness, and in developing at each area of this progress out of the primitive economic and political conditions of the frontier into the complexity of city life. Said Calhoun[1] in 1817, "We are great, and rapidly—I was about to say fearfully—growing!" So saying, he touched the distinguishing feature of American life. All peoples show development; the germ theory[2] of politics has been sufficiently emphasized. In the case of most nations, however, the development has occurred in a limited area; and if the nation has expanded, it has met other growing peoples whom it has conquered. But in the case of the United States we have a different phenomenon. Limiting our attention to the Atlantic coast, we have the familiar phenomenon of the evolution of institutions in a limited area, such as the rise of representative government; the differentiation of simple colonial governments into complex organs; the progress from primitive industrial society, without division of labor, up to manufacturing civilization. But we have in addition to this a recurrence of the process of evolution in each western area reached in the process of expansion. Thus American development has exhibited not merely advance along a single line, but a return to primitive conditions on a continually advancing frontier line, and a new development for that area. American social development has been continually beginning over again on the frontier. This perennial rebirth, this fluidity of American life, this expansion westward with its new opportunities, its continuous touch with the simplicity of primitive society, furnish the forces dominating American character. The true point of view in the history of this nation is not the Atlantic coast, it is the Great West. Even the slavery struggle, which is made so exclusive an object of attention by writers like Professor von Holst, occupies its important place in American history because of its relation to westward expansion.

3 In this advance, the frontier is the outer edge of the wave—the meeting point between savagery and civilization. Much has been written about the frontier from the point of view of border warfare and the chase, but as a field for the serious study of the economist and the

historian it has been neglected.

4 The American frontier is sharply distinguished from the European frontier—a fortified boundary line running through dense populations. The most significant thing about the American frontier is, that it lies at the hither edge of free land. In the census reports it is treated as the margin of that settlement which has a density of two or more to the square mile. The term is an elastic one, and for our purposes does not need sharp definition. We shall consider the whole frontier belt, including the Indian country and the outer margin of the "settled area" of the census reports. This paper will make no attempt to treat the subject exhaustively; its aim is simply to call attention to the frontier as a fertile field for investigation, and to suggest some of the problems which arise in connection with it.

5 In the settlement of America we have to observe how European life entered the continent, and how America modified and developed that life and reacted on Europe. Our early history is the study of European germs developing in an American environment. Too exclusive attention has been paid by institutional students to the Germanic origins, too little to the American factors. The frontier is the line of most rapid and effective Americanization. The wilderness masters the colonist. It finds him a European in dress, industries, tools, modes of travel, and thought. It takes him from the railroad car and puts him in the birch canoe. It strips off the garments of civilization and arrays him in the hunting shirt and the moccasin. It puts him in the log cabin of the Cherokee and Iroquois and runs an Indian palisade around him. Before long he has gone to planting Indian corn and plowing with a sharp stick; he shouts the war cry and takes the scalp in orthodox Indian fashion. In short, at the frontier the environment is at first too strong for the man. He must accept the conditions which it furnishes, or perish, and so he fits himself into the Indian clearings and follows the Indian trails. Little by little he transforms the wilderness, but the outcome is not the old Europe, not simply the development of Germanic germs, any more than the first phenomenon was a case of reversion to the Germanic mark. The fact is, that here is a new product that is American. At first, the frontier was the Atlantic coast. It was the frontier of Europe in a very real sense. Moving westward, the frontier became more and more American. As successive terminal moraines result from successive glaciations, so each frontier leaves its traces behind it, and when it becomes a settled area the region still partakes of the frontier characteristics. Thus the advance of the frontier has meant a steady movement away from the influence of Europe, a steady growth of independence on American lines. And to study

this advance, the men who grew up under these conditions, and the political, economic, and social results of it, is to study the really American part of our history.

Composite Nationality

First, we note that the frontier promoted the formation of a composite nationality for the American people. The coast was preponderantly English, but the later tides of continental immigration flowed across to the free lands. This was the case from the early colonial days. The Scotch-Irish and the Palatine Germans, or "Pennsylvania Dutch," furnished the dominant element in the stock of the colonial frontier. With these peoples were also the freed indented servants, or redemptioners, who at the expiration of their time of service passed to the frontier. Governor Spotswood of Virginia writes in 1717, "The inhabitants of our frontiers are composed generally of such as have been transported hither as servants, and, being out of their time, settle themselves where land is to be taken up and that will produce the necessarys of life with little labour." Very generally these redemptioners were of non-English stock. In the crucible of the frontier the immigrants were Americanized, liberated, and fused into a mixed race, English in neither nationality nor characteristics. The process has gone on from the early days to our own. Burke[3] and other writers in the middle of the eighteenth century believed that Pennsylvania was "threatened with the danger of being wholly foreign in language, manners, and perhaps even inclinations." The German and Scotch-Irish elements in the frontier of the South were only less great. In the middle of the present century the German element in Wisconsin was already so considerable that leading publicists looked to the creation of a German state out of the commonwealth by concentrating their colonization. Such examples teach us to beware of misinterpreting the fact that there is a common English speech in America into a belief that the stock is also English.

Intellectual Traits

From the conditions of frontier life came intellectual traits of profound importance. The works of travelers along each frontier from colonial days onward describe certain common traits, and these traits have, while softening down, still persisted as survivals in the place of their origin, even when a higher social organization succeeded. The result is that to the frontier the American intellect owes its striking characteristics. That coarseness and strength combined with acuteness and inquisitiveness; that practical, inventive turn of mind, quick to find expedients; that masterful grasp of material things, lacking in the artistic but powerful to effect great ends; that restless, nervous energy; that dominant individualism, working for good and for evil, and withal that buoyancy and exuberance which comes with freedom—these are traits of the frontier, or traits called out elsewhere because of the existence of the frontier. Since the days when the fleet of Columbus sailed into the waters of the New World, America has been another name for opportunity, and the people of the United States have taken their tone from the incessant expansion which has not only been open but has even been forced upon them. He would be a rash prophet who should assert that the expansive character of American life has now entirely ceased. Movement has been its dominant fact, and, unless this training has no effect upon a people, the American energy will continually demand a wider field for its exercise. But never again will such gifts of free land offer themselves. For a moment, at the frontier, the bonds of custom are broken and unrestraint is triumphant. There is not *tabula rasa*. The stubborn American environment is there with its imperious summons to accept its conditions; the inherited ways of doing things are also there; and yet, in spite of environment, and in spite of custom, each frontier did indeed furnish a new field of opportunity, a gate of escape from the bondage of the past; and freshness, and confidence, and scorn of older society, impatience of its restraints and its ideas, and indifference to its lessons, have accompanied the frontier. What the Mediterranean Sea was to the Greeks, breaking the bond of custom, offering new experiences, calling out new institutions and activities, that, and more, the ever retreating frontier has been to the United States directly[4], and to the nations of Europe more remotely. And now, four centuries from the discovery of America, at the end of a hundred years of life under the Constitution, the frontier has gone, and with its going has closed the first period of American history.

Notes

1. Calhoun：卡尔洪(John Caldwell Calhoun, 1782—1850)，政治家，曾任美国副总统、国务卿。
2. germ theory：原意为微生物理论或细菌理论，指小小的微生物或细菌蔓延扩散而导致疾病。本文用于政治领域，可以理解为政治起源理论。
3. Burke：伯克(Edmund Burke, 1729—1797)，英国著名政治家和保守主义政治理论家，生于爱尔兰。
4. What the Mediterranean Sea was to the Greeks, breaking the bond of custom... the ever retreating frontier has been to the United States directly...

此句为长难句，主干部分为以上部分，句型可以看作：What A is to B，C is to D. 意思是：C 与 D 的关系就像 A 与 B 的关系。

Vocabulary

superintendent *n.* 主管部门
census *n.* 普查，统计
recurrence *n.* 复发
perennial *adj.* 重复出现的
fluidity *n.* 流动性
fortify *v.* 加强，增强
hither *adj.* 向这边的
elastic *adj.* 有弹力的；灵活的
birch canoe 桦木独木舟
garment *n.* 服装，衣服
moccasin *n.* 软帮平底鞋
Cherokee，Iroquois 均为印第安部落名称
palisade *n.* 尖木栅栏
scalp *n.* 头皮
orthodox *adj.* 正统的，规范的
moraine *n.* 冰碛
glaciation *n.* 冻结成冰，冰河作用
partake of 带有几分
composite *adj.* 混合的
indented servant 契约奴
redemptioner *n.* 用劳力抵偿债务的人
crucible *n.* 熔炉
fuse *v.* 融合；融化
coarseness *n.* 粗鲁
acuteness *n.* 敏锐
inquisitiveness *n.* 求知欲
expedient *n.* 应急对策
withal *adv.* 此外
buoyancy *n.* 愉快；乐观；恢复力
exuberance *n.* 精神焕发，兴高采烈
incessant *adj.* 不停的，持续不断的
rash *adj.* 轻率的，鲁莽的
tabula rasa 白板
imperious *adj.* 蛮横的

Reading comprehension exercises

I. Decide whether the following statements are True or False according to the text.

1. (　　) The westward movement ended in 1890.
2. (　　) According to the author, one peculiar feature of American development is that the frontier keeps the pace of fast growth toward the west.
3. (　　) Slavery is also an important issue in the westward expansion.
4. (　　) The major difference between the American frontier and the European frontier lies in that the European frontier tried to protect its border while the American frontier was open to the wilderness.
5. (　　) The European colonists changed the wilderness of the American west into a new world with European civilization.

6.（　　）The European colonists managed to keep their own cultural traits despite the completely different environment of the American west.

7.（　　）The author mentioned "germ theory"（Paragraph 2）in which German and Irish immigrants were the main source of germs.

8.（　　）The author stressed that the American frontier is of great significance to the first period of American history, just like the significant role of the Mediterranean Sea to Greek civilization.

II. Comprehension questions

1. How were European colonists transformed into a new nation—American?
2. Write about the influence of German and Irish immigrants on America.
3. What are the relations between the traits of Americans and those of the American frontier?

第三节　延伸阅读

——《最后的莫希干人》节选

一、文本导读

《最后的莫希干人》是美国作家库珀于1826年创作的长篇小说，被认为是库珀代表作《皮袜子故事集》(*Leatherstocking Tales*，1823—1841)五部曲中最有代表性的一部。

这部故事集被美国历史学家艾伦·内文斯誉为"迄今为止最接近美国史诗"的作品。在《最后的莫希干人》中库珀通过塑造形形色色的人物令美国人意识到自己的过去，令欧洲人意识到美国的存在。库珀作为作家敏锐地观察到美国无与伦比的大森林在拓疆者手中的斧下一片片倒下，这些拓疆者既是建设者，也是毁灭者，这些观察都被作家记录在他的作品中。

《最后的莫希干人》创作于1826年，正值英国和法国之间于北美进行七年战争的第三年，故事发生在18世纪中叶位于现纽约州的原始森林、遍布瀑布和山洞的崇山峻岭中，情节以英国上校军官Munro的两个女儿Cora和Alice去探望父亲途中被劫持又被营救的过程为主线而展开，人物涉及英国人、法国人和印第安人，真实反映了当时美国西部边疆的矛盾冲突；描写了白人的种族优越感，茂密神秘的森林衬托出印第安莫西干酋长"大蟒蛇"Chingachgook和儿子"快鹿腿"Uncas的骁勇、善战、正直、慷慨、忠诚，但同时又野蛮、残忍的丰富的人物性格。故事最终以爱上混血出身Cora的Uncas在营救Cora时二人不幸双双被敌人杀死结束，Uncas 作为莫希干部落最后的勇士的悲剧结局反映并预示了土著印第安人在北美殖民进程中的悲惨遭遇和命运，同时揭示了人性的复杂性。

另外，小说中还有一个人物 David Gamut，随着情节剧烈冲突的发展，这位白人宗教歌手从一个充满喜剧色彩的人物逐渐变得越来越坚强勇敢，最后居然用心爱的乐器交换武器加入战斗，其性格转换自然可信、层次丰富，让读者感悟到拓疆初期边疆的自然环境以及人类之间的冲突对拓疆者的巨大影响。

本节文本选自小说最后一章(第 33 章)的最后部分。前一章(第 32 章)为高潮部分，主要描述在解救姐妹俩的过程中 Uncas 如何为爱而奋不顾身，最后 Uncas 和 Cora 二人不幸双双被杀。最后一章详细描述了二人的印第安式葬礼，以及葬礼中主要人物的心理活动，聚焦 Chingachgook 对失去儿子，同时失去部落希望的悲伤，唯一聊以慰藉的是，Chingachgook 将会在 Hawkeye 兄弟般的陪伴下度过余生。

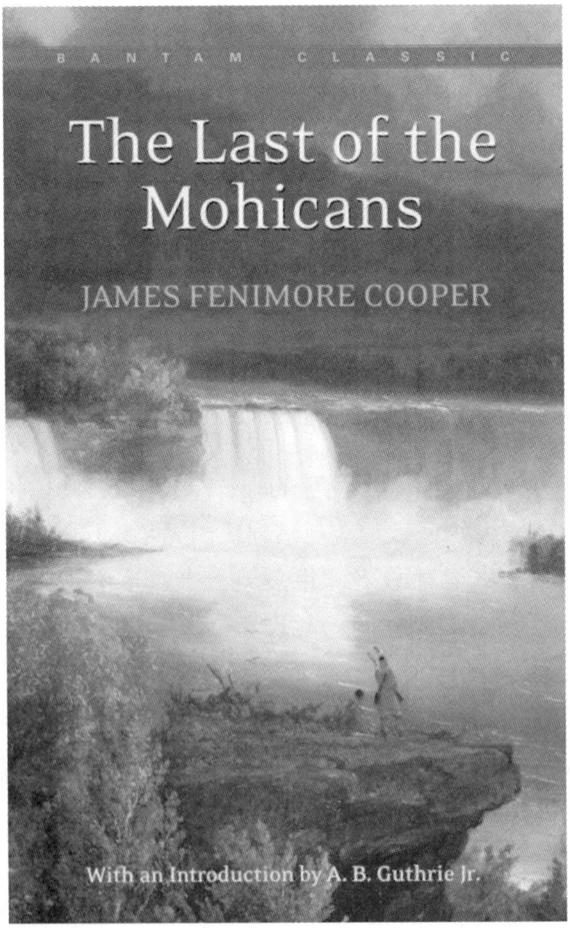

二、原文节选

The Last of the Mohicans

James Fenimore Cooper

Chapter 33 (Excerpt)

The sun rose on the Lenape a nation of mourners. No shouts of success, no songs of triumph, were heard, in rejoicings for their victory. The latest straggler had returned from his fell employment, only to strip himself of the terrific emblems of his bloody calling, and to join in the lamentations of his countrymen, as a stricken people. Pride and exultation were supplanted by humility, and the fiercest of human passions was already succeeded by the most profound and unequivocal demonstrations of grief.

Six Delaware girls, with their long, dark, flowing tresses falling loosely across their bosoms, stood apart, and only gave proof of their existence as they occasionally strewed sweet-scented herbs and forest flowers on a litter of fragrant plants that, under a pall of Indian robes, supported all that now remained of the ardent, high-souled, and generous Cora. Her form was concealed in many wrappers of the same simple manufacture, and her face was shut forever from the gaze of men. At her feet was seated the desolate Munro. His aged head was bowed nearly to the earth, in compelled submission to the stroke of Providence; but a hidden anguish struggled about his furrowed brow, that was only partially concealed by the careless locks of gray that had fallen, neglected, on his temples. Gamut stood at his side, his meek head bared to the rays of the sun, while his eyes, wandering and concerned, seemed to be equally divided between that little volume, which contained so many quaint but holy maxims, and the being in whose behalf his soul yearned to administer consolation. Heyward was also nigh, supporting himself against a tree, and endeavoring to keep down those sudden risings of sorrow that it required his utmost manhood to subdue.

But sad and melancholy as this group may easily be imagined, it was far less touching than another, that occupied the opposite space of the same area. Seated, as in life, with his form and limbs arranged in grave and decent composure, Uncas appeared, arrayed in the most gorgeous ornaments that the wealth of the tribe could furnish. Rich plumes nodded above his head;

wampum, gorgets, bracelets, and medals, adorned his person in profusion; though his dull eye and vacant lineaments too strongly contradicted the idle tale of pride they would convey.

Directly in front of the corpse Chingachgook was placed, without arms, paint or adornment of any sort, except the bright blue blazonry of his race, that was indelibly impressed on his naked bosom. During the long period that the tribe had thus been collected, the Mohican warrior had kept a steady, anxious look on the cold and senseless countenance of his son. So riveted and intense had been that gaze, and so changeless his attitude, that a stranger might not have told the living from the dead, but for the occasional gleamings of a troubled spirit, that shot athwart the dark visage of one, and the deathlike calm that had forever settled on the lineaments of the other. The scout was hard by, leaning in a pensive posture on his own fatal and avenging weapon; while Tamenund, supported by the elders of his nation, occupied a high place at hand, whence he might look down on the mute and sorrowful assemblage of his people.

The day was drawing to the close of its first quarter, and yet had the multitude maintained its breathing stillness since its dawn.

At length, the sage of the Delawares stretched forth an arm, and leaning on the shoulders of his attendants, he arose with an air as feeble as if another age had already intervened between the man who had met his nation the preceding day, and him who now tottered on his elevated stand.

"Men of the Lenape!" he said, in low, hollow tones, that sounded like a voice charged with some prophetic mission: "the face of the Manitou is behind a cloud! His eye is turned from you; His ears are shut; His tongue gives no answer. You see him not; yet His judgments are before you. Let your hearts be open and your spirits tell no lie. Men of the Lenape! the face of the Manitou is behind a cloud."

A girl, selected for the task by her rank and qualifications, commenced by modest allusions to the qualities of the deceased warrior, embellishing her expressions with those oriental images that the Indians have probably brought with them from the extremes of the other continent, and which form of themselves a link to connect the ancient histories of the two worlds. She called him the "panther of his tribe"; and described him as one whose moccasin left no trail on the dews; whose bound was like the leap of a young fawn; whose eye was brighter than a star in the dark night; and whose voice, in battle, was loud as the thunder of the Manitou. She reminded him of the mother who bore him, and dwelt forcibly on the happiness she must feel in possessing such a son. She bade him tell her, when they met in the world of spirits, that the Delaware girls had shed tears above the grave of her child, and had called her blessed.

Then, they who succeeded, changing their tones to a milder and still more tender strain, alluded, with the delicacy and sensitiveness of women, to the stranger maiden, who had left the upper earth at a time so near his own departure, as to render the will of the Great Spirit too manifest to be disregarded. They admonished him to be kind to her, and to have consideration for her ignorance of those arts which were so necessary to the comfort of a warrior like himself. They dwelled upon her matchless beauty, and on her noble resolution, without the taint of envy, and as angels may be thought to delight in a superior excellence; adding, that these endowments should prove more than equivalent for any little imperfection in her education.

Then, with another transition in voice and subject, allusions were made to the virgin who wept in the adjacent lodge. They compared her to flakes of snow; as pure, as white, as brilliant, and as liable to melt in the fierce heats of summer, or congeal in the frosts of winter. They doubted not that she was lovely in the eyes of the young chief, whose skin and whose sorrow seemed so like her own; but though far from expressing such a preference, it was evident they deemed her less excellent than the maid they mourned. Still they denied her no need her rare charms might properly claim. Her ringlets were compared to the exuberant tendrils of the vine, her eye to the blue vault of heavens, and the most spotless cloud, with its glowing flush of the sun, was admitted to be less attractive than her bloom.

During these and similar songs nothing was audible but the murmurs of the music; relieved, as it was, or rather rendered terrible, by those occasional bursts of grief which might be called its choruses. The Delawares themselves listened like charmed men; and it was very apparent, by the variations of their speaking countenances, how deep and true was their sympathy. Even David was not reluctant to lend his ears to the tones of voices so sweet; and long ere the chant was ended, his gaze announced that his soul was enthralled.

The scout, to whom alone, of all the white men, the words were intelligible, suffered himself to be a little aroused from his meditative posture, and bent his face aside, to catch their meaning, as the girls proceeded. But when they spoke of the future prospects of Cora and Uncas, he shook his head, like one who knew the error of their simple creed, and resuming his reclining attitude, he maintained it until the ceremony, if that might be called a ceremony, in which feeling was so deeply imbued, was finished. Happily for the self-command of both Heyward and Munro, they knew not the meaning of the wild sounds they heard.

Chingachgook was a solitary exception to the interest manifested by the native part of the audience. His look never changed throughout the whole of the scene, nor did a muscle move in his rigid countenance, even at the wildest or the most pathetic parts of the lamentation. The cold and senseless remains of his son was all to him, and every other sense but that of sight seemed frozen, in order that his eyes might take their final gaze at those lineaments he had so long loved, and which were now about to be closed forever from his view.

"Why hast thou left us, pride of the Wapanachki?" he said, addressing himself to the dull ears of Uncas, as if the empty clay retained the faculties of the animated man; "thy time has been like that of the sun when in the trees; thy glory brighter than his light at noonday. Thou art gone, youthful warrior, but a hundred Wyandots are clearing the briers from thy path to the world of the spirits. Who that saw thee in battle would believe that thou couldst die? Who before thee has ever shown Uttawa the way into the fight? Thy feet were like the wings of eagles; thine arm heavier than falling branches from the pine; and thy voice like the Manitou when He speaks in the clouds. The tongue of Uttawa is weak," he added, looking about him with a melancholy gaze, "and his heart exceeding heavy. Pride of the Wapanachki, why hast thou left us?"

The lips of Chingachgook had so far parted, as to announce that it was the monody of the father. Though not an eye was turned toward him nor the smallest sign of impatience exhibited, it was apparent, by the manner in which the multitude elevated their heads to listen, that they drank in the sounds with an intenseness of attention, that none but Tamenund himself had ever before commanded. But they listened in vain. The strains rose just so loud as to become intelligible, and then grew fainter and more trembling, until they finally sank on the ear, as if borne away by a passing breath of wind. The lips of the Sagamore closed, and he remained silent in his seat, looking with his riveted eye and motionless form, like some creature that had been turned from the Almighty hand with the form but without the spirit of a man. The Delawares who knew by these symptoms that the mind of their friend was not prepared for so mighty an effort of fortitude, relaxed in their attention; and, with an innate delicacy, seemed to bestow all their thoughts on the obsequies of the stranger maiden.

The place which had been chosen for the grave of Cora was a little knoll, where a cluster of young and healthful pines had taken root, forming of themselves a melancholy and appropriate shade over the spot. On reaching it the girls deposited their burden, and continued for many minutes waiting, with characteristic patience, and native timidity, for some evidence that they whose feelings were most concerned were content with the arrangement. At length the scout, who alone understood their habits, said, in their own language:

"My daughters have done well; the white men thank them."

Satisfied with this testimony in their favor, the girls proceeded to deposit the body in a shell, ingeniously, and not inelegantly, fabricated of the bark of the birch; after which they lowered it into its dark and final abode. The ceremony of covering the remains, and concealing the marks of the fresh earth, by leaves and other natural and customary objects, was conducted with the same simple and silent forms. But when the labors of the kind beings who had performed these sad and friendly offices were so far completed, they hesitated, in a way to show that they knew not how much further they might proceed. It was in this stage of the rites that the scout again addressed them:

"My young women have done enough," he said: "the spirit of the pale face has no need of food or raiment, their gifts being according to the heaven of their color. I see," he added, glancing an eye at David, who was preparing his book in a manner that indicated an intention to lead the way in sacred song, "that one who better knows the Christian fashions is about to speak."

The females stood modestly aside, and, from having been the principal actors in the scene, they now became the meek and attentive observers of that which followed. During the time David occupied in pouring out the pious feelings of his spirit in this manner, not a sign of surprise, nor a look of impatience, escaped them. They listened like those who knew the meaning of the strange words, and appeared as if they felt the mingled emotions of sorrow, hope, and resignation, they were intended to convey.

But the tie which, through their common calamity, had united the feelings of these simple dwellers in the woods with the strangers who had thus transiently visited them, was not so easily broken. Years passed away before the traditionary tale of the white maiden, and of the young warrior of the Mohicans ceased to beguile the long nights and tedious marches, or to animate their youthful and brave with a desire for vengeance. Neither were the secondary actors in these momentous incidents forgotten. Through the medium of the scout, who served for years afterward as a link between them and civilized life, they learned, in answer to their inquiries, that the "Gray Head" was speedily gathered to his fathers—borne down, as was erroneously believed, by his military misfortunes; and that the "Open Hand" had conveyed his surviving daughter far into the settlements of the pale faces, where her tears had at last ceased to flow, and had been succeeded by the bright smiles which were better suited to her joyous nature.

But these were events of a time later than that which concerns our tale. Deserted by all of his color, Hawkeye returned to the spot where his sympathies led him, with a force that no ideal bond of union could destroy. He was just in time to catch a parting look of the features of Uncas, whom the Delawares were already inclosing in his last vestment of skins. They paused to permit the longing and lingering gaze of the sturdy woodsman, and when it was ended, the body was enveloped, never to be unclosed again. Then came a procession like the other, and the whole nation was collected about the temporary grave of the chief—temporary, because it was proper that, at some future day, his bones should rest among those of his own people.

Chingachgook became once more the object of the common attention. He had not yet spoken, and something consolatory and instructive was expected from so renowned a chief on an occasion of such interest. Conscious of the wishes of the people, the stern and self-restrained warrior raised his face, which had latterly been buried in his robe, and looked about him with a steady eye. His firmly compressed and expressive lips then severed, and for the first time during the long ceremonies his voice was distinctly audible. "Why do my brothers mourn?" he said, regarding the dark race of dejected warriors by whom he was environed; "why do my daughters weep? that a young man has gone to the happy hunting-grounds; that a chief has filled his time with honor? He was good; he was dutiful; he was brave. Who can deny it? The Manitou had need of such a warrior, and He has called him away. As for me, the son and the father of

Uncas, I am a blazed pine, in a clearing of the pale faces. My race has gone from the shores of the salt lake and the hills of the Delawares. But who can say that the serpent of his tribe has forgotten his wisdom? I am alone—"

"No, no," cried Hawkeye, who had been gazing with a yearning look at the rigid features of his friend, with something like his own self-command, but whose philosophy could endure no longer; "no, Sagamore, not alone. The gifts of our colors may be different, but God has so placed us as to journey in the same path. I have no kin, and I may also say, like you, no people. He was your son, and a red-skin by nature; and it may be that your blood was nearer—but, if ever I forget the lad who has so often fou't at my side in war, and slept at my side in peace, may He who made us all, whatever may be our color or our gifts, forget me! The boy has left us for a time; but, Sagamore, you are not alone."

Chingachgook grasped the hand that, in the warmth of feeling, the scout had stretched across the fresh earth, and in an attitude of friendship these two sturdy and intrepid woodsmen bowed their heads together, while scalding tears fell to their feet, watering the grave of Uncas like drops of falling rain.

In the midst of the awful stillness with which such a burst of feeling, coming as it did, from the two most renowned warriors of that region, was received, Tamenund lifted his voice to disperse the multitude.

"It is enough," he said. "Go, children of the Lenape, the anger of the Manitou is not done. Why should Tamenund stay? The pale faces are masters of the earth, and the time of the red men has not yet come again. My day has been too long. In the morning I saw the sons of Unamis happy and strong; and yet, before the night has come, have I lived to see the last warrior of the wise race of the Mohicans."

Comprehension questions

1. What impresses you most after reading this passage?
2. Can you describe some details of the rites of Mohican funerals?
3. Hawkeye comforted and assured Sagamore by saying that "you are not alone", do you believe so? Why or why not?

第四章
美国内战

第一节　时代背景

一、内战爆发前的美国南方

(一)南方经济

1793年轧棉机(cotton gin)的引入彻底改变了棉花的生产方式，使得棉花迅速取代烟草、稻米和甘蔗成为南方最主要的作物。1840年后棉花占据美国出口总额的一半价值，南方提供了全球棉花需求总量的一半。英国是当时的工业大国，棉纺业是英国最重要的产业，而其75%的棉花需求量由美国南方提供。在南方领导人看来，棉花就是王(Cotton was King)。

棉花种植在南方的井喷导致对劳动力的极大需求，黑人奴隶离不开轧棉机，而种植园主则离不开奴隶。如此一来，美国南北方的经济很大程度上都依赖于南方的黑人奴隶。

但是种植园农业对土地的消耗和浪费巨大，导致南方人口向西部和北部流失，从而导致南方滑向越来越单一化经济形式的危险局面。

而南方又不得不充满怨恨地看着自己的利润流向北方的银行家、航运商，从而吸引了大量欧洲移民去到北方，使北方的劳动力和财富激增。

(二)种植园奴隶制

美国国会1808年规定禁止进口奴隶，从此以后，美国黑人奴隶的数量全部依靠本土奴隶的繁衍。奴隶主把奴隶看成自己的财产，并投入大量资金。至 1860 年，南方的奴隶主要集中在南方腹地(Deep South)的“黑色地带”(black belt)，从南卡罗来纳州到佐治亚州再纵深向新成立的西南部诸州：亚拉巴马、密西西比、路易斯安那，这些州处于南方的前沿地带，在随后的几十年迅速发展成为棉花王国。

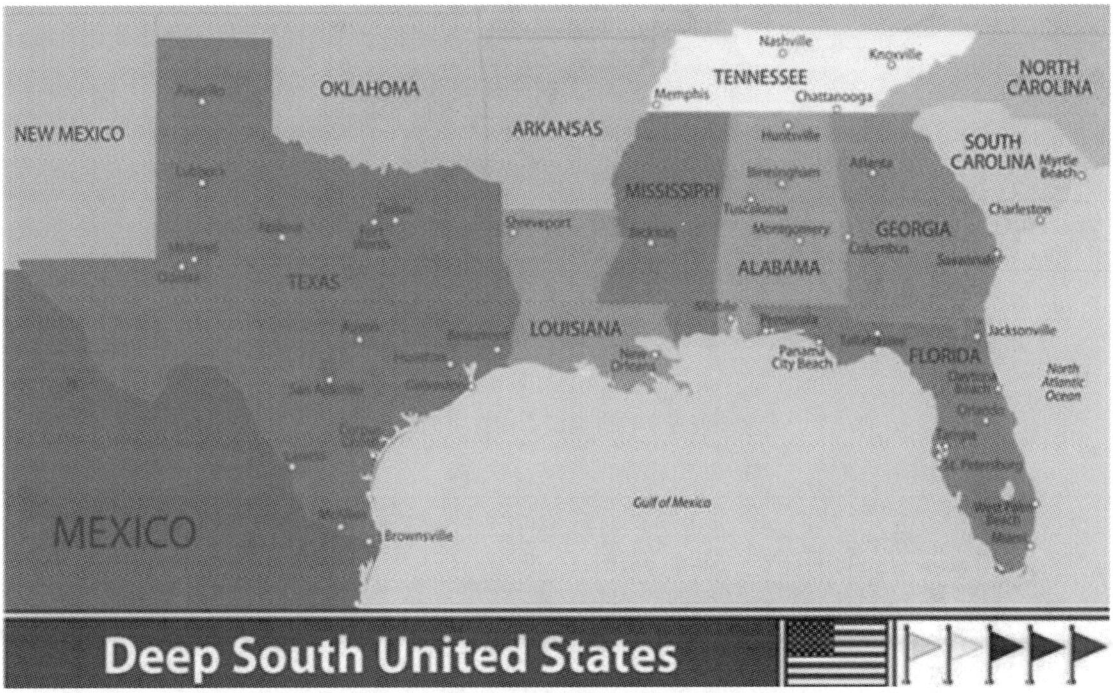

美国南部诸州

(三)黑人奴隶

南方黑人奴隶的处境十分悲惨，他们没有尊严，没有独立自主权，被剥夺了受教育的权利，在美国内战初期，近九成的成年奴隶属于文盲。至 1860 年，所有的南方黑人奴隶都是出生在美国的非洲后裔，形成了独特的美国黑人历史和文化。

二、南北冲突

19 世纪 50 年代南方经济占上风，他们在国会的投票席也多于北方，15 个奴隶制州可以左右政策的制定。南方诸州反感北方废奴的呼声，尤其反感北方通过所谓的“地下铁路”

协助奴隶逃跑至北方，每年会损失一千奴隶。

由美国画家 Eastman Johnson 于 1862 年创作的著名画作《自由之旅——逃亡奴隶》
生动展现了奴隶渴望奔向自由的心情。

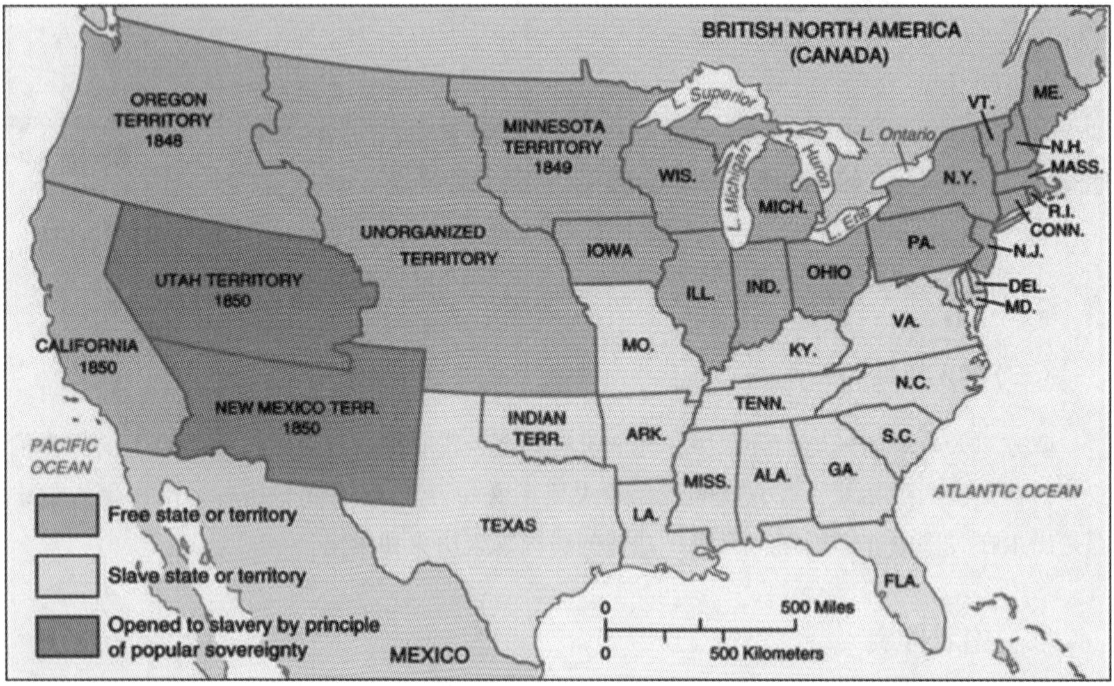

浅灰色区域为奴隶制州，中灰色区域为自由州，深灰色(现犹他州和新墨西哥州)区域尚未归属美国领土。

1849 年南方人宣布将于次年(1850 年)在田纳西州纳什维尔开会商议退出联邦的计划。1850 年通过了新的《逃亡奴隶法案》，将给予庇护奴隶逃跑的北方人高额罚款或判刑，引发北方人的强烈不满，甚至将原先的一部分保守派推向了反奴隶制的一边。

北方在发展工业、多种作物和水陆交通的过程中逐渐积累了人力和财力，他们决心不惜一切代价阻止南方脱离联邦的任何尝试。

南北方之间的水火不容通过 1850 年达成的奴隶制妥协协议暂时得到缓解，该妥协协议同意北纬 36 度 30 分以北的地区禁止奴隶制。

三、林肯当选总统

1860 年新成立不久的共和党提名公开反对奴隶制的亚伯拉罕·林肯为总统候选人，拉开了内战的序幕。1860 年的总统竞选结果对美国历史来说至关重要，决定了这个国家是继续维持和平还是卷入战争，尽管林肯仇恨奴隶制，但他本人并不是坚定的废奴主义者(abolitionist)。

南方虽然输掉了总统竞选，但仍然在参众两院占有优势，林肯的当选并不能废除奴隶制，因为只有修宪才能改变奴隶制，而这种修宪在南方投票权占优的情况下是不可能实现的。

林肯在极其困难的环境下推迟到 1861 年 3 月 4 日才正式上任，在他上任之前，美国已经开始分裂了。

阿伯拉罕·林肯(1809—1865)，美国第十六任总统

四、南方脱离联邦

1860 年 12 月南卡罗来纳州投票一致同意退出联邦，之后的几周时间内 11 个南方州宣布脱离联邦。其中的 7 个州于 1861 年 2 月在亚拉巴马州首府蒙哥马利成立了自己的政府，取名为“美利坚联盟国”(The Confederate States of America)，推选杰弗逊·戴维斯(Jefferson Davis)任总统。

矛盾激化且不可调和，内战一触即发。

五、内战进程(1861—1865)

1861 年 4 月 12 日，杰弗逊·戴维斯下令南方部队炮击萨姆特堡要塞(Fort Sumter)，美国内战(亦称南北战争)正式爆发。

战争初期南方占据着地理位置、军队及民众士气等明显优势，而且拥有常胜将军李将军(Robert E. Lee，1807—1870)为总元帅，确保了多场战斗的胜利。

但是随着战争进程的推移，南方的致命弱点逐渐显现出来：由于交通线被北方摧毁，南方的补给严重短缺，士兵缺衣少药、食物短缺，民众和士兵都不得不挨饿挨冻。

而南方的致命弱点却恰好是北方的优势。

北方拥有种植多种作物的巨大农场提供食物；还拥有大量工厂生产物资；美国当时四分之三的铁路线在北方；而且北方还控制着海上运输。

北方的劣势在于战斗力，虽然不缺人力，但成分复杂，军队由各行各业的手艺人临时组建，又缺乏得力的指挥官，所以在战争之初北方并不占优。但是“业余”士兵们逐渐调整适应战斗，尤其是指挥官换为格兰特将军(Ulysses Simpson Grant，1822—1885)之后，北方的战斗力大大提升，战争进入白热化阶段。1862 年，李将军率领南方部队经过激烈交战取得了半岛战斗的胜利。

六、《解放黑人奴隶宣言》

林肯总统下决心改变策略争取早日结束战争局面，之前并不坚定废除奴隶制的他曾说道，叛军不能长期试图破坏联邦政府失败后，再全身而退地回归。他不顾众人的反对决定起草《解放黑人奴隶宣言》(*The Emancipation Proclamation*)，该宣言于 1863 年 1 月 1 日正式生效。这份文件改变了战争性质，吸引了大量黑人奴隶逃到北方并加入军队与南方作战，大大削弱了南方的实力，而且切断了英法等国支持南方的可能，孤立了南方，是北方最终取得胜利的重要举措。

七、葛底斯堡战役

1863年生效的《解放黑人奴隶宣言》不仅改变了美国内战的战争性质，也排除了南方企图与北方和谈以达到各据一方的可能性，战争必须进行到底，南方开始处于不利局面，他们最后的胜利希望在于1863年7月1—3日宾夕法尼亚州葛底斯堡附近小山谷的战役，北方军队9.2万名士兵在米德(George G. Meade)将军的指挥下对垒李将军率领的7.6万名南方部队，在三天的激烈拉锯战中，双方共伤亡5万多人，但是北方军队笑到了最后，南方赢得战争的希望不复存在。

5个月后，林肯总统来到了葛底斯堡战士公墓，发表了2分钟的《葛底斯堡演讲》，宣传了“三民”政府的诠释：民有、民治、民享。

八、战争结局

葛底斯堡战役之后，林肯断然拒绝了南方想保持独立的和谈条件，战争持续进行。1865年4月，北方军队攻占了南方大本营里士满，格兰特将军代表联邦军队接受了李将军代表南方的投降，并给予南方优厚的投降条件，美国内战正式结束。

1865年4月南方撤出里士满后烧毁了这座城市。

1865 年 4 月 14 日，南方投降仅 5 天后，在首都华盛顿的福特剧院，林肯总统正在包厢观剧的时候，一名狂热支持南方的演员约翰·威尔克斯·布斯潜到林肯的身后朝他的头部开了枪，林肯总统于次日清晨不幸去世。

1865 年 4 月 25 日林肯总统的遗体到达纽约，16 万人上街哀悼。

九、美国内战的意义

内战的结束给美国带来了很多巨大的变化：

(1)第 13 项宪法修正案正式终结了奴隶制的合法化，第 14 项宪法修正案给予所有在美国出生的人以公民权，极大程度地扩大了联邦政权。

(2)脱离联邦闹分裂成为永远不可能实现的议题。

(3)工业产业进一步得到发展。

(4)联邦政府在征税、发展国家银行、印发钞票、招募军队等方面的权力进一步增强。

(5)美国终于成为一个单一的国家，而不是各个州的组合；美国也从此成为一个现代国家。

第二节 文本阅读

——《解放黑人奴隶宣言》

一、文本导读

《解放黑人奴隶宣言》是林肯总统签署的军事法令，因为林肯作为总统不能命令各州结束奴隶制，所以根据《美国宪法》第二条第二款，他以军队战时总指挥的身份签署文件，适用范围仅限于叛乱南方各州的约350万黑人奴隶，一旦他们逃脱南方政府的管辖，他们将获得永久的自由。在结束部分林肯称此宣言为“正义的行为”(an act of justice)，并祈求上帝保佑。

作为公文性质，《解放黑人奴隶宣言》的语言风格较枯燥乏味，但是作为战时措施，该宣言有效地利用南方的人力资源补充了北方的军队力量；宣言还成功阻止了南方获得英法等反奴隶制国家的国际支持。

林肯在内战之初只有一个目的：阻止南方脱离联邦，维护美国联邦的完整性，而《解放黑人奴隶宣言》的颁布拓展了战争的目标，增强了战争的道德色彩，改变了战争性质，成功阻止了境外英法势力的干预。

1863年1月1日《解放黑人奴隶宣言》颁布施行之后，南方约七分之一的黑人奴隶逃到了北方阵营，并且根除了南方想和谈与北方各据一方的可能性，战争必须进行到底。

为了确保废除奴隶制，林肯敦促国会修宪，于1865年1月31日以获得符合规定三分之二的票数通过宪法第13项修订案，于同年12月6日正式实施，宣告奴隶制在美国合法化的终结。

二、《解放黑人奴隶宣言》原文

THE EMANCIPATION PROCLAMATION

By the President of the United States of America:

A Proclamation.

Whereas, on the twenty-second day of September, in the year of our Lord one thousand eight hundred and sixty-two, a proclamation was issued by the President of the United States, containing, among other things, the following, to wit[1]:

"That on the first day of January, in the year of our Lord one thousand eight hundred and sixty-three, all persons held as slaves within any State or designated part of a State, the people whereof shall then be in rebellion against the United States, shall be then, thenceforward, and forever free; and the Executive Government of the United States, including the military and naval authority thereof, will recognize and maintain the freedom of such persons, and will do no act or acts to repress such persons, or any of them, in any efforts they may make for their actual freedom."

"That the Executive will, on the first day of January aforesaid, by proclamation, designate the States and parts of States, if any, in which the people thereof, respectively, shall then be in rebellion against the United States; and the fact that any State, or the people thereof, shall on that day be, in good faith, represented in the Congress of the United States by members chosen thereto at elections wherein a majority of the qualified voters of such State shall have participated, shall, in the absence of strong countervailing testimony, be deemed conclusive evidence that such State, and the people thereof, are not then in rebellion against the United States."

Now, therefore I, Abraham Lincoln, President of the United States, by virtue of the power in me vested as Commander-in-Chief, of the Army and Navy of the United States in time of actual armed rebellion against the authority and government of the United States, and as a fit and necessary war measure for suppressing said rebellion, do, on this first day of January, in the year of our Lord one thousand eight hundred and sixty-three, and in accordance with my purpose so to do publicly proclaimed for the full period of one hundred days, from the day first above mentioned, order and designate as the States and parts of States wherein the people thereof respectively, are this day in rebellion against the United States, the following, to wit:

Arkansas, Texas, Louisiana (except the Parishes of St. Bernard, Plaquemines, Jefferson, St. John, St. Charles, St. James Ascension, Assumption, Terrebonne, Lafourche, St. Mary, St. Martin, and Orleans, including the City of New Orleans), Mississippi, Alabama, Florida, Georgia, South Carolina, North Carolina, and Virginia (except the forty-eight counties designated as West Virginia, and also the counties of Berkley, Accomac, Northampton,

Elizabeth City, York, Princess Ann, and Norfolk, including the cities of Norfolk and Portsmouth), and which excepted parts, are for the present, left precisely as if this proclamation were not issued.

And by virtue of the power, and for the purpose aforesaid, I do order and declare that all persons held as slaves within said designated States, and parts of States, are, and henceforward shall be free; and that the Executive government of the United States, including the military and naval authorities thereof, will recognize and maintain the freedom of said persons.

And I hereby enjoin upon the people so declared to be free to abstain from all violence, unless in necessary self-defence; and I recommend to them that, in all cases when allowed, they labor faithfully for reasonable wages.

And I further declare and make known, that such persons of suitable condition, will be received into the armed service of the United States to garrison forts, positions, stations, and other places, and to man vessels of all sorts in said service.

And upon this act, sincerely believed to be an act of justice, warranted by the Constitution, upon military necessity, I invoke the considerate judgment of mankind, and the gracious favor of Almighty God.

In witness whereof, I have hereunto set my hand and caused the seal of the United States to be affixed.

Done at the City of Washington, this first day of January, in the year of our Lord one thousand eight hundred and sixty three, and of the Independence of the United States of America the eighty-seventh.

By the President: ABRAHAM LINCOLN
WILLIAM H. SEWARD, Secretary of State.

Note

1. to wit:(正式，老式说法)也就是说，即，相当于(to be more exact about something)。

Vocabulary

emancipation *n.* 解放
proclamation *n.* 宣言；公告；生命
whereof *adv.* 关于什么；关于那事物；关于那人
thereof *adv.* 在其中，由此
thereto *adv.* （formal or law 法律）附之；随之
countervailing *adj.* 抗衡的；抵消的
deem *vt.* 认为，视为
by virtue of 凭借，依靠
vest *v.* 给予；授予某人某种权利(头衔、财产等)
wherein *adv.* /*conj.* （formal）其中
enjoin *v.* 命令
garrison *n.* 卫戍部队
invoke *v.* 祈求

Reading comprehension exercises

I. Decide whether the following statements are True or False.

1. (　　) *The Emancipation* Proclamation was issued on January 1, 1863.
2. (　　) *The Emancipation Proclamation* was issued by Abraham Lincoln, who was not only President, but also Commander in Chief of the Armed Forces.
3. (　　) All slaves in the United States were proclaimed freedom by *The Emancipation Proclamation.*
4. (　　) One of the major functions of *The Emancipation Proclamation* is that slaves in the rebellious Southern states were encouraged to join the Union troops.
5. (　　) Lincoln had been always against slavery, he was determined to abolish slavery at the beginning of the Civil War.

II. Comprehension questions

1. What factors made Lincoln determined to draft *The Emancipation Proclamation*?
2. What roles did *The Emancipation Proclamation* play in the process of the Civil War?
3. Consider the problems and difficult situations the slaves might probably encounter after they gained freedom legally.

——《葛底斯堡演讲》

一、文本导读

《葛底斯堡演讲》是美国第 16 任总统亚伯拉罕·林肯于葛底斯堡战役结束四个多月之后的 1863 年 11 月 19 日前往位于战场附近的国家公墓参加公墓落成典礼时发表的讲话。

这篇讲话不到 300 词，演讲时间不到 3 分钟，开头引用《独立宣言》提醒人们美国的立国原则，结尾部分表达了林肯的政府理念：民有、民治、民享(of the people，by the people，for the people)，以赢得所有人对国家政府的认同，成为美国历史上乃至世界上最著名的经典演讲之一。其政府理念直接被之后的法国宪法借用；其中的一些经典语句被后世多次引用，例如马丁·路德·金的《我有一个梦想》。

葛底斯堡演讲属于纪念性演讲(commemorative speech)，虽然篇幅很短，但作者运用了平行结构、重复、对偶、比喻、渐进、押头韵等多种修辞手法，使得该演说凝练精悍、朗朗上口、令人回味、令人难忘。

二、葛底斯堡演讲原文

Gettysburg Address

Abraham Lincoln

(November 19, 1863 on the battlefield near Gettysburg, Pennsylvania, USA)

Four score and seven years ago[1], our fathers brought forth upon this continent a new nation: conceived in liberty, and dedicated to the proposition that all men are created equal.

Now we are engaged in a great civil war... testing whether that nation, or any nation so conceived and so dedicated...can long endure. We are met on a great battlefield of that war.

We have come to dedicate a portion of that field as a final resting place for those who here gave their lives that this nation might live. It is altogether fitting and proper that we should do this.

But, in a larger sense, we cannot dedicate... we cannot consecrate... we cannot hallow this ground. The brave men, living and dead, who struggled here have consecrated it, far above our poor power to add or detract. The world will little note, nor long remember, what we say here, but it can never forget what they did here.

It is for us the living, rather, to be dedicated here to the unfinished work which they who fought here have thus far so nobly advanced. It is rather for us to be here dedicated to the great task remaining before us...that from these honored dead we take increased devotion to that cause for which they gave the last full measure of devotion...that we here highly resolve that these dead shall not have died in vain...that this nation, under God, shall have a new birth of freedom...and that government of the people...by the people...for the people...shall not perish from this earth.

Note

1. Four score and seven years ago：score 的意思是 20，4 个 20 再加 7 即 87，林肯于 1863 年发表这个演讲，87 年前就是 1776 年，亦即《独立宣言》的发布年代。

Vocabulary

address *n.* 演说，演讲
conceive *v.* 怀孕；设想，构想
consecrate *v.* （formal）把……奉为神圣；（为宗教）奉献，献身
hallow *v.* 把……视为神圣

Reading comprehension exercises

I. Match the rhetoric devices used in each of the following sentences or phrases.

A. alliteration（头韵）　B. antithesis（对偶，对照）　C. climax（渐进法）
D. metaphor　E. parallelism　F. repetition

1. ...we take increased devotion to that cause for which they gave the last full measure of devotion...（　　）
2. But, in a larger sense, we cannot dedicate...we cannot consecrate...we cannot hallow this ground.（　　）
3. The brave men, living and dead, who struggled here have consecrated it, far above our poor power to add or detract.（　　）
4. ...our fathers brought forth upon this continent a new nation: conceived in liberty, and

dedicated to the proposition that all men are created equal. (　　)

5. ...government of the people...by the people...for the people...(　　)

6. Four score and seven years ago (　　)

II. Fill in the blanks without referring to the text.

1. Four ________ and seven years ago, our fathers brought forth upon this continent a new nation: ________ in liberty, and dedicated to the proposition that ________ ________ ________ ________ ________.

2. It is rather for us to be here ________ to the great task remaining before us...that from these honored dead we take increased ________ to that cause for which they gave the last full measure of ________...that we here highly resolve that these dead shall not have died in vain...that this nation, under God, shall have a new birth of ________...and that government ________ the people...________ the people...________ the people...shall not ________ from this earth.

III. Comprehension questions

1. Why do you think that the Gettysburg Address could become a classic speech in the world?

2. Do you think that the present US government is that of the people, by the people, and for the people? Why or why not? Please give your reasons.

第三节　延伸阅读

——《汤姆叔叔的小屋》节选

一、文本导读

《汤姆叔叔的小屋》是美国女作家哈里特·比彻·斯托（Harriet Beecher Stowe, 1811—1896，通常称为斯托夫人）于1852年，即美国内战约十年前发表的一部长篇小说。

小说情节分为两条主线展开：黑奴 George Harris 及其妻子 Eliza 和大约五岁的儿子 Harry（其妻、子与汤姆同为奴隶主 Arthur Shelby 拥有）的逃亡经历；汤姆叔叔的悲惨遭遇。汤姆叔叔无疑是小说的绝对主角，他能干、善良、仁慈、宽厚，但是几经辗转被卖给了凶残的奴隶主 Simon Legree，最终被 Legree 毒打致死。

斯托夫人由于对1850年通过的《逃亡奴隶法案》感到失望，决心创作一部作品揭露奴隶制的恐怖、罪恶和不道德，以激发北方民众看清奴隶制的真面目，唤起人们的良知，并采取相应行动。她在小说中通过细腻形象的细节描写，通过对汤姆叔叔和Legree的善恶鲜明对照，通过描述奴隶家庭被拆散、母亲失去孩子、恶劣的生活劳动条件等，成功地达到了写作目的。

小说一经出版，引起巨大的轰动。

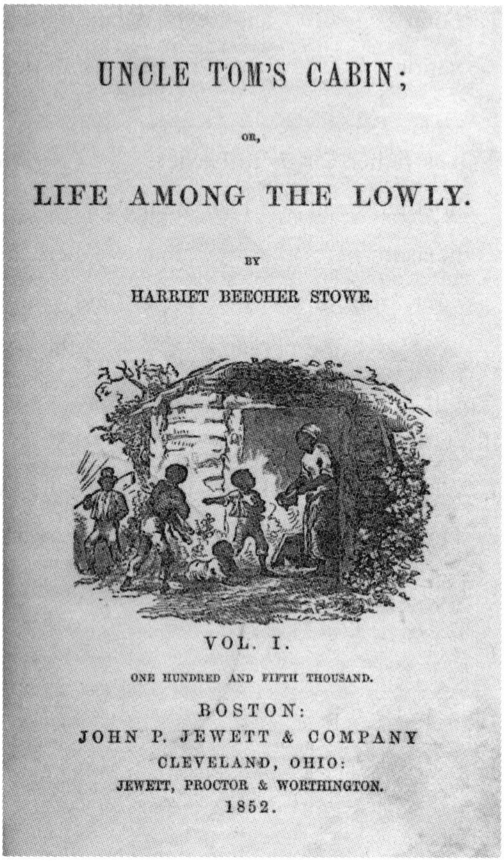
UNCLE TOM'S CABIN;

OR,

LIFE AMONG THE LOWLY.

BY

HARRIET BEECHER STOWE.

VOL. I.

ONE HUNDRED AND FIFTH THOUSAND.

BOSTON:
JOHN P. JEWETT & COMPANY
CLEVELAND, OHIO:
JEWETT, PROCTOR & WORTHINGTON.
1852.

《汤姆叔叔的小屋》首版的扉页插图

在美国国内，该书当年的销量达到创纪录的30万册，还不包括盗版、借阅、听人朗读等，之后又再版无数，还被改编为多种形式的舞台剧在美国各地上演。小说对奴隶苦难的生动写照引发了世界各地被剥削劳苦大众的共鸣，被翻译成多国语言远销世界各地，受到广泛欢迎，尤其是欧洲。

《汤姆叔叔的小屋》在当时的历史背景下所起的作用远远超出了小说的范畴：它不仅争取了美国国内更多的人同情奴隶痛恨奴隶制，更让全世界人民了解奴隶制的罪恶，阻止了英法欲干涉支持南方的企图，保证了北方取得战争的胜利。因此，从政治意义层面讲，没有哪部文学作品能超过《汤姆叔叔的小屋》，像这样改变历史的进程。1862年林肯见到斯托夫人时曾打趣道："你就是那位引发了一场大战的小妇人。"

《汤姆叔叔的小屋》以其对奴隶处境的生动刻画和对奴隶制的鞭笞批判，不仅具有巨大的现实意义，而且至今仍长盛不衰，被无数次改编成各种艺术形式，包括舞台剧、插画、电影等。但是，这部作品从诞生之日起也备受争议，不少人指出作者虽然批判奴隶制，但仍然把黑人奴隶描写成低于白人的种群，主角汤姆也过于顺从软弱，缺乏反抗精神。这些都值得我们在阅读时细细品味。

下文节选自《汤姆叔叔的小屋》第33章，描写了善良能干的汤姆来到新主人Legree的棉花种植园之后与那里的奴隶一起摘棉花的悲惨遭遇，尤其是汤姆因帮助女奴Cassy而与Legree产生激烈冲突，并惨遭毒打，突出反映了两人之间善与恶的鲜明对照，让读者充分体会到奴隶制的残忍和奴隶们的无助与悲凉。

文中对话采用了很多口语化形式，更加真实生动，也不会影响读者的理解。

二、原文节选

IT took but a short time to familiarize Tom with all that was to be hoped or feared in his new way of life. He was an expert and efficient workman in whatever he undertook; and was, both from habit and principle, prompt and faithful. Quiet and peaceable in his disposition, he hoped, by unremitting diligence, to avert from himself at least a portion of the evils of his condition. He saw enough of abuse and misery to make him sick and weary; but he determined to toil on, with religious patience, committing himself to Him that judgeth righteously, not without hope that some way of escape might yet be opened to him.

Legree took silent note of Tom's availability. He rated him as a first-class hand; and yet he felt a secret dislike to him, —the native antipathy of bad to good. He saw, plainly, that when, as was often the case, his violence and brutality fell on the helpless, Tom took notice of it; for, so subtle is the atmosphere of opinion, that it will make itself felt, without words; and the opinion even of a slave may annoy a master. Tom in various ways manifested a tenderness of feeling, a commiseration for his fellow-sufferers, strange and new to them, which was watched with a jealous eye by Legree. He had purchased Tom with a view of eventually making him a sort of overseer, with whom he might, at times, intrust his affairs, in short absences; and, in his view, the first, second, and third requisite for that place, was *hardness*. Legree made up his mind, that, as Tom was not hard to his hand, he would harden him forthwith; and some few weeks after Tom had been on the place, he determined to commence the process.

One morning, when the hands were mustered for the field, Tom noticed, with surprise, a new comer among them, whose appearance excited his attention. It was a woman, tall and slenderly formed, with remarkably delicate hands and feet, and dressed in neat and respectable garments. By the appearance of her face, she might have been between thirty-five and forty; and it was a face that, once seen, could never be forgotten, —one of those that, at a glance, seem to convey to us an idea of a wild, painful, and romantic history. Her forehead was high, and her eyebrows marked with beautiful clearness. Her straight, well-formed nose, her finely-cut mouth, and the graceful contour of her head and neck, showed that she must once have been beautiful; but her face was deeply wrinkled with lines of pain, and of proud and bitter endurance. Her complexion was sallow and unhealthy, her cheeks thin, her features sharp, and her whole form emaciated. But her eye was the most remarkable feature, —so large, so heavily black, overshadowed by long lashes of equal darkness, and so wildly, mournfully despairing. There was a fierce pride and defiance in every line of her face, in every curve of the flexible lip, in every motion of her body; but in her eye was a deep, settled night of anguish, —an expression so hopeless and unchanging as to contrast fearfully with the scorn and pride expressed by her whole demeanor.

Where she came from, or who she was, Tom did not know. The first he did know, she was walking by his side, erect and proud, in the dim gray of the dawn. To the gang, however she was known; for there was much looking and turning of heads, and a smothered yet apparent exultation among the miserable, ragged, half starved creatures by whom she was surrounded.

"Got to come to it, at last, —glad of it!" said one.

"He! he! he!" said another; "you'll know how good it is, Misse!"

"We'll see her work!"

"Wonder if she'll get a cutting up, at night, like the rest of us!"

"I'd be glad to see her down for a flogging, I'll bound!" said another.

The woman took no notice of these taunts, but walked on, with the same expression of angry scorn, as if she heard nothing. Tom had always lived among refined and cultivated people, and he felt intuitively, from her air and bearing, that she belonged to that class; but how or why she could be fallen to those degrading circumstances, he could not tell. The woman neither looked at him nor spoke to him, though, all the way to the field, she kept close at his side.

Tom was soon busy at his work; but, as the woman was at no great distance from him, he often glanced an eye to her, at her work. He saw, at a glance, that a native adroitness and handiness made the task to her an easier one than it proved to many. She picked very fast and very clean, and with an air of scorn, as if she despised both the work and the disgrace and humiliation of the circumstances in which she was placed.

In the course of the day, Tom was working near the mulatto woman who had been bought in the same lot with himself. She was evidently in a condition of great suffering, and Tom often heard her praying, as she wavered and trembled, and seemed about to fall down. Tom silently, as he came near to her, transferred several handfuls of cotton from his own sack to hers.

"O, don't, don't!" said the woman, looking surprised; "it'll get you into trouble."

Just then Sambo came up. He seemed to have a special spite against this woman; and, flourishing his whip, said, in brutal, guttural tones, "What dis yer, Luce, —foolin'a'?" and, with the word, kicking the woman with his heavy cowhide shoe, he struck Tom across the face with his whip.

Tom silently resumed his task; but the woman, before at the last point of exhaustion, fainted.

"I'll bring her to!" said the driver, with a brutal grin. "I'll give her something better than camphire!" and, taking a pin from his coat-sleeve, he buried it to the head in her flesh. The woman groaned, and half rose. "Get up, you beast, and work, will yer, or I'll show yer a trick more!"

The woman seemed stimulated, for a few moments, to an unnatural strength, and worked with desperate eagerness.

"See that you keep to dat ar," said the man, "or yer'll wish yer's dead to-night, I reckin!"

"That I do now!" Tom heard her say; and again he heard her say, "O, Lord, how long! O, Lord, why don't you help us?"

At the risk of all that he might suffer, Tom came forward again, and put all the cotton in his sack into the woman's.

"O, you must n't! you donno what they'll do to ye!" said the woman.

"I can bar it!" said Tom, "better'n you;" and he was at his place again. It passed in a moment.

Suddenly, the stranger woman whom we have described, and who had, in the course of her work, come near enough to hear Tom's last words, raised her heavy black eyes, and fixed them, for a second, on him; then, taking a quantity of cotton from her basket, she placed it in his.

"You know nothing about this place," she said, "or you would n't have done that. When you've been here a month, you'll be done helping anybody; you'll find it hard enough to take care of your own skin!"

"The Lord forbid, Missis!" said Tom, using instinctively to his field companion the respectful form proper to the high bred with whom he had lived.

"The Lord never visits these parts," said the woman, bitterly, as she went nimbly forward with her work; and again the scornful smile curled her lips.

But the action of the woman had been seen by the driver, across the field; and, flourishing his whip, he came up to her.

"What! what!" he said to the woman, with an air of triumph, "YOU a foolin'? Go along! yer under me now, —mind yourself, or yer'll cotch it!"

A glance like sheet-lightning suddenly flashed from black eyes; and, facing about, with quivering lip and dilated nostrils, she drew herself up, and fixed a glance, blazing with rage and scorn, on the driver.

"Dog!" she said, "touch *me*, if you dare! I've power enough, yet, to have you torn by the dogs, burnt alive, cut to inches! I've only to say the word!"

"What de devil you here for, den?" said the man, evidently cowed, and sullenly retreating a step or two. "Did n't mean no harm, Misse Cassy!"

"Keep your distance, then!" said the woman. And, in truth, the man seemed greatly inclined to attend to something at the other end of the field, and started off in quick time.

The woman suddenly turned to her work, and labored with a despatch that was perfectly astonishing to Tom. She seemed to work by magic. Before the day was through, her basket was filled, crowded down, and piled, and she had several times put largely into Tom's. Long after dusk, the whole weary train, with their baskets on their heads, defiled1 up to the building appropriated to the storing and weighing the cotton. Legree was there, busily conversing with the two drivers.

"Dat ar Tom's gwine to make a powerful deal o'trouble; kept a puttin'into Lucy's basket. — One o'these yer dat will get all der niggers to feelin"bused, if Mas'r don't watch him!" said Sambo.

"Hey-dey! The black cuss!" said Legree. "He'll have to get a breakin'in, won't he, boys?"

Both negroes grinned a horrid grin, at this intimation.

"Ay, ay! let Mas'r Legree alone, for breakin'in! De debil heself could n't beat Mas'r at dat!" said Quimbo.

"Wal, boys, the best way is to give him the flogging to do, till he gets over his notions. Break him in!"

"Lord, Mas'r'll have hard work to get dat out o'him!"

"It'll have to come out of him, though!" said Legree, as he rolled his tobacco in his mouth.

"Now, dar's Lucy, —de aggravatinest, ugliest wench on de place!" pursued Sambo.

"Take care, Sam; I shall begin to think what's the reason for your spite agin Lucy."

"Well, Mas'r knows she sot herself up agin Mas'r, and wouldn't have me, when he telled her to."

"I'd a flogged her into't," said Legree, spitting, "only there's such a press o'work, it don't seem wuth a while to upset her jist now. She's slender; but these yer slender gals will bear half killin'to get their own way!"

"Wal, Lucy was real aggravatin'and lazy, sulkin'round; would n't do nothin', —and Tom he tuck up for her."

"He did, eh! Wal, then, Tom shall have the pleasure of flogging her. It'll be a good practice for him, and he won't put it on to the gal like you devils, neither."

"Ho, ho! haw! haw! haw!" laughed both the sooty wretches; and the diabolical sounds seemed, in truth, a not unapt expression of the fiendish character which Legree gave them.

"Wal, but, Mas'r, Tom and Misse Cassy, and dey among'em, filled Lucy's basket. I ruther guess der weight's in it, Mas'r!"

"*I do the weighing*!" said Legree, emphatically.

Both the drivers again laughed their diabolical laugh.

"So!" he added, "Misse Cassy did her day's work."

"She picks like de debil and all his angels!"

"She's got'em all in her, I believe!" said Legree; and, growling a brutal oath, he proceeded to the weighing-room.

Slowly the weary, dispirited creatures, wound their way into the room, and, with crouching reluctance, presented their baskets to be weighed.

Legree noted on a slate, on the side of which was pasted a list of names, the amount.

Tom's basket was weighed and approved; and he looked, with an anxious glance, for the success of the woman he had befriended.

Tottering with weakness, she came forward, and delivered her basket. It was of full weight, as Legree well perceived; but, affecting anger, he said,

"What, you lazy beast! short again! stand aside, you'll catch it, pretty soon!"

The woman gave a groan of utter despair, and sat down on a board.

The person who had been called Misse Cassy now came forward, and, with a haughty, negligent air, delivered her basket. As she delivered it, Legree looked in her eyes with a sneering yet inquiring glance.

She fixed her black eyes steadily on him, her lips moved slightly, and she said something in French. What it was, no one knew; but Legree's face became perfectly demoniacal in its expression, as she spoke; he half raised his hand, as if to strike, —a gesture which she regarded with fierce disdain, as she turned and walked away.

"And now," said Legree, "come here, you Tom. You see, I telled ye I did n't buy ye jest for the common work; I mean to promote ye, and make a driver of ye; and to-night ye may jest as well begin to get yer hand in. Now, ye jest take this yer gal and flog her; ye've seen enough on't to know how."

"I beg Mas'r's pardon," said Tom; "hopes Mas'r won't set me at that. It's what I an't used to, —never did, —and can't do, no way possible."

"Ye'll larn a pretty smart chance of things ye never did know, before I've done with ye!" said Legree, taking up a cow-hide, and striking Tom a heavy blow across the cheek, and following up the infliction by a shower of blows.

"There!" he said, as he stopped to rest; "now, will ye tell me ye can't do it?"

"Yes, Mas'r," said Tom, putting up his hand, to wipe the blood that trickled down his face. "I'm willin'to work night and day, and work while there's life and breath in me; but this yer thing I can't feel it right to do; —and, Mas'r, I *never* shall do it, — *never*!"

Tom had a remarkably smooth, soft voice, and a habitually respectful manner, that had given Legree an idea that he would be cowardly, and easily subdued. When he spoke these last words, a thrill of amazement went through every one; the poor woman clasped her hands, and said, "O Lord!" and every one involuntarily looked at each other and drew in their breath, as if to prepare for the storm that was about to burst.

Legree looked stupefied and confounded; but at last burst forth, —

"What! ye blasted black beast! tell *me* ye don't think it *right* to do what I tell ye! What have any of you cussed cattle to do with thinking what's right? I'll put a stop to it! Why, what do ye think ye are? May be ye think ye'r a gentleman master, Tom, to be a telling your master what's right, and what an't! So you pretend it's wrong to flog the gal!"

"I think so, Mas'r," said Tom; "the poor crittur's sick and feeble; 't would be downright cruel, and it's what I never will do, nor begin to. Mas'r, if you mean to kill me, kill me; but, as to my raising my hand agin any one here, I never shall, —I'll die first!"

Tom spoke in a mild voice, but with a decision that could not be mistaken. Legree shook with anger; his greenish eyes glared fiercely, and his very whiskers seemed to curl with passion; but, like some ferocious beast, that plays with its victim before he devours it, he kept back his strong impulse to proceed to immediate violence, and broke out into bitter raillery.

"Well, here's a pious dog, at last, let down among us sinners! —a saint, a gentleman, and no less, to talk to us sinners about our sins! Powerful holy critter, he must be! Here, you rascal, you make believe to be so pious, —did n't you never hear, out of yer *Bible*, 'Servants, obey yer masters'? An't I yer master? Did n't I pay down twelve hundred dollars, cash, for all there is inside yer old cussed black shell? An't yer mine, now, body and soul?" he said, giving Tom a violent kick with his heavy boot; "tell me!"

In the very depth of physical suffering, bowed by brutal oppression, this question shot a gleam of joy and triumph through Tom's soul. He suddenly stretched himself up, and, looking earnestly to heaven, while the tears and blood that flowed down his face mingled, he exclaimed,

"No! no! no! my soul an't yours, Mas'r! You have n't bought it, —ye can't buy it! It's been bought and paid for, by one that is able to keep it; —no matter, no matter, you can't harm me!"

"I can't!" said Legree, with a sneer; "we'll see, —we'll see! Here, Sambo, Quimbo, give this dog such a breakin'in as he won't get over, this month!"

The two gigantic negroes that now laid hold of Tom, with fiendish exultation in their faces, might have formed no unapt personification of powers of darkness. The poor woman screamed with apprehension, and all rose, as by a general impulse, while they dragged him unresisting from the place.

Comprehension questions

1. What kind of person do you think Uncle Tom is, after reading this chapter? Give your reasons.
2. What kind of person do you think Legree is, after reading this passage? Give your reasons.
3. What kind of person do you think Cassy is, after reading this passage? Give your reasons.
4. Do you agree that Uncle Tom could have had avoided such a tragic ending if he had not been sold to Legree?

第五章
民权运动与女权运动

第一节　时 代 背 景

一、《解放黑人奴隶宣言》

1862 年 9 月 22 日，美国总统亚伯拉罕·林肯(Abraham Lincoln)发表了《解放黑人奴隶宣言》(*The Emancipation Proclamation*)，在宣言中表示截至 1863 年 1 月 1 日，仍在叛乱中的各州以及各州内叛乱地区的奴隶将获得自由。100 天后，《解放黑人奴隶宣言》正式生效。赢得连任后，林肯力促国会通过宪法修正案，禁止美国国土上任何的畜奴行为。《解放黑人奴隶宣言》为最终废除全美奴隶制度奠定了基础。然而奴隶制的废除只是让黑人获得了法律意义上的自由，却没有赋予他们和白人一样的权力，种族主义在美国社会根深蒂固，种族隔离制度使得黑人和白人不能通婚，不能乘同一辆公交车，不能一起上学，不能在一个餐厅吃饭等。这些不公正的对待，最终引发了美国 20 世纪五六十年代的民权运动。

二、非暴力不合作运动

非暴力不合作运动(Satyagraha Movement)是由甘地领导的印度人民反抗英国殖民统治的非暴力抵抗运动。莫罕达斯·卡拉姆昌德·甘地(Mohandas Karamchand Gandhi)，尊称“圣雄甘地”(Mahatma Gandhi)，是印度民族解放运动的领导人、印度国民大会党领袖，也是提倡非暴力抵抗的现代政治学说——甘地主义的创始人。甘地倡导的“不合作”运动包括抵制立法机构选举，抵制在政府机关和法院工作，拒绝在英国学校读书，提倡手纺车运动以抵制英国货物泛滥，拒绝纳税等。“非暴力不合作运动”打击了英国的殖民统治，反映了印度人民要求独立的愿望，促进了印度人民的团结，为印度的独立奠定了基础。甘地的“非暴力”主张影响了全世界的民族主义者，使全世界受压迫的人们看到了可以通过合法的、和平的群众运动获得民主权利的可能性，美国黑人民权运动就是其中的典型代表。

圣雄甘地(1869—1948)

三、民权运动

20世纪五六十年代的民权运动(Civil Right Movement)是美国历史上规模最大的群众运动，是非裔美国人和其他有色人种反对种族歧视和种族压迫，争取政治、经济和社会平等权利而进行的抗争。奴隶制被废除近一百年后，种族隔离、歧视、剥夺公民权利和出于种族动机的暴力在美国社会依旧普遍存在，比如南方各州实行的《吉姆·克劳法案》(*Jim Crow Laws*)禁止非裔美国人进入教室、浴室、剧院、火车车厢、陪审团和立法机构。为了扭转这种歧视和不公正现象，非裔美国人举行了大规模示威活动及非暴力抗议行为，如蒙哥马利巴士抵制和格林斯伯罗·伍尔沃思静坐等。同时，不同种族、宗教和社会团体加入这一运动，表达自己的诉求，争取平等和自由的权利。1964年《民权法》(*Civil Rights Act*)通过，它禁止限制投票的选举策略，保证种族和宗教少数群体平等获得公共设施，禁止基于种族、肤色、宗教、性别或国籍的工作歧视，建立美国公民权利委员会，并成立了平等就业机会委员会。马丁·路德·金是美国民权运动的灵魂人物，他也因领导美国黑人的民权运动而获得了1964年诺贝尔和平奖。1968年马丁·路德·金在田纳西州孟菲斯遇刺身亡，历时二十年的民权运动进入尾声。

塞尔玛游行(1965年)

四、马丁·路德·金

马丁·路德·金(Martin Luther King, Jr., 1929年1月15日—1968年4月4日)，非裔美国人，出生于美国佐治亚州亚特兰大，美国牧师、社会活动家、民权主义者，美国民权运动领袖，毕生致力于用非暴力手段追求种族平等。从莫尔豪斯学院、克罗泽神学院和波士顿大学毕业后，他成为一名牧师。1954年，他成为全国有色人种协会蒙哥马利分会的领导人之一，并帮助创建了南方基督教领袖会议(Southern Christian Leadership Conference)。1955年他领导了蒙哥马利巴士抵制运动，揭开了美国民权运动的序幕。1963年4月，马丁·路德·金参与领导了亚拉巴马州伯明翰大规模群众示威游行。1963年8月参与组织了华盛顿“工作与自由”大游行，并在林肯纪念堂前发表了著名的《我有一个梦想》的演讲。1964年，马丁·路德·金获得了诺贝尔和平奖。1965年，帮助组织了塞尔玛到蒙哥马利游行。此后，他将注意力扩展到解决黑人贫困问题和越南战争。1968年，马丁·路德·金在田纳西州的孟菲斯(Memphis)遇刺身亡，时年39岁。

马丁·路德·金在华盛顿大游行中发表《我有一个梦想》的演讲

五、蒙哥马利巴士抵制运动

蒙哥马利巴士抵制运动(Montgomery Bus Boycott)是美国民权运动历史上的一座里程碑。1955年12月1日，在美国亚拉巴马州州府蒙哥马利市，非裔女裁缝罗莎·帕克斯(Rosa Parks)因拒绝给白人让座而被警察逮捕，从而引发了长达381天的巴士抵制运动。在巴士抵制运动的第一天夜晚，马丁·路德·金发表了鼓舞人心的演讲，说道“除了抵抗我们没有选择”(“...there was no alternative but to protest”)，同时他号召人们采取非暴力的

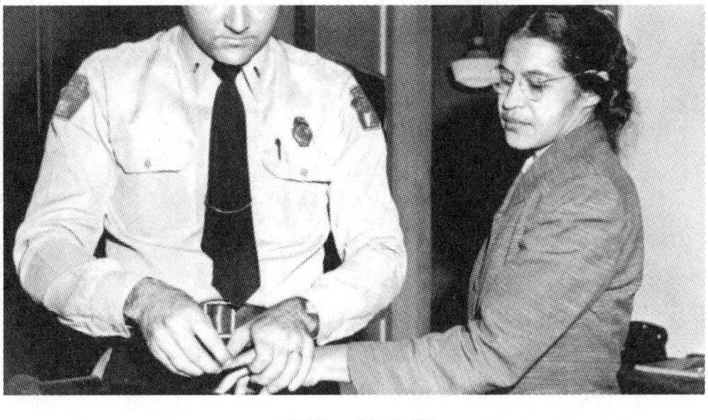

罗莎·帕克斯

形式抵抗。1956 年 6 月 4 日，蒙哥马利地区联邦法庭作出裁决，裁定亚拉巴马州的公交种族隔离法违宪。1956 年 11 月 13 日，美国最高法院支持了联邦地区法庭的裁决，认定蒙哥马利市的公交种族隔离法违宪。蒙哥马利巴士抵制运动展现了非暴力运动的力量。在蒙哥马利巴士抵制运动之后，非暴力主义在美国迅速发展，成了美国民权运动的中流砥柱。

六、华盛顿大游行

1963 年 8 月 28 日，25 万美国民众(其中 1/4 为白人)聚集在首都华盛顿市中心国家广场(National Mall)的大草坪上，呼吁结束一切形式的歧视，让非裔美国人享有与白人一样的公民权利和经济权利。这场大游行的口号是“为了工作与自由而在华盛顿游行(March on Washington for Jobs and Freedom)”，是由众多民权、劳工以及宗教团体共同组织的，马丁·路德·金在位于华盛顿的林肯纪念堂前，发表了著名的演讲——《我有一个梦想》。华盛顿大游行为推动 1964 年《民权法案》和 1965 年《投票权法案》的通过作出了巨大贡献。1964 年，约翰逊(Lyndon Baines Johnson)总统签署了具有历史意义的《民权法》(*Civil Rights Act*)，禁止在就业、公共场所以及其他生活领域实行歧视。马丁·路德·金参加了法案的签署仪式。

1963 年华盛顿大游行中的马丁·路德·金与其他民权运动领袖

七、美国南部诸州(Deep South)

马丁·路德·金在《我有一个梦想》的演讲中提及的佐治亚(Georgia)、亚拉巴马(Alabama)、密西西比(Mississippi)、路易斯安那(Louisiana)和南卡罗来纳州(South Carolina)，在美国也被称为深南诸州(Deep South)。深南诸州早期是典型的奴隶制农业经济，以种植园为生产单位，以棉花、糖、烟草为主要农作物，以非洲黑奴为主要劳动力，黑人被作为商品任意奴役、买卖和伤害。早期的深南诸州充斥着白人至上的思想，是美国种族歧视和种族隔离最严重的地区，也是美国最保守的地区。

八、美国第二次女权主义运动浪潮

美国的第二次女权主义运动浪潮(the second wave of American feminism)从20世纪60年代开始到80年代末结束。第一次美国女权主义运动主要是争取选举权的女权斗争，而第二次美国女权主义运动则更多地关注女性在社会和家庭受到的不公正待遇。“二战”以后，男性重新成为劳动力的主力，而女性被期望回归家庭，重新担当家庭主妇和母亲角色。然而，战争期间，女性通过工作获得了独立与尊严，不愿意再次回到男性的统治之下，这导致了第二次女权主义运动的爆发。1963年贝蒂·弗里丹(Betty Friedan)出版了《女性的奥秘》(*The Feminine Mystique*)一书，讨论了20世纪60年代美国白人中产阶级女性普遍的不快乐这个“没有名字的问题(unnamed problem)”，指出广告业和教育系统的缺陷将女性困据于家庭生活中，使她们丧失了自己的身份和个性。这本书深深触动了广大女性，成千上万的白人中产阶级妇女投身到女权主义运动中，这标志着第二次女权主义运动浪潮的开始。第二次女权主义运动关注的问题主要有同工同酬、生殖权利、家庭暴力和工作场所安全等问题。此后，一系列法案的颁布标志着这场运动取得了巨大的成功：1963年的《同工同酬法》(the *Equal Pay Act*)、1964年的《民权法》第七章(*Title VII of the Civil Rights Act*)、1972年和1974年的《妇女教育公平法》(*The Women's Educational Equity Act*)、1970年的《民权法》第十章(*Title X of the Civil Rights Act*)，1974年的《平等信贷机会法》(*The Equal Credit Opportunity Act*)和1978年的《怀孕歧视法》(*Pregnancy Discrimination Act*)等。这些法令为更大程度地实现男女平等提供了保障。美国的第二次女权主义运动浪潮使得妇女在许多领域成为主流，但同时也带来了一些问题，比如片面和偏激地对待男女差别、贫困单身母亲增加、居高不下的离婚率等。

第二节　文本阅读

——《我有一个梦想》

一、文本导读

1963年8月28日，马丁·路德·金在华盛顿特区林肯纪念堂的台阶上面对25万民众发表了著名演讲《我有一个梦想》，呼吁结束对美国黑人的歧视，实现真正的种族平等。这次演讲无疑是美国民权运动的高光时刻，表达了美国黑人对自由和平等的强烈愿望。马丁·路德·金在演讲一开始就谈到了亚伯拉罕·林肯(Abraham Lincoln)的《解放黑人奴隶宣言》为黑人提供了“伟大的希望之光”，让他们摆脱奴隶制的束缚。但是美国黑人没有结束“漫长的囚禁之夜”的生活，没有获得真正意义上的自由，而是“在美国社会的角落里苦苦挣扎”，所以他梦想建立一个真正意义上的所有公民，无论肤色、种族，都享有自由和平等的国家，一个充满公平和正义的国家，一个不是以肤色而以品格评价优劣的国家，而美国要想成为一个伟大的国家，这些梦想就一定要实现。

这篇演讲不仅以其历史重要性而闻名，而且以其卓越的演说技巧而闻名。在演讲中马丁·路德·金熟练地运用象征、隐喻、比喻、重复、典故及其他修辞手段，该演讲被认为是20世纪最伟大、最著名的演讲之一，同时也是一篇优秀的文学作品。演讲中大量运用了隐喻，比如银行的“支票”。这里的银行是美国的隐喻，也是美国向其公民提供的正义的隐喻，而美国黑人因为肤色，而被以“资金不足”为由拒绝从银行“兑现”支票。其他隐喻，如岛屿、海洋、山谷、岩石、夏天、秋天、梦想等都反映了美国社会的现状。演讲中也大量用到了象征的手法。“光明”象征希望，“黑暗”象征绝望，“美国”象征着“对黑人的隔离和歧视”，“黑人”象征着“被迫害和歧视”，“林肯”象征着解放，“梦”象征着美国民族的梦想。同时重复和排比的运用使得演讲铿锵有力、掷地有声，极具号召力和感染力。

二、《我有一个梦想》原文①

I am happy to join with you today in what will go down in history as the greatest demonstration

① https://www.usconstitution.net/dream.html.

for freedom in the history of our nation.

Five score years ago, a great American, in whose symbolic shadow we stand today, signed the Emancipation Proclamation. This momentous decree came as a great beacon light of hope to millions of Negro slaves who had been seared in the flames of withering injustice. It came as a joyous daybreak to end the long night of their captivity.

But one hundred years later, the Negro still is not free. One hundred years later, the life of the Negro is still sadly crippled by the manacles of segregation and the chains of discrimination. One hundred years later, the Negro lives on a lonely island of poverty in the midst of a vast ocean of material prosperity. One hundred years later, the Negro is still languishing in the corners of American society and finds himself an exile in his own land. So we have come here today to dramatize a shameful condition.

In a sense we have come to our nation's capital to cash a check. When the architects of our republic wrote the magnificent words of the *Constitution* and the *Declaration of Independence*, they were signing a promissory note to which every American was to fall heir. This note was a promise that all men, yes, black men as well as white men, would be guaranteed the unalienable rights of life, liberty, and the pursuit of happiness.

It is obvious today that America has defaulted on this promissory note insofar as her citizens of color are concerned. Instead of honoring this sacred obligation, America has given the Negro people a bad check, a check which has come back marked "insufficient funds". But we refuse to believe that the bank of justice is bankrupt. We refuse to believe that there are insufficient funds in the great vaults of opportunity of this nation. So we have come to cash this check — a check that will give us upon demand the riches of freedom and the security of justice. We have also come to this hallowed spot to remind America of the fierce urgency of now. This is no time to engage in the luxury of cooling off or to take the tranquilizing drug of gradualism. Now is the time to make real the promises of democracy. Now is the time to rise from the dark and desolate valley of segregation to the sunlit path of racial justice. Now is the time to lift our nation from the quick sands of racial injustice to the solid rock of brotherhood. Now is the time to make justice a reality for all of God's children.

It would be fatal for the nation to overlook the urgency of the moment. This sweltering summer of the Negro's legitimate discontent will not pass until there is an invigorating autumn of freedom and equality. Nineteen sixty-three is not an end, but a beginning. Those who hope that the Negro needed to blow off steam and will now be content will have a rude awakening if the nation returns to business as usual. There will be neither rest nor tranquility in America until the Negro is granted his citizenship rights. The whirlwinds of revolt will continue to shake the foundations of our nation until the bright day of justice emerges.

But there is something that I must say to my people who stand on the warm threshold which leads into the palace of justice. In the process of gaining our rightful place we must not be guilty of wrongful deeds. Let us not seek to satisfy our thirst for freedom by drinking from the cup of bitterness and hatred.

We must forever conduct our struggle on the high plane of dignity and discipline. We must not allow our creative protest to degenerate into physical violence. Again and again we must rise to the majestic heights of meeting physical force with soul force. The marvelous new militancy which has engulfed the Negro community must not lead us to a distrust of all white people, for many of our white brothers, as evidenced by their presence here today, have come to realize that their destiny is tied up with our destiny. They have come to realize that their freedom is inextricably bound to our freedom. We cannot walk alone.

As we walk, we must make the pledge that we shall always march ahead. We cannot turn back. There are those who are asking the devotees of civil rights, "When will you be satisfied?"

We can never be satisfied as long as the Negro is the victim of the unspeakable horrors of police brutality. We can never be satisfied, as long as our bodies, heavy with the fatigue of travel, cannot gain lodging in the motels of the highways and the hotels of the cities. We cannot be satisfied as long as the Negro's basic mobility is from a smaller ghetto to a larger one. We can never be satisfied as long as our children are stripped of their selfhood and robbed of their dignity by signs stating "For Whites Only". We cannot be satisfied as long as a Negro in Mississippi cannot vote and a Negro in New York believes he has nothing for which to vote. No, no, we are not satisfied, and we will not be satisfied until justice rolls down like waters and righteousness like a mighty stream.

I am not unmindful that some of you have come here out of great trials and tribulations. Some of you have come fresh from narrow jail cells. Some of you have come from areas where your quest for freedom left you battered by the storms of persecution and staggered by the winds of police brutality. You have been the veterans of creative suffering. Continue to work with the faith that unearned suffering is redemptive.

Go back to Mississippi, go back to Alabama, go back to South Carolina, go back to Georgia, go back to Louisiana, go back to the slums and ghettos of our northern cities, knowing that somehow this situation can and will be changed. Let us not wallow in the valley of despair.

I say to you today, my friends, so even though we face the difficulties of today and tomorrow, I still have a dream. It is a dream deeply rooted in the American dream.

I have a dream that one day this nation will rise up and live out the true meaning of its creed: "We hold these truths to be self-evident: that all men are created equal."

I have a dream that one day on the red hills of Georgia the sons of former slaves and the sons of former slave owners will be able to sit down together at the table of brotherhood.

I have a dream that one day even the state of Mississippi, a state sweltering with the heat of injustice, sweltering with the heat of oppression, will be transformed into an oasis of freedom and justice.

I have a dream that my four little children will one day live in a nation where they will not be judged by the color of their skin but by the content of their character.

I have a dream today.

I have a dream that one day, down in Alabama, with its vicious racists, with its governor having his lips dripping with the words of interposition and nullification; one day right there in Alabama, little black boys and black girls will be able to join hands with little white boys and white girls as sisters and brothers.

I have a dream today.

I have a dream that one day every valley shall be exalted, every hill and mountain shall be made low, the rough places will be made plain, and the crooked places will be made straight, and the glory of the Lord shall be revealed, and all flesh shall see it together.

This is our hope. This is the faith that I go back to the South with. With this faith we will be able to hew out of the mountain of despair a stone of hope. With this faith we will be able to transform the jangling discords of our nation into a beautiful symphony of brotherhood. With this faith we will be able to work together, to pray together, to struggle together, to go to jail together, to stand up for freedom together, knowing that we will be free one day.

This will be the day when all of God's children will be able to sing with a new meaning, "My country, 'tis of thee, sweet land of liberty, of thee I sing. Land where my fathers died, land of the pilgrim's pride, from every mountainside, let freedom ring."

And if America is to be a great nation this must become true. So let freedom ring from the prodigious hilltops of New Hampshire. Let freedom ring from the mighty mountains of New York. Let freedom ring from the heightening Alleghenies of Pennsylvania!

Let freedom ring from the snowcapped Rockies of Colorado!

Let freedom ring from the curvaceous slopes of California!

But not only that; let freedom ring from Stone Mountain of Georgia!

Let freedom ring from Lookout Mountain of Tennessee!

Let freedom ring from every hill and molehill of Mississippi. From every mountainside, let freedom ring.

And when this happens, when we allow freedom to ring, when we let it ring from every village and every hamlet, from every state and every city, we will be able to speed up that day when all of God's children, black men and white men, Jews and Gentiles, Protestants and Catholics, will be able to join hands and sing in the words of the old Negro spiritual, "Free at last! Free at last! Thank God Almighty, we are free at last!"

Vocabulary

batter *v.* 连续猛击；殴打
beacon *n.* 灯塔；指路明灯；指引者；楷模
decree *n.* 法令；政令
discord *n.* 不协和音；不和；纷争
engulf *v.* 吞没；吞噬；吞食
exile *n.* 被流放者；背井离乡者
gradualism *n.* (社会改革上的)渐进主义，渐进主义政策
hew *v.* 砍，劈
inalienable *adj.* 不可剥夺(或分割)的
inextricably *adv.* 密不可分地，息息相关地
interposition *n.* 提出(异议)；干预
invigorating *adj.* 焕发精神的；精力充沛的
languish *v.* 长期受苦；受煎熬；变得衰弱
manacle *n.* 手铐；脚镣；镣铐
momentous *adj.* 具有历史意义的；重大的；重要的
nullification *n.* 无效，废除，废弃；(美)州对国会法令的拒绝执行
persecution *n.* 迫害；逼迫
quicksand *n.* 流沙；难以摆脱的困境；危险局面
redemptive *adj.* 赎回的；救赎的；拯救的
sear *v.* 烧灼；灼伤
segregation *n.* (对不同种族、宗教或性别的人所采取的)隔离并区别对待
sweltering *adj.* 闷热的；炎热的；热得难受的
tranquility *n.* 平和；平静；镇静；宁静
tribulation *n.* 大灾难；患难；苦难
vault *n.* (尤指银行的)金库，保险库

Reading comprehension exercises

I. Choose the best answer to the following questions.

1. The main focus of Martin Luther King's speech is on
   A) Celebrating the anniversary of *The Emancipation Proclamation.*
   B) Convincing everyone to live in peace and tranquility.
   C) Ending segregation and racial injustice in America.
   D) Getting more money for America's black population.
2. Which meaning is not what the term "Dream" refers to in Martin Luther King's speech?
   A) "Dream" refers to the American dream.
   B) It means his expectation and needs to avoid racial discrimination between white and black peoples.
   C) He has a dream of equality and justice, brotherhood and freedom and serenity.
   D) He wants to win Nobel Prize.
3. What analogy does Martin Luther King use in order to illustrate America's broken promise of life, liberty, and the pursuit of happiness to "her citizens of color"?
   A) A check that has come back marked "insufficient funds".
   B) A bucket tied to a frayed rope over a bottomless well.
   C) A crossroads in a dark forest.
   D) A vast stretch of sand occasionally interrupted by lakes.
4. "... many of our white brothers... have come to realize that their freedom is inextricably bound to our freedom." What does "inextricably bound" mean here?
   A) Unable to be excused or pardoned.
   B) Unable to be separated or disconnected.
   C) Unable to be solved or explained.
   D) Unable to be forgotten or unseen.
5. In Paragraph 11, Martin Luther King addresses those in the audience who have been unjustly imprisoned and "battered by...police brutality". What advice does he offer to these people?
   A) Seek revenge at all costs.
   B) Recruit lawyers and sue your local police departments.
   C) Return home and continue to work for justice.
   D) Pray that God will forgive those who persecuted you.

II. Comprehension questions

1. What dream does Martin Luther King have? How does he want to fulfill it?
2. How is Martin Luther King's dream connected with the "American Dream"?
3. What is the historical significance of Martin Luther King's speech?
4. Do you think that Martin Luther King's goal for America has been reached? Why or why not?

第三节 延伸阅读

——《女性的奥秘》节选

一、文本导读

贝蒂·弗里丹(Betty Friedan)是美国第二次女权主义运动浪潮的领军人物，她于1963年出版的《女性的奥秘》(*The Feminine Mystique*)是女权主义里程碑式的著作。贝蒂·弗里丹在《女性的奥秘》一书中分析和讨论了美国20世纪五六十年代社会推崇的幸福的家庭主妇形象(upper-middle-class-suburban-homemaker-mother housewife)，即女性满足于妻子和母亲的社会角色，或者说可以通过家务、婚姻、性被动和独自抚养孩子来获得女性气质(femininity)或者是女性的神秘感(feminine mystique)。美国社会的专栏、书籍、文章、广告都在强化这种妥善履行家务职责的家庭主妇形象，使得女性也以获得这种女性的神秘感为人生目标。

然而弗里丹通过访谈和调查发现，很多看上去幸福的家庭主妇们并不快乐，她们身心疲惫，甚至抑郁成疾，需要求助于心理医生、镇静剂和酒精来缓解空虚感。家庭主妇们不快乐的主要原因是为了迎合社会塑造的女性气质或者说女性的神秘感，这种不快乐是"没有名字的问题"，是难以言说的痛苦。

弗里丹指出女性的神秘感是一种错误的观念，女性在社会中的角色不是仅仅成为妻子、母亲和家庭主妇。这种神秘感赋予美国女性的新形象是一个陈旧的形象："家庭主妇"，而成为家庭主妇其实是一种社会的倒退。在20世纪20年代，甚至更早，(资产阶级)女性就开始摆脱维多利亚时代的旧价值观，走出家庭，拥有独立的职业和生活。"二战"期间，因为数百万男性参军，女性接管了许多男性的职业，在各种工作中扮演了重要的角色。然而50年代以后，独立的女性形象被弱化，取而代之的是幸福的家庭主妇的形象和女性神秘感的概念，女性从广阔的社会退回到了家庭，把成为贤妻良母当作人生目标，美国妇女几十年来为自由和平等做出的努力和牺牲又回到了原点。

弗里丹受亚伯拉罕·马斯洛(Abraham Maslow)心理需求理论的影响，认为女性的神秘感否定了女性基本的人类成长需求，正是这种被抑制的需求使得女性不快乐，孩子们也因为母亲们的不满足感和神经质而受到影响。弗里丹认为个人成就感来自身份的认同，而职业是获得身份认同的主要途径，无论是男性还是女性。她呼吁社会恢复20世纪20至40年代独立的职业女性形象。

《女性的奥秘》一书唤醒了许多读者，让他们意识到，社会舆论塑造的中产阶级郊区家庭妇女形象是一种伤害妇女、家庭和社会的错误观念，它剥夺了女性发挥自己潜力的机会，使女性陷入苦闷和彷徨。《女性的奥秘》促使了新一代美国妇女的觉醒，极大地推动了20世纪六七十年代美国妇女解放运动的发展，是美国女权主义的代表作。

本文节选的是《女性的奥秘》第一章的部分内容。在这一章中，弗里丹通过调查，列举了大量的数据和实例，包括自身的经历，描述和讨论了这个普遍存在于美国中产阶级白人妇女中的"没有名字的问题"。文章一开始就谈到20世纪50年代末，1400万女孩在17岁之前订婚，平均结婚年龄已降至20岁，女性接受高度教育的比例从1920年的47%下降到1958年的35%，而上大学的目标也多是为婚姻增加筹码。整个社会舆论和教育系统塑造出美国女性梦寐以求的形象——郊区家庭主妇，而数以百万计的妇女则按照那些描述中的家庭妇女们的完美生活而生活："她们唯一的理想是当贤妻良母；她们最大的抱负是生5个孩子和拥有一幢漂亮的房子；她们的唯一战斗是找到一位丈夫，并牢牢拴住他(Their only dream was to be perfect wives and mothers; their highest ambition to have five children and a beautiful house; their only fight to get and keep their husbands)。"①但是弗里丹通过调查发现，很多妇女都会感觉空虚，不完整，被"没有名字的问题"困扰。然而当美国妇女实际上不幸福这一事实被《纽约时报》《新闻周刊》等媒体公开以后，几乎每一个谈论这件事的人都认为它不值一提。人们提出了各种理由，比如家政服务不到位，接送孩子路途太远，以及接受教育使得女性在担任家庭主妇这一角色时感到不快乐等。人们还为此提供了各种解决方案，比如提供更实际的家政培训，取消大学对女性的招生等。最终这个问题不了了之，人们甚至批判女性有舒适的生活却依然不满足。

弗里丹不能接受那种认为美国妇女能享受其他时代、其他国家的妇女连做梦也没有想到的生活，因而女性就不存在问题的回答。她认为这个无法明言的问题，并不是女性气质丧失或接受教育太多或家庭生活要求过高的问题，而是她们思想中的那些对女性气质、女性奥秘的错误思想以及对事实错误的理解导致的，这些错误的思想和理解成为了束缚她们

① Friedan, B. The Feminine Mystique[M]. New York: W. W. Norton & Company, 2001: 47.

的锁链。这些锁链很难被发现，也很难摆脱。在本章的最后一段，弗里丹呼吁人们关注女性的内心呼声，对于广大女性而言，“我想要的不仅仅是我的丈夫、我的孩子和我的家(I want something more than my husband and my children and my home)”。

二、原文节选

Excerpts from *The Feminine Mystique* (1963)①

Betty Friedan

The problem lay buried, unspoken, for many years in the minds of American women. It was a strange stirring, a sense of dissatisfaction, a yearning that women suffered in the middle of the twentieth century in the United States. Each suburban wife struggled with it alone. As she made the beds, shopped for groceries, matched slipcover material, ate peanut butter sandwiches with her children, chauffeured Cub Scouts and Brownies, lay beside her husband at night — she was afraid to ask even of herself the silent question — "Is this all?"

For over fifteen years there was no word of this yearning in the millions of words written about women, for women, in all the columns, books and articles by experts telling women their role was to seek fulfillment as wives and mothers. Over and over women heard in voices of tradition and of Freudian sophistication that they could desire no greater destiny than to glory in their own femininity. Experts told them how to catch a man and keep him, how to breastfeed children and handle their toilet training, how to cope with sibling rivalry and adolescent rebellion; how to buy a dishwasher, bake bread, cook gourmet snails, and build a swimming pool with their own hands; how to dress, look, and act more feminine and make marriage more exciting; how to keep their husbands from dying young and their sons from growing into delinquents. They were taught to pity the neurotic, unfeminine, unhappy women who wanted to be poets or physicists or presidents. They learned that truly feminine women do not want careers, higher education, political rights — the independence and the opportunities that the old-fashioned feminists fought for. Some women, in their forties and fifties, still remembered painfully giving up those dreams, but most of the younger women no longer even thought about them. A thousand expert voices applauded their femininity, their adjustment, their new maturity. All they had to do was

① Friedan, B. The Feminine Mystique [M]. W. W. Norton & Company, 2001: 57-78.

devote their lives from earliest girlhood to finding a husband and bearing children.

By the end of the nineteen-fifties, the average marriage age of women in America dropped to 20, and was still dropping, into the teens. Fourteen million girls were engaged by 17. The proportion of women attending college in comparison with men dropped from 47 percent in 1920 to 35 percent in 1958. A century earlier, women had fought for higher education; now girls went to college to get a husband. By the mid-fifties, 60 percent dropped out of college to marry, or because they were afraid too much education would be a marriage bar. Colleges built dormitories for "married students," but the students were almost always the husbands. A new degree was instituted for the wives—"Ph. T." (Putting Husband Through).

Then American girls began getting married in high school. And the women's magazines, deploring the unhappy statistics about these young marriages, urged that courses on marriage, and marriage counselors, be installed in the high schools. Girls started going steady at twelve and thirteen, in junior high....

By the end of the fifties, the United States birthrate was overtaking India's. The birth-control movement, renamed Planned Parenthood, was asked to find a method whereby women who had been advised that a third or fourth baby would be born dead or defective might have it anyhow. Statisticians were especially astounded at the fantastic increase in the number of babies among college women. Where once they had two children, now they had four, five, six. Women who had once wanted careers were now making careers out of having babies....

In a New York hospital, a woman had a nervous breakdown when she found she could not breastfeed her baby. In other hospitals, women dying of cancer refused a drug which research had proved might save their lives: its side effects were said to be unfeminine. "If I have only one life, let me live it as a blonde," a larger-than-life- sized picture of a pretty, vacuous woman proclaimed from newspaper, magazine, and drugstore ads. And across America, three out of every ten women dyed their hair blonde. They ate a chalk called Metrecal, instead of food, to shrink to the size of the thin young models. Department-store buyers reported that American women, since 1939, had become three and four sizes smaller. "Women are out to fit the clothes, instead of vice-versa," one buyer said.

Interior decorators were designing kitchens with mosaic murals and original paintings, for kitchens were once again the center of women's lives. Home sewing became a million-dollar industry. Many women no longer left their homes, except to shop, chauffeur their children, or attend a social engagement with their husbands. Girls were growing up in America without ever having jobs outside the home. In the late fifties, a sociological phenomenon was suddenly remarked: a third of American women now worked, but most were no longer young and very few were pursuing careers. They were married women who held part-time jobs, selling or secretarial, to put their husbands through school, their sons through college, or to help pay the mortgage. Or they were widows supporting families. Fewer and fewer women were entering professional work. The shortages in the nursing, social work, and teaching professions caused crises in almost every American city. Concerned over the Soviet Union's lead in the space race, scientists noted that America's greatest source of unused brain-power was women. But girls would not study physics: it was "unfeminine." A girl refused a science fellowship at Johns Hopkins to take a job in a real-estate office. All she wanted, she said, was what every other American girl wanted—to get married, have four children and live in a nice house in a nice suburb.

The suburban housewife — she was the dream image of the young American women and the envy, it was said, of women all over the world. The American housewife — freed by science and labor-saving appliances from the drudgery, the dangers of childbirth and the illnesses of her grandmother. She was healthy, beautiful, educated, concerned only about her husband, her children, her home. She had found true feminine fulfillment. As a housewife and mother, she was respected as a full and equal partner to man in his world. She was free to choose automobiles, clothes, appliances, supermarkets; she had everything that women ever dreamed of.

In the fifteen years after World War II, this mystique of feminine fulfillment became the cherished and self-perpetuating core of contemporary American culture. Millions of women lived their lives in the image of those pretty pictures of the American suburban housewife, kissing their husbands goodbye in front of the picture window, depositing their stationwagonsful of children at school, and smiling as they ran the new electric waxer over the spotless kitchen floor. They baked their own bread, sewed their own and their children's clothes, kept their new washing machines and dryers running all day. They changed the sheets on the beds twice a week instead of once, took the rughoolag class in adult education, and pitied their poor frustrated mothers, who had dreamed of having a career. Their only dream was to be perfect wives and mothers; their highest ambition to have five children and a beautiful house, their only fight to get and keep their husbands. They had no thought for the unfeminine problems of the world outside the home; they wanted the men to make the major decisions. They gloried in their role as women, and wrote proudly on the census blank: "Occupation: housewife."

For over fifteen years, the words written for women, and the words women used when they talked to each other, while their husbands sat on the other side of the room and talked shop or politics or septic tanks, were about problems with their children, or how to keep their husbands happy, or improve their children's school, or cook chicken or make slipcovers. Nobody argued whether women were inferior or superior to men; they were simply different. Words like "emancipation" and "career" sounded strange and embarrassing; no one had used them for years. When a Frenchwoman named Simone de Beauvoir wrote a book called *The Second Sex*, an American critic commented that she obviously "didn't know what life was all about," and besides, she was talking about French women. The "woman problem" in America no longer existed.

If a woman had a problem in the 1950's and 1960's, she knew that something must be wrong with her marriage, or with herself. Other women were satisfied with their lives, she thought. What kind of a woman was she if she did not feel this mysterious fulfillment waxing the kitchen floor? She was so ashamed to admit her dissatisfaction that she never knew how many other women shared it. If she tried to tell her husband, he didn't understand what she was talking about. She did not really understand it herself....

But on an April morning in 1959, I heard a mother of four, having coffee with four other mothers in a suburban development fifteen miles from New York, say in a tone of quiet desperation, "the problem." And the others knew, without words, that she was not talking about a problem with her husband, or her children, or her home. Suddenly they realized they all shared the same problem, the problem that has no name. They began, hesitantly, to talk about it. Later, after they had picked up their children at nursery school and taken them home to nap, two of the women cried, in sheer relief, just to know they were not alone.

Gradually I came to realize that the problem that has no name was shared by countless women in America. As a magazine writer I often interviewed women about problems with their children, or their marriages, or their houses, or their communities. But after a while I began to recognize the telltale signs of this other problem. I saw the same signs in suburban ranch houses and split-levels on Long Island and in New Jersey and Westchester County; in colonial houses in a small Massachusetts town; on patios in Memphis; in suburban and city apartments; in living rooms in the Midwest. Sometimes I sensed the problem, not as a reporter, but as a suburban housewife, for during this time I was also bringing up my own three children in Rockland County, New York. I heard echoes of the problem in college dormitories and semiprivate maternity wards, at PTA meetings and luncheons of the League of Women Voters, at suburban cocktail parties, in station wagons waiting for trains, and in snatches of conversation overheard at Schrafft's. The groping words I heard from other women, on quiet afternoons when children were at school or on quiet evenings when husbands worked late, I think I understood first as a woman long before I understood their larger social and psychological implications.

Just what was this problem that has no name? What were the words women used when they tried to express it? Sometimes a woman would say "I feel empty somehow... incomplete." Or she would say, "I feel as if I don't exist."...

A mother of four who left college at nineteen to get married told me:

> *I've tried everything women are supposed to do — hobbies, gardening, pickling, canning, being very social with my neighbors, joining committees, running PTA teas. I can do it all, and I like it, but it doesn't leave you anything to think about—any feeling of who you are. I never had any career ambitions. All I wanted was to get married and have four children. I love the kids and Bob and my home. There's no problem you can even put a name to. But I'm desperate. I begin to feel I have no personality. I'm a server of food and putter-on of pants and a bed maker, somebody who can be called on when you want something. But who am I?*

In 1960, the problem that has no name burst like a boil through the image of the happy American housewife.... The actual unhappiness of the American housewife was suddenly being reported — from *the New York Times* and *Newsweek* to *Good Housekeeping* and CBS Television

(“The Trapped Housewife”), although almost everybody who talked about it found some superficial reason to dismiss it. It was attributed to incompetent appliance repairmen (*New York Times*), or the distances children must be chauffeured in the suburbs (*Time*), or too much PTA (*Redbook*). Some said it was the old problem — education: more and more women had education, which naturally made them unhappy in their role as housewives....

Home economists suggested more realistic preparation for housewives, such as high-school workshops in home appliances. College educators suggested more discussion groups on home management and the family, to prepare women for the adjustment to domestic life....

A male humorist joked in Harper’s Bazaar (July, 1960) that the problem could be solved by taking away woman’s right to vote....

A number of educators suggested seriously that women no longer be admitted to the four-year colleges and universities: in the growing college crisis, the education which girls could not use as housewives was more urgently needed than ever by boys to do the work of the atomic age.

The problem was dismissed by telling the housewife she doesn’t realize how lucky she is — her own boss, no time clock, no junior executive gunning for her job. What if she isn’t happy — does she think men are happy in this world? Does she really, secretly, still want to be a man? Doesn’t she know yet how lucky she is to be a woman?

The problem was also, and finally, dismissed by shrugging that there are NO solutions: this is what being a woman means, and what is wrong with American women that they can’t accept their role gracefully?...

Even so, most men, and some women, still did not know that this problem was real. But those who had faced it honestly knew that all the superficial remedies, the sympathetic advice, the scolding words and the cheering words were somehow drowning the problem in unreality. A bitter laugh was beginning to be heard from American women. They were admired, envied, pitied, theorized over until they were sick of it, offered drastic solutions or silly choices that no one could take seriously. They got all kinds of advice from the growing armies of marriage and child-guidance counselors, psychotherapists, and armchair psychologists, on how to adjust to their role as housewives. No other road to fulfillment was offered to American women in the middle of the twentieth century. Most adjusted to their role and suffered or ignored the problem that has no name. It can be less painful for a woman, not to hear the strange, dissatisfied voice stirring within her.

It is NO longer possible to ignore that voice, to dismiss the desperation of so many American women. This is not what being a woman means, no matter what the experts say. For human suffering there is a reason; perhaps the reason has not been found because the right questions have not been asked, or pressed far enough. I do not accept the answer that there is no problem because American women have luxuries that women in other times and lands never dreamed of; part of the strange newness of the problem is that it cannot be understood in terms of the age-old material problems of man: poverty, sickness, hunger, cold. The women who suffer this problem have a hunger that food cannot fill. It persists in women whose husbands are struggling intern and law clerks, or prosperous doctors and lawyers; in wives of workers and executives who make $5,000 a year or $50,000. It is not caused by lack of material advantages; it may not even be felt by women preoccupied with desperate problems of hunger, poverty or illness. And women who think it will be solved by more money, a bigger house, a second car, moving to a better suburb, often discover it gets worse.

It is no longer possible today to blame the problem on loss of femininity: to say that education and independence and equality with men have made American women unfeminine. I have heard so many women try to deny this dissatisfied voice within themselves because it does not fit the pretty picture of femininity the experts have given them. I think, in fact, that this is the first clue to the mystery; the problem cannot be understood in the generally accepted terms by which scientists have studied women, doctors have treated them, counselors have advised them, and writers have written about them. Women who suffer this problem, in whom this voice is stirring, have lived their whole lives in the pursuit of feminine fulfillment. They are not career women (although career women may have other problems); they are women whose greatest ambition has been marriage and children. For the oldest of these women, these daughters of the American middle class, no other dream was possible. The ones in their forties and fifties who once had other dreams gave them up and threw themselves joyously into life as housewives. For the youngest, the new wives and mothers, this was the only dream. They are the ones who quit high school and college to marry, or marked time in some job in which they had no real interest until they married. These women are very "feminine" in the usual sense, and yet they still suffer the problem....

The fact is that NO one today is muttering angrily about "women's rights," even though more and more women have gone to college....

It is easy to see the concrete details that trap the suburban housewife, the continual demands on her time. But the chains that bind her in her trap are chains in her own mind and spirit. They are chains made up of mistaken ideas and misinterpreted facts, of incomplete truths and unreal choices. They are not easily seen and not easily shaken off.

How can any woman see the whole truth within the bounds of her own life? How can she believe that voice inside herself, when it denies the conventional, accepted truths by which she has been living? And yet the women I have talked to, who are finally listening to that inner voice, seem in some incredible way to be groping through to a truth that has defied the experts.

I think the experts in a great many fields have been holding pieces of that truth under their microscopes for a long time without realizing it. I found pieces of it in certain new research and theoretical developments in psychological, social and biological science whose implications for women seem never to have been examined. I found many clues by talking to suburban doctors, gynecologists, obstetricians, child-guidance clinicians, pediatricians, high-school guidance counselors, college professors, marriage counselors, psychiatrists and ministers-questioning them not on their theories, but on their actual experience in treating American women. I became aware of a growing body of evidence, much of which has not been reported publicly because it does not fit current modes of thought about women — evidence which throws into question the standards of feminine normality, feminine adjustment, feminine fulfillment, and feminine maturity by which most women are still trying to live.

I began to see in a strange new light the American return to early marriage and the large families that are causing the population explosion; the recent movement to natural childbirth and breastfeeding; suburban conformity, and the new neuroses, character pathologies and sexual problems being reported by the doctors. I began to see new dimensions to old problems that have long been taken for granted among women: menstrual difficulties, sexual frigidity, promiscuity, pregnancy fears, childbirth depression, the high incidence of emotional breakdown and suicide among women in their twenties and thirties, the menopause crises, the so-called passivity and immaturity of American men, the discrepancy between women's tested intellectual abilities in childhood and their adult achievement, the changing incidence of adult sexual orgasm in American women, and persistent problems in psychotherapy and in women's education.

If I am right, the problem that has no name stirring in the minds of so many American women today is not a matter of loss of femininity or too much education, or the demands of domesticity. It is far more important than anyone recognizes. It is the key to these other new and old problems which have been torturing women and their husbands and children, and puzzling their doctors and educators for years. It may well be the key to our future as a nation and a culture. We can no longer ignore that voice within women that says: "I want something more than my husband and my children and my home."

Comprehension questions

1. What is "the problem that has no name" of which Friedan writes?
2. Why does Friedan believe that women in America in the 1950s and early 1960s, despite the era's prosperity and stability, are fundamentally unhappy?
3. Are the ideas promoted in the book *The Feminine Mystique* popular in China today?
4. If you were a female student, would you like to be a housewife after graduation from college? Why or Why not?
5. If you were a male student, would you like your future wife to be a housewife? Why or why not?
6. Someone says that too much education brings about "the problem of unknown"? Do you agree with this idea? Why or why not?
7. If you were a policy-maker, what measures would you take to help women keep the balance between being a career woman and being a mother?

第六章
美国的环保运动

第一节 时 代 背 景

一、蕾切尔·卡逊(Rachel Carson)

蕾切尔·卡逊，美国海洋生物学家、作家、现代环保主义奠基人，美国《时代周刊》评选的20世纪最有影响力的一百人之一。蕾切尔·卡逊1907年出生于美国宾夕法尼亚州，1932年获得约翰斯·霍普金斯大学生物学硕士，后入职美国渔业局(后更名为美国渔业和

海洋生物学家及环保主义者蕾切尔·卡逊

野生动物管理署)，并开始了她的写作生涯。蕾切尔·卡逊的作品以兼顾科学性和文学性著称，其主要作品有《海风下》(*Under the Sea-Wind*, 1941)，《我们周围的海洋》(*The Sea Around Us*, 1952)、《海之边缘》(*The Edge of the Sea*, 1955)，而1962年出版的《寂静的春天》(*Silent Spring*)无疑是她最具影响力的作品，引发了全球对于环境保护的关注，蕾切尔·卡逊本人也因此被誉为环保主义之母。蕾切尔·卡逊的作品细腻传神地描绘了大自然的勃勃生机，深刻揭露了人类活动对于大自然的伤害，更反思了人类该如何与环境和平共处，而不是去征服自然、控制自然。1963年蕾切尔·卡逊入选美国艺术与科学学院院士。1964年4月蕾切尔·卡逊因癌症去世。1980年美国政府追授她总统自由勋章。

二、《寂静的春天》

1962年出版的《寂静的春天》是公认的世界环保主义的奠基之作，引发了全美，乃至全世界对于环境保护的关注。蕾切尔·卡逊通过翔实的调查和实例揭示了过度使用DDT等杀虫剂导致的生态灾难，没有绿树，没有花香，没有鸟鸣，春天一片死寂。《寂静的春天》唤醒了民众及政府的环境保护意识，环保法案陆续出台，环保组织纷纷建立，环保运动如火如荼。1967年，美国建立了环境保护基金，1969年美国国会通过《联邦环境政策法案》，并于1970年成立了环保局。同时，联合国建立了联合国环境规划署、联合国可持续发展委员会等机构，其他知名的环保组织还包括绿色和平组织、世界自然保护基金会、世界自然保护联盟等。霍顿·米夫林出版公司(Houghton Mifflin Company)1994年再版了《寂

《寂静的春天》50周年纪念版(Houghton Mifflin Company)

静的春天》，美国前副总统、著名环保主义人士艾伯特·戈尔（Albert Arnold Gore Jr.）在为其撰写的序言中写道："1964年春天，蕾切尔·卡逊逝世后，一切都很清楚了，她的声音永远不会寂静。她惊醒的不但是我们国家，甚至是整个世界。《寂静的春天》的出版应该恰当地被看成现代环境运动的肇始。"①虽然蕾切尔·卡逊所倡导的环境保护意识已经深入人心，但是经济发展和环境保护之间的矛盾从未消除，人口增长、城市化、工业化给环境带来的压力日益增长，人性的贪婪使得环境保护在利益面前不堪一击，环境保护的道路依旧漫长。

三、DDT

在《寂静的春天》中被反复提到的白色粉末叫DDT，中文名为"滴滴涕"，学名为双对氯苯基三氯乙烷（Dichloro-Diphenyl-Trichloroethane），是一种有机氯类杀虫剂。1874年，奥地利化学家欧特马·勤德勒（Othmar Zeidler）首次合成了DDT。1939年，瑞士化学家保罗·米勒（Paul Muller）发现DDT能迅速杀死蚊子、虱子和农作物害虫。时值第二次世界大战和战后时期，伤寒、霍乱、疟疾等通过蚊虫传染的疾病流行，DDT的使用令蚊虫、苍蝇和虱子得到有效的控制，并使疟疾、伤寒和霍乱等疾病的发病率急剧下降，拯救了成千上万人的生命，于是人们开始大量使用DDT。但在20世纪60年代科学家们发现DDT在环境中非常难降解，并可以在动物脂肪内蓄积。1962年，美国科学家蕾切尔·卡逊在其著作《寂静的春天》中怀疑DDT进入食物链是导致一些食肉和食鱼的鸟接近灭绝的主要原因，因此从20世纪70年代后DDT逐渐被世界各国明令禁止生产和使用，我国也从2007年开始停止生产DDT。

四、西奥多·罗斯福

西奥多·罗斯福（Theodore Roosevelt，1858—1919），美国军事家、政治家、外交家、环保主义者、作家，美国第26任总统。

1882年，西奥多·罗斯福成为纽约州议员，正式踏入政坛。1897年，西奥多·罗斯福任美国海军部副部长，大力推进美国海军现代化建设。在此后爆发的美西战争中，他战功卓著。1898年11月他当选了纽约州长，1900年成为美国副总统，1901年总统麦金莱（William McKinley）遇刺身亡，西奥多·罗斯福继任总统，成为美国史上最年轻的总统，1905年连任。

① 蕾切尔·卡森. 寂静的春天[M]. 吕瑞兰，李长生，译. 上海：上海译文出版社，2014.

西奥多·罗斯福担任总统期间为20世纪初快速发展的美国制定了一系列强有力的政策，为美国成为世界强国奠定了基础，被认为是美国历史上最伟大的总统之一。在内政上，西奥多·罗斯福是一个强势的改革者，打击腐败，强调政府监管，推行公平交易法案，反对行业垄断，推动劳资和解，倡导社会公平，推进食品安全立法和自然资源保护政策。在外交上，西奥多·罗斯福奉行“门罗主义”，实行扩张政策，建设强大军队，干涉南美事务。

在美国，西奥多·罗斯福总统又被称为“自然保护总统”。在任期间致力于保护森林、矿产、石油等资源，制定了一系列环境资源保护政策和措施，成立了国家林业局，初步构建了国家公园体系，建立了大量的自然资源保护区，其中包括5个国家公园、51个联邦鸟类保护区、4个国家野生动物保护区、1亿多英亩的国家森林、18个国家纪念碑等。西奥多·罗斯福总统推行这些自然资源保护的措施，使得自然资源的保护逐步纳入政府的管理之下。

伴随着工业革命的进程，经济发展和环境保护的直接矛盾成为世界性的难题，对快速发展中的中国亦然，西奥多·罗斯福政府对自然资源的保护措施对于我们也有一定的启发和借鉴意义。

西奥多·罗斯福(1858—1919)

第二节 文本阅读

——《寂静的春天》节选

一、文本导读

《寂静的春天》全书共十七章，通过丰富翔实的实例和数据向民众展示了以DDT为代表的人造合成化学药物对水资源、土壤、生物以及人类造成的巨大伤害，以及大自然的报复。因为篇幅的原因我们选取了本书的第一章——“明天的寓言”。在这个寓言里，蕾切尔·卡逊创造了一个宁静的小镇，在这里，所有生命似乎都与周围环境和谐相处(“all life seemed to live in harmony with its surroundings”)，然而小镇的美丽与安宁突然被一种导致死亡和疾病的“奇怪的枯萎病(strange blight)”打破了，而导致这可怕的枯萎病的正是人们自己，是人们的无知和贪婪让无数美国小镇的春天陷入寂静(“silenced the voices of spring in countless towns in America”)。蕾切尔·卡逊在结束这一章时解释说到，这本书将试图探索到底是什么让人们如此彻底地破坏了他们的自然栖息地，以此吸引读者继续阅读后面的章节。在本书的最后一章，蕾切尔·卡逊指出我们必须与其他生物共同分享我们的地球，“控制自然”是一个妄自尊大的产物，如果我们任由合成化学物质在对付昆虫之余来伤害整个环境，那“明天的寓言”就会变成活生生的现实了。

二、原文节选

A Fable for Tomorrow①

Rachel Carson

THERE WAS ONCE a town in the heart of America where all life seemed to live in harmony with its surroundings. The town lay in the midst of a checkerboard of prosperous farms, with fields of grain and hillsides of orchards where, in spring, white clouds of bloom drifted above the green fields. In autumn, oak and maple and birch set up a blaze of color that flamed and flickered across a backdrop of pines. Then foxes barked in the hills and deer silently crossed the fields, half hidden in the mists of the fall mornings.

Along the roads, laurel, viburnum and alder, great ferns and wildflowers delighted the traveler's eye through much of the year. Even in winter the roadsides were places of beauty, where countless birds came to feed on the berries and on the seed heads of the dried weeds rising above the snow. The countryside was, in fact, famous for the abundance and variety of its bird life, and when the flood of migrants was pouring through in spring and fall, people traveled from great distances to observe them. Others came to fish the streams, which flowed clear and cold out of the hills and contained shady pools where trout lay. So it had been from the days many

① Carson, R. Silent Spring[M]. Crest Books: 1964: 10-11.

years ago when the first settlers raised their houses, sank their wells, and built their barns.

Then a strange blight crept over the area and everything began to change. Some evil spell had settled on the community: mysterious maladies swept the flocks of chickens; the cattle and sheep sickened and died. Everywhere was a shadow of death. The farmers spoke of much illness among their families. In the town the doctors had become more and more puzzled by new kinds of sickness appearing among their patients. There had been several sudden and unexplained deaths, not only among adults but even among children, who would be stricken suddenly while at play and die within a few hours. There was a strange stillness. The birds, for example—where had they gone? Many people spoke of them, puzzled and disturbed. The feeding stations in the backyards were deserted. The few birds seen anywhere were moribund; they trembled violently and could not fly. It was a spring without voices. On the mornings that had once throbbed with the dawn chorus of robins, catbirds, doves, jays, wrens, and scores of other bird voices there was now no sound; only silence lay over the fields and woods and marsh.

On the farms the hens brooded, but no chicks hatched. The farmers complained that they were unable to raise any pigs—the litters were small and the young survived only a few days. The apple trees were coming into bloom but no bees droned among the blossoms, so there was no pollination and there would be no fruit.

The roadsides, once so attractive, were now lined with browned and withered vegetation as though swept by fire. These, too, were silent, deserted by all living things. Even the streams were now lifeless. Anglers no longer visited them, for all the fish had died.

In the gutters under the eaves and between the shingles of the roofs, a white granular powder still showed a few patches; some weeks before it had fallen like snow upon the roofs and the lawns, the fields and streams.

No witchcraft, no enemy action had silenced the rebirth of new life in this stricken world. The people had done it themselves....

This town does not actually exist, but it might easily have a thousand counterparts in America or elsewhere in the world. I know of no community that has experienced all the misfortunes I describe. Yet every one of these disasters has actually happened somewhere, and many real communities have already suffered a substantial number of them. A grim specter has crept upon us almost unnoticed, and this imagined tragedy may easily become a stark reality we all shall know.

What has already silenced the voices of spring in countless towns in America? This book is an attempt to explain.

Vocabulary

prosperous *adj.* 繁荣的，富足的
migrant *n.* 移民；移居者；候鸟
blight *n.* 枯萎病；荒芜
malady *n.* 弊病；疾病；腐败
stricken *adj.* 受灾的，患病的，受困扰的；极其忧伤的
stillness *n.* 静止；沉静
deserted *adj.* 空旷的；被遗弃的，被抛弃的；废弃的
moribund *adj.* 垂死的；停滞不前的
brood *v.* 孵蛋；沉思，担忧
drone *v.* 嗡嗡作声；混日子；唠叨
withered *adj.* 枯萎的；憔悴的；凋谢了的
anglers *n.* 钓鱼；琵琶鱼；钓鱼者
granular *adj.* 颗粒的；粒状的
grim *adj.* 严肃的，坚定的；令人不快的，令人沮丧的；阴森的，凄凉的
specter *n.* 幽灵；妖怪；恐怖之物
stark *adj.* 明显的，鲜明的

Reading comprehension exercises

I. Choose the best answer to the following questions.

1. What is not described in the first chapter of *Silent Spring*?

   A) A quiet town in America where "all life seemed to live in harmony with its surroundings".

   B) The sudden destroy of the beauty and peace of the town by a "strange blight".

   C) The death and illness of plants and animals.

D) The history of life on earth.

2. What silenced the voices of spring in countless towns in America?

   A) The people had done it themselves.

   B) The Second War II.

   C) The factories producing chemicals.

   D) The Cold War.

3. What does checkerboard (Paragraph 1) refer to?

   A) The arrangement of field.

   B) The board for checkers.

   C) The diagram like the checkerboard.

   D) The patterns of the cloth.

4. Why do you think Carson calls this chapter a "fable"?

   A) Carson uses a fable to document what had happened in the towns in America.

   B) Carson recalls the beautiful scenery in her hometown which was destroyed by DDT.

   C) Carson uses it as a horror story to scare people.

   D) Carson uses a fictitious town to serve as a warning for the overuse of pesticides in the ecosystem.

II. Comprehension questions

1. Compare the two scenarios in the first chapter of *Silent Spring* and explain why the author called it "silent spring" and her purpose of writing the book.
2. *Silent Spring* raises difficult questions about power of science and technology: magic bullets that produce wondrous solutions to big problems as well as unchecked powers whose inventions now exceed human control. How might this book help us rethink the relationship between environmental protection and scientific and technological development?
3. *Silent Spring* raises questions about the relationship between human prosperity and environmental protection. Do you think humans possess higher value than non-humans? How do we balance the welfare of humans with that of nature? How do we sustain good quality of life while also protecting nature?
4. Besides what have mentioned in *Silent Spring*, what are the other reasons that cause environmental problems?
5. Make a list of top environmental problems you think in China now, then discuss about the strategies the government should do to protect the environment.
6. List the strategies that could be taken to inform the public the importance of protecting the

environment and conserving the variety.

第三节　延伸阅读

——西奥多·罗斯福在国会发表的有关保护自然资源的演讲节选

一、文本导读

19 世纪中后期到 20 世纪初，美国工业迅速发展的同时，人们对包括森林、土地、矿产在内的自然资源进行了疯狂的掠夺性的开发，自然环境遭到了严重的破坏。针对这一情况，西奥多·罗斯福总统提出保护环境是最根本的问题，只有解决了保护自然资源的问题才有可能解决其他的问题。西奥多·罗斯福在任内推行了一系列保护森林、土地、水资源、野生动植物和矿产资源的举措，使得自然资源的管理从自由放任的状态逐步转向积极的管理和保护，为 20 世纪美国的环境保护和经济发展奠定了坚实的基础。以下是他在 1907 年 12 月 3 日向国会发表的第七次年度讲话中有关自然资源保护部分的摘录。

在最长的时间内为最多的人带来最大的利益(for the greatest good of the greatest number for the longest time)，这是吉福·平肖(Gifford Pinchot)，西奥多·罗斯福最重要的环保顾问、美国首任林业局局长在定义保护区(conservation)时指出的保护自然环境的重要意义，也是西奥多·罗斯福这段讲话中始终贯彻的观点。在讲话的开始，他就指出保护和合理有效地利用自然资源是国民生活所有问题中最根本的问题，是保持文明发展的物质基础，浪费和破坏自然资源、耗尽土地资源等短视的行为会使得我们的子孙后代无法继续享有我们该传递给他们的繁荣与富庶。接着他提到建设从五大湖区到密西西比河的深水航道问题、灌溉问题、复垦问题、填海及处理公共土地、限制过度放牧等问题。他指出乐观是一种好品质，但过分乐观就是愚蠢。"我们"总是乐观地说"我国"的资源取之不尽用之不竭，但事实并非如此。国家的矿藏如煤、铁、石油、天然气等都是不可再生的，因此最后必将枯竭。如果"我们"现在任意浪费这些资源，"我们"的后代会比正常情况下提前一两代就感受到资源的匮乏。接着西奥多·罗斯福强调了森林过度砍伐的问题，指出如果森林的消耗量与生长量继续不变的话，国家的森林资源很快就会枯竭。同时他强烈谴责了那些为了一时的私利(通过伐木业破坏森林获取巨大的经济利益)而牺牲了全体人民的利益以及整个国家的未来的人。最后他指出政府应该将森林资源置于自己的管理之下以为国家所用，土地和河流也是如此，它们都是国家财富，理应归国家所有。

二、原文节选

Excerpts from "The Conservation of Natural Resources" (1907) ①

Theodore Roosevelt

To the Senate and House of Representatives:

The conservation of our natural resources and their proper use constitute the fundamental problem which underlies almost every other problem of our National life. We must maintain for our civilization the adequate material basis without which that civilization can not exist. We must show foresight, we must look ahead. As a nation we not only enjoy a wonderful measure of present prosperity but if this prosperity is used aright it is an earnest of future success such as no other nation will have. The reward of foresight for this Nation is great and easily foretold. But there must be the look ahead, there must be a realization of the fact that to waste, to destroy, our natural resources, to skin and exhaust the land instead of using it so as to increase its usefulness, will result in undermining in the days of our children the very prosperity which we ought by right to hand down to them amplified and developed.

For the last few years, through several agencies, the Government has been endeavoring to get our people to look ahead and to substitute a planned and orderly development of our resources in place of a haphazard striving for immediate profit. Our great river systems should be developed as National water highways, the Mississippi, with its tributaries, standing first in importance, and the Columbia second, although there are many others of importance on the Pacific, the Atlantic and the Gulf slopes. The National Government should undertake this work, and I hope a beginning will be made in the present Congress; and the greatest of all our rivers, the Mississippi, should receive especial attention. From the Great Lakes to the mouth of the Mississippi there should be a deep waterway, with deep waterways leading from it to the East and the West. Such a waterway would practically mean the extension of our coast line into the

① Roosevelt, T. The Conservation of Natural Resources (1907) [EB/OL]. https://millercenter.org/the-presidency/presidential-speeches/december-3-1907-seventh-annual-message.

very heart of our country. It would be of incalculable benefit to our people. If begun at once it can be carried through in time appreciably to relieve the congestion of our great freight-carrying lines of railroads. The work should be systematically and continuously carried forward in accordance with some well-conceived plan. The main streams should be improved to the highest point of efficiency before the improvement of the branches is attempted; and the work should be kept free from every faint of recklessness or jobbery. The inland waterways which lie just back of the whole eastern and southern coasts should likewise be developed. Moreover, the development of our waterways involves many other important water problems, all of which should be considered as part of the same general scheme. The Government dams should be used to produce hundreds of thousands of horsepower as an incident to improving navigation; for the annual value of the unused water-power of the United States perhaps exceeds the annual value of the products of all our mines. As an incident to creating the deep waterways down the Mississippi, the Government should build along its whole lower length levees which taken together with the control of the headwaters, will at once and forever put a complete stop to all threat of floods in the immensely fertile Delta region. The territory lying adjacent to the Mississippi along its lower course will thereby become one of the most prosperous and populous, as it already is one of the most fertile, farming regions in all the world. I have appointed an Inland Waterways Commission to study and outline a comprehensive scheme of development along all the lines indicated. Later I shall lay its report before the Congress.

Irrigation should be far more extensively developed than at present, not only in the States of the Great Plains and the Rocky Mountains, but in many others, as, for instance, in large portions of the South Atlantic and Gulf States, where it should go hand in hand with the reclamation of swamp land. The Federal Government should seriously devote itself to this task, realizing that utilization of waterways and water-power, forestry, irrigation, and the reclamation of lands threatened with overflow, are all interdependent parts of the same problem. The work of the Reclamation Service in developing the larger opportunities of the western half of our country for irrigation is more important than almost any other movement. The constant purpose of the Government in connection with the Reclamation Service has been to use the water resources of the public lands for the ultimate greatest good of the greatest number; in other words, to put upon the land permanent home-makers, to use and develop it for themselves and for their children and children's children. There has been, of course, opposition to this work; opposition from some interested men who desire to exhaust the land for their own immediate profit without regard to the welfare of the next generation, and opposition from honest and well-meaning men who did not fully understand the subject or who did not look far enough ahead. This opposition is, I think, dying away, and our people are understanding that it would be utterly wrong to allow a few individuals to exhaust for their own temporary personal profit the resources which ought to be developed through use so as to be conserved for the permanent common advantage of the people as a whole.

The effort of the Government to deal with the public land has been based upon the same principle as that of the Reclamation Service. The land law system which was designed to meet the needs of the fertile and well-watered regions of the Middle West has largely broken down when applied to the dryer regions of the Great Plains, the mountains, and much of the Pacific slope, where a farm of 160 acres is inadequate for self-support. In these regions the system lent itself to fraud, and much land passed out of the hands of the Government without passing into the hands of the home-maker. The Department of the Interior and the Department of Justice joined in prosecuting the offenders against the law; and they have accomplished much, while where the administration of the law has been defective it has been changed. But the laws themselves are defective. Three years ago a public lands commission was appointed to scrutinize the law, and defects, and recommend a remedy. Their examination specifically showed the existence of great fraud upon the public domain, and their recommendations for changes in the law were made with the design of conserving the natural resources of every part of the public lands by putting it to its best use. Especial attention was called to the prevention of settlement by the passage of great areas of public land into the hands of a few men, and to the enormous waste caused by unrestricted grazing upon the open range. The recommendations of the Public Lands Commission are sound, for they are especially in the interest of the actual homemaker; and where the small home-maker can not at present utilize the land they provide that the Government shall keep control of it so that it may not be monopolized by a few men. The Congress has not yet acted upon these recommendations; but they are so just and proper, so essential to our National welfare, that I feel confident, if the Congress will take time to consider them, that they will ultimately be adopted.

Some such legislation as that proposed is essential in order to preserve the great stretches of public grazing land which are unfit for cultivation under present methods and are valuable only for the forage which they supply. These stretches amount in all to some 300, 000, 000 acres, and are open to the free grazing of cattle, sheep, horses and goats, without restriction. Such a system, or lack of system, means that the range is not so much used as wasted by abuse. As the West settles the range becomes more and more over-grazed. Much of it can not be used to advantage unless it is fenced, for fencing is the only way by which to keep in check the owners of nomad flocks which roam hither and thither, utterly destroying the pastures and leaving a waste behind so that their presence is incompatible with the presence of home-makers. The existing fences are all illegal. Some of them represent the improper exclusion of actual settlers, actual home-makers, from territory which is usurped by great cattle companies. Some of them represent what is in itself a proper effort to use the range for those upon the land, and to prevent its use by nomadic outsiders. All these fences, those that are hurtful and those that are beneficial, are alike illegal and must come down. But it is an outrage that the law should necessitate such action on the part of the Administration. The unlawful fencing of public lands for private grazing must be stopped, but the necessity which occasioned it must be provided for. The Federal Government should have control of the range, whether by permit or lease, as local necessities may determine. Such control could secure the great benefit of legitimate fencing, while at the same time securing and promoting the settlement of the country. In some places it may be that the tracts of range adjacent to the homesteads of actual settlers should be allotted to them severally or in common for the summer grazing of their stock. Elsewhere it may be that a lease system would serve the purpose; the leases to be temporary and subject to the rights of settlement, and the amount charged being large enough merely to permit of the efficient and beneficial control of the range by the Government, and of the payment to the county of the equivalent of what it would otherwise receive in taxes. The destruction of the public range will continue until some such laws as these are enacted. Fully to prevent the fraud in the public lands which, through the joint action of the Interior Department and the Department of Justice, we have been endeavoring to prevent, there must be further legislation, and especially a sufficient appropriation to permit the Department of the Interior to examine certain classes of entries on the ground before they pass into private ownership. The Government should part with its title only to the actual home-maker, not to the profit-maker who does not care to make a home. Our prime object is to secure the rights and guard the interests of the small ranchman, the man who plows and pitches hay for himself. It is this small ranchman, this actual settler and homemaker, who in the long run is most hurt by permitting thefts of the public land in whatever form.

Optimism is a good characteristic, but if carried to an excess it becomes foolishness. We are prone to speak of the resources of this country as inexhaustible; this is not so. The mineral wealth of the country, the coal, iron, oil, gas, and the like, does not reproduce itself, and therefore is certain to be exhausted ultimately; and wastefulness in dealing with it today means that our descendants will feel the exhaustion a generation or two before they otherwise would. But there are certain other forms of waste which could be entirely stopped — the waste of soil by washing, for instance, which is among the most dangerous of all wastes now in progress in the United States, is easily preventable, so that this present enormous loss of fertility is entirely unnecessary. The preservation or replacement of the forests is one of the most important means of preventing this loss. We have made a beginning in forest preservation, but it is only a beginning. At present lumbering is the fourth greatest industry in the United States; and yet, so rapid has been the rate of exhaustion of timber in the United States in the past, and so rapidly is the remainder being exhausted, that the country is unquestionably on the verge of a timber famine which will be felt in every household in the land. There has already been a rise in the price of lumber, but there is certain to be a more rapid and heavier rise in the future. The present annual consumption of lumber is certainly three times as great as the annual growth; and if the consumption and growth continue unchanged, practically all our lumber will be exhausted in another generation, while long before the limit to complete exhaustion is reached the growing scarcity will make itself felt in many blighting ways upon our National welfare. About 20 per cent of our forested territory is now reserved in National forests; but these do not include the most valuable timber lauds, and in any event the proportion is too small to expect that the reserves can accomplish more than a mitigation of the trouble which is ahead for the nation. Far more drastic action is needed. Forests can be lumbered so as to give to the public the full use of their mercantile timber without the slightest detriment to the forest, any more than it is a detriment to a farm to furnish a harvest; so that there is no parallel between forests and mines, which can only be completely used by exhaustion. But forests, if used as all our forests have been used in the past and as most of them are still used, will be either wholly destroyed, or so damaged that many decades have to pass before effective use can be made of them again. All these facts are so obvious that it is extraordinary that it should be necessary to repeat them. Every business man in the land, every writer in the newspapers, every man or woman of an ordinary school education, ought to be able to see that immense quantities of timber are used in the country, that the forests which supply this timber are rapidly being exhausted, and that, if no change takes place, exhaustion will come comparatively soon, and that the effects of it will be felt severely in the everyday life of our people. Surely, when these facts are so obvious, there should be no delay in taking preventive measures. Yet we seem as a nation to be willing to proceed in this matter with happy-go-lucky indifference even to the immediate future. It is this attitude which permits the self-interest of a very few persons to weigh for more than the ultimate interest of all our people. There are persons who find it to their immense pecuniary benefit to destroy the forests by lumbering. They are to be blamed for thus sacrificing the future of the Nation as a whole to their own self-interest of the moment; but heavier blame attaches to the people at large for permitting such action, whether in the White Mountains, in the southern Alleghenies, or in the Rockies and Sierras. A big lumbering company, impatient for immediate returns and not caring to look far enough ahead, will often deliberately destroy all the good timber in a region, hoping afterwards to move on to some new country. The shiftless man of small means, who does not care to become an actual home-maker but would like immediate profit, will find it to his advantage to take up timber land simply to turn it over to such a big company, and leave it valueless for future settlers. A big mine owner, anxious only to develop his mine at the moment, will care only to cut all the timber that he wishes without regard to the future — probably net looking ahead to the condition of the country when the forests are exhausted, any more than he does to the condition when the mine is worked out. I do not blame these men nearly as much as I blame the supine public opinion, the indifferent public opinion, which permits their action to go unchecked. Of course to check the waste of timber means that there must be on the part of the public the acceptance of a temporary restriction in the lavish use of the timber, in order to prevent the total loss of this use in the future. There are plenty of men in public and private life who actually advocate the continuance of the present system of unchecked and wasteful extravagance, using as an argument the fact that to check it will of course mean interference with the ease and comfort of certain people who now get lumber at less cost than they ought to pay, at the expense of the future generations. Some of these persons actually demand that the present forest reserves be thrown open to destruction, because, forsooth, they think that thereby the price of lumber could be put down again for two or three or more years. Their attitude is precisely like that of an agitator protesting against the outlay of money by farmers on manure and in taking care of their farms generally. Undoubtedly, if the average farmer were content absolutely to ruin his farm, he could for two or three years avoid spending any money on it, and yet make a good deal of money out of it. But only a savage would, in his private affairs, show such reckless disregard of the future; yet it is precisely this reckless disregard of the future which the opponents of the forestry system are now endeavoring to get the people of the United States to show. The only trouble with the movement for the preservation of our forests is that it has not gone nearly far enough, and was not begun soon enough. It is a most fortunate thing, however, that we began it when we did. We should acquire in the Appalachian and White Mountain regions all the forest lands that it is possible to acquire for the use of the Nation. These lands, because they form a National asset, are as emphatically national as the rivers which they feed, and which flow through so many States before they reach the ocean.

Comprehension questions

1. President Theodore Roosevelt regarded "Conservation as a National Duty". What did he advocate to do to protect the natural resources in this speech?
2. Roosevelt's legacy reflected the approach of Pinchot, who emphasized efficiency and utility, more than that of naturalist John Muir (with whom Roosevelt worked to preserve Yosemite), who sought to keep such landscapes relatively unspoiled and pristine. What is your opinion on the two ways of protecting the wilderness and natural resources?
3. The end of 19th century and the beginning of the 20th century witnessed fast development in industry, science and technology in the United States. What were the costs and benefits of such development? What lessons can we draw from it?
4. Chinese government advocates environment protection and sustainable development. What can we learn from Roosevelt's legacy on natural source protection? What measures can we take to establish an eco-friendly society?
5. Today, the extinction of several species or loss of biodiversity is a much debated issue among the environmentalists at international level. What is the meaning of protecting biodiversity? What can we do to protect biodiversity?

第七章
美　国　梦

第一节　时 代 背 景

从殖民时代开始，美洲新大陆一直是移民眼中的梦想之地、机会之地（land of opportunity）。不少欧洲移民在本国受到宗教压迫，怀抱追求宗教自由与个人发展的梦想远渡重洋移民美国。新航线、新大陆的开辟也意味着新的资源、新的机会，发财致富的梦想吸引了大量旧大陆居民尤其是贫困阶层的到来。也正是基于这样共同的梦想，《独立宣言》宣称“人人生而平等”，并享有“生命、自由和追求幸福的权利”。在美国梦的指引之下，几个世纪以来美国一直是最大移民输入国。

一、美国殖民时期（1607—1790 年）的移民

1607 年，在伦敦弗吉尼亚公司的组织下，百余名英国人分乘三艘船只抵达美洲大陆。他们持有英国国王詹姆斯一世的特许状，意在开辟殖民地寻求黄金以获利，同时也契合英国开辟新航线并与其他欧洲殖民国家相抗衡的政策。依据英王的名字，这些殖民者将当地注入大西洋的河流命名为詹姆斯河，第一个定居点就叫詹姆斯敦。头两年的时间，詹姆斯敦在饥荒、疾病以及与印第安人的冲突中风雨飘摇。随着烟草种植业的发展以及与印第安人关系的改善，詹姆斯敦逐步稳定扩张，17 世纪一直都是弗吉尼亚殖民地的首府。

1619 年，约 20 名黑人从非洲乘船抵达弗吉尼亚，随后更多的黑人被运往美洲殖民地。早期的黑人跟许多欧裔移民一样同为契约劳工，工作四至七年即可获得自由。17 世纪四五十年代，部分黑人在詹姆斯敦附近购买了自己的农田，少数黑人家庭生活富足，还拥有

自己的契约劳工。

1620年，上百名清教徒怀着追求宗教自由的理想，乘坐“五月花号”抵达美洲东海岸，建立了第二个英国殖民地，并以英国西南部城市普利茅斯命名。在印第安人的帮助下，清教徒们度过了第一年的寒冬，并在第二年获得了丰收。1621年11月下旬的星期四，清教徒们和印第安人欢聚一堂，庆祝了美国历史上第一个感恩节。大量的英国移民随后纷至沓来，在美洲东北部地区定居。移民以农业、渔业、造船业及贸易为生，人口不断增长，殖民地范围不断扩大，到1790年新英格兰地区(缅因州、佛蒙特州、新罕布什尔州、马萨诸塞州、罗得岛州、康涅狄格州)人口总数达到九十万。

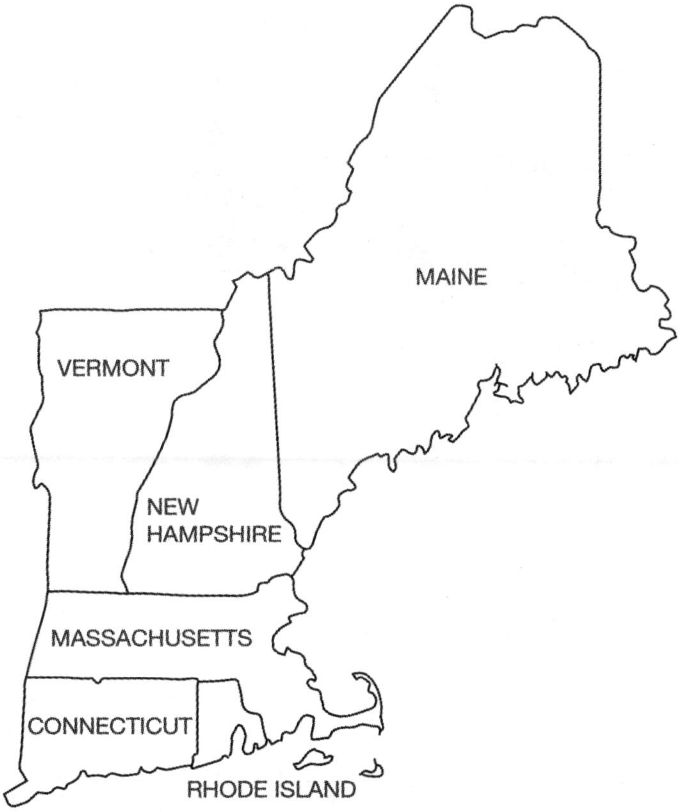

新英格兰地图

1607—1733年，英国在北美洲大西洋沿岸建立了13个殖民地：特拉华、宾夕法尼亚、新泽西、佐治亚、康涅狄格、马萨诸塞、马里兰、南卡罗来纳、新罕布什尔、弗吉尼亚、纽约、北卡罗来纳和罗德岛。每个殖民地都建立并发展了自治体制，居民大多数是拥有自己土地的独立农民，人口从当初的2000人增长至独立战争前的2400万人。这13个殖民地成为美国建国之初的13个州，在美国国旗——星条旗上体现为13道红白相间的宽条。这些殖民地最终成为美国独立时的组成部分，即后来的美利坚合众国。

1775年大西洋沿岸的13个殖民地

美洲早期移民除了英国人，多为德国人与荷兰人。1624年在荷兰西印度公司的组织下，30户荷兰家庭乘船抵达美洲，在现在的曼哈顿岛定居下来。他们按荷兰首都阿姆斯特丹的名字，将此处命名为新阿姆斯特丹。1664年9月英国人占领新阿姆斯特丹，英国国王查理二世将这片地方交给弟弟约克公爵(后来的詹姆斯二世)管辖，地名也随之以约克公爵的领地约克郡而改为纽约，即“新约克”。

1625年，荷兰西印度公司将11名黑奴运往新阿姆斯特丹。随着美洲种植园的发展，黑奴贸易逐步走向高潮。70%的黑奴被送往新大陆种植糖，其余的则种植咖啡、棉花和香烟。到1790年黑人总人口达到76万余人，占美国总人口的19.3%。

1790年美国人口普查数据显示总人口为390万人，其中白人近320万人。86%的白人为英国人后裔，9%为德国人后裔，3.4%为荷兰人后裔，2.1%为法国人后裔，0.25%为瑞典人后裔。

美国1790年人口数据(印第安人未计入)	
祖籍	人口
非洲	757000
英格兰	2100000
阿尔斯特(今爱尔兰北部及北爱尔兰)	300000
德国	270000
苏格兰	15000
荷兰	100000
威尔士	10000
法国	15000
犹太人(散居欧洲各国)	2000
瑞典	6000
其他	200000
英国合计	2560000
合计	3900000

二、美国1790—1860年的移民

1820—1850年迎来了美国历史上第一次移民大潮。大量的爱尔兰人因为大饥荒和革命失败的原因移民美国，因身无长技，他们大多定居城市，以苦工身份谋生，参与修建运河和铁路，或到纺织厂和码头打工。德国移民则被低廉的农田价格吸引，其中一半人直奔中西部和得克萨斯州的农田，另一半成为城市工匠。由于宗教信仰的差异，这些信仰天主教的爱尔兰和德国移民融入美国的过程并不容易。

1848年，加利福尼亚州发现黄金的消息不胫而走，海内外的淘金者蜂拥而至。在淘金热期间约有30万人来到加利福尼亚，大多数淘金者来自美国东部，海外移民则来自拉丁美洲、欧洲、澳大利亚和中国。中国的淘金者多来自广东台山，他们来此淘金，因此将这

里称为“金山”，后来又改称“旧金山”。

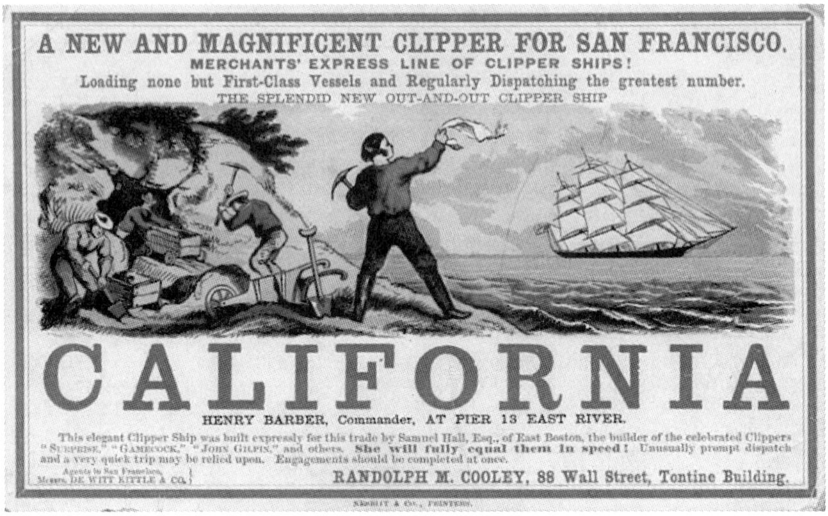

1850 年前后乘船赴加利福尼亚的广告

这一时期的美国梦以本杰明·富兰克林为代表人物，是典型的“清教徒的梦想”。富兰克林是英国移民的后裔，家境贫困，只上过两年学即辍学帮工。经过不懈努力，他成为著名的美国政治家、物理学家、印刷商和出版商、作家、发明家和科学家。富兰克林白手起家的故事激励了无数后来人修身立德，辛勤工作，靠自己的双手一点点积攒财富。随着 19 世纪 40 年代末淘金热的兴起，一夜暴富的“加利福尼亚梦”赢得了越来越多的拥趸。在美国梦的衡量标准中，物质财富的权重逐步增大。

三、美国 1850—1930 年的移民

1850—1930 年，约 500 万德国人移居美国，其中 100 万人在中西部定居下来。除了传统的德国、英国和爱尔兰移民，越来越多的南欧和东欧地区居民也加入了移民大军。蒸汽船替代帆船导致船票降价，欧洲铁路系统逐步扩展，抵达海港乘船出海对他们来说变得更加便捷。这些移民来自意大利、希腊、匈牙利和波兰等斯拉夫语国家，其中不少人信奉天主教或者犹太教，同讲英语信新教的美国人不免有所摩擦。但总体而言，不同民族文化不断地相互影响、同化和融合，形成了大熔炉（melting pot）这一独特的新的共同文化的社会。1924 年，美国通过《移民法》，对移民人数进行限制。该法案基于 1890 年的人口普查，规定每年来自任何国家的移民只能占 1890 年时那个国家已经生活在美国的人数的

2%。美国历史上的大规模移民暂告一段落。

1908 年美国戏剧《大熔炉》

这一时期美国梦的代表人物为亨利·福特。作为爱尔兰移民的后裔，福特 16 岁就离家做学徒工。经过多年奋斗，他创立了福特汽车公司，引进福特 T 型车，带来了运输业及美国工业的革命，自己也成为当时世界上最有钱及知名度最高的人物。

四、20 世纪 20 年代的美国

1918 年第一次世界大战结束后，欧洲一直致力于战后重建并解决因战争而造成的劳动力消减问题。美国则进入高速发展时期，经济规模开始凌驾于欧洲之上。整个 20 世纪 20 年代发生了数不胜数的激动人心的事件，沉浸在喧嚣、狂热、绚丽多彩的气氛中，因此被后人称为“咆哮的二十年代”(the Roaring Twenties)。

20世纪20年代工业化批量生产的发展使科技产品及各种消费品的价格大为降低，开始走入寻常家庭。“一战”前汽车还是典型的奢侈品，到了20世纪20年代物美价廉的汽车在美国随处可见，1929年美国汽车保有量接近2700万辆，其中仅福特公司生产的T型车到1927年就总共卖出了1500万辆。汽车工业迅速成为首屈一指的支柱产业，钢铁、石油、轮胎、公路建设等产业随之兴起，加油站、连锁店、汽车旅馆等相关服务业也迅猛发展。

1925年款的福特T型车

1920年美国诞生了第一个电台节目和第一个商业电台，无线电收音机日益普及：1925年19%的美国家庭拥有收音机，1930年这一比例达到40%(城市家庭拥有收音机的比例更远高于此)。电台成为影响力巨大的大众传媒，美国进入“广播黄金时代”(the Golden Age of Radio)。

音乐节目迅速成为最受欢迎的广播形式，爵士乐赢得了越来越多的听众。爵士乐原本于19世纪末至20世纪初起源于美国新奥尔良的非裔美国人社区，随着广播节目的推广，这种音乐形式被主流的中产阶级白人所接受，尤其受到年轻人的喜爱。美国作家弗朗西斯·斯科特·菲茨杰拉德将20世纪20年代称作“爵士年代”(the Jazz Age)，并将它用在1922年短篇小说集《爵士时代的故事》(*Tales of the Jazz Age*)的标题上。

"一战"时期直至"咆哮的二十年代"中成年的一代人尤其是作家常常被称作"迷惘的一代"（the Lost Generation）。这一名称出自作家格特鲁德·斯坦，海明威在1926年的小说《太阳照常升起》中使用了"迷惘的一代"作为题词，从而使这一名称广为人知。海明威、菲茨杰拉德等代表作家常常基于自己的亲身经历，或描绘富裕阶层纸醉金迷的生活方式，或展现美国梦的破碎，流露出浓厚的悲观情调。

五、近代美国梦的变迁

1931年在《美国史诗》一书中，亚当斯将"美国梦"定义为"无论每个人的社会阶层或出生环境如何，生活都应该变得更好，更丰富，更丰裕，每个人都有机会根据能力或成就而定"。美国梦的概念自此广为人知，其核心内容为机会均等与社会流动：每个人都享有成功的机遇，只要努力即可发家致富提升自己的社会地位，而不必依赖于家世和背景。1963年马丁·路德·金提出民权运动的根源即非裔美国人对美国梦的追求，他的演讲《我有一个梦想》激励了无数美国人争取真正的自由平等。

近年来随着美国贫富差距日益扩大，越来越多的美国人对美国梦抱以悲观的态度。对代际流动的横向研究表明，在经合组织十几个发达国家中，美国已远远落后于丹麦、瑞典、法国、德国等国家，如今美国劳工家庭的孩子很难过上比父母更好的生活。2020年沃拉克等学者在《美国政治科学期刊》上发表论文，纵向分析了1973—2018年美国梦的变迁，得出的结论是：美国人越来越难相信美国梦了。

第二节　文本阅读

——《了不起的盖茨比》节选

一、文本导读

《了不起的盖茨比》（*The Great Gatsby*）出版于1925年，是美国作家弗朗西斯·斯科特·基·菲茨杰拉德创作的中篇小说，被公认为美国文学的经典著作。1998年，现代图书馆编辑委员会投票，将其评选为最伟大的美国小说第二名，2005年又入选《时代》周刊百本最佳英文小说，成为美国中学和大学文学课的必读作品。

《了不起的盖茨比》的背景设在1922年纽约附近的长岛，小说的叙述者尼克身上有着作者菲茨杰拉德的影子：来自中西部，毕业于常青藤盟校，"一战"期间从军，战后来到纽约发展。尼克在长岛的西卵租房而居，附近住着一位神秘的百万富翁盖茨比，他的生活极尽奢侈，豪宅里常常笙歌鼎沸、觥筹交错，他自己却鲜有露面。隔着海湾相望的东卵住着尼克的表亲黛西，她嫁给了尼克的校友汤姆，生活优渥闲适。

不久尼克得知盖茨比和黛西其实是旧相识，五年前盖茨比还在军中服役时两人就坠入爱河。盖茨比被派往海外后，黛西转而嫁给了世家子弟汤姆。盖茨比之所以在黛西家对岸买下豪宅并夜夜笙歌，正是为了引起黛西的注意从而再续前缘。在尼克的助力下，两人果真旧情复燃。很快汤姆发现了此事，三人就此对质。汤姆宣称盖茨比的财富来源不法，黛西于是选择留在汤姆身边。

心慌意乱的黛西在回家路上开车撞死了汤姆的情妇，盖茨比决意保护黛西，由自己担下罪责。然而汤姆刻意误导死者的丈夫，导致盖茨比被仇杀身亡。葬礼过后，心灰意冷的尼克决定离开纽约，重返中西部故乡生活。

英国学者皮尔森认为，20 世纪的小说中菲兹杰拉德的作品最为贴合美国梦的概念。从殖民地时期开始，美国人就笃信美国充满了机会，只要努力不懈地奋斗就一定能达成目标，获得更好的生活。盖茨比一生追求金钱与爱情，坚信只要获取了财富就能赢回旧爱。他常常凝望黛西家码头上的绿灯，因为绿灯就象征着他的梦想与爱情。然而与之前美国作家截然不同的是，菲兹杰拉德对美国梦主题的展现不再是一派乐观，而是充满了幻灭感。可望而不可即的绿灯恰恰意味着盖茨比的梦想无法达成。

本书节选的原文来自《了不起的盖茨比》第九章，整部小说的结尾部分。在举办完盖茨比的葬礼，即将离开纽约之际，尼克重返盖茨比的豪宅，不禁思绪万千。“我们就这样奋力前进，逆水行舟，而浪潮不断地将我们推回到过去。”(So we beat on, boats against the current, borne back ceaselessly into the past.)这句结束语含义深刻、意象生动，逆水行舟的暗喻即代表着美国人对梦想的追寻，一方面不懈努力，一方面又充满了无力感。语言表达上的安排则近似于莎士比亚常用的五步抑扬格，听起来起伏跌宕、抑扬顿挫，形成了诗歌的节奏。头韵法的使用更是增加了韵律感：几个以 b 开头的单词“beat”“boats”“borne”和“back”如同潮汐起伏，与句尾不送气的 p 音(past)交相呼应。这句结束语因此广为流传，并作为墓志铭镌刻于菲兹杰拉德的墓碑之上。

二、原文节选

Gatsby's house was still empty when I left—the grass on his lawn had grown as long as mine. One of the taxi drivers in the village never took a fare past the entrance gate without stopping for a minute and pointing inside; perhaps it was he who drove Daisy and Gatsby over to East Egg[1] the night of the accident and perhaps he had made a story about it all his own. I didn't want to hear it and I avoided him when I got off the train.

I spent my Saturday nights in New York because those gleaming, dazzling parties of his were with me so vividly that I could still hear the music and the laughter faint and incessant from his garden and the cars going up and down his drive. One night I did hear a material car there and saw its lights stop at his front steps. But I didn't investigate. Probably it was some final guest who had been away at the ends of the earth and didn't know that the party was over.

On the last night, with my trunk packed and my car sold to the grocer, I went over and looked at that huge incoherent failure of a house once more. On the white steps an obscene word, scrawled by some boy with a piece of brick, stood out clearly in the moonlight and I erased it, drawing my shoe raspingly along the stone. Then I wandered down to the beach and sprawled out on the sand.

Most of the big shore places were closed now and there were hardly any lights except the shadowy, moving glow of a ferryboat across the Sound. And as the moon rose higher the inessential houses began to melt away until gradually I became aware of the old island here that flowered once for Dutch sailors'[2] eyes—a fresh, green breast of the new world. Its vanished trees, the trees that had made way for Gatsby's house, had once pandered in whispers to the last and greatest of all human dreams; for a transitory enchanted moment man must have held his breath in the presence of this continent, compelled into an aesthetic contemplation he neither understood nor desired, face to face for the last time in history with something commensurate to his capacity for wonder.

And as I sat there brooding on the old, unknown world, I thought of Gatsby's wonder when he first picked out the green light at the end of Daisy's dock. He had come a long way to this blue lawn and his dream must have seemed so close that he could hardly fail to grasp it. He did not know that it was already behind him, somewhere back in that vast obscurity beyond the city, where the dark fields of the republic rolled on under the night.

Gatsby believed in the green light, the orgastic future that year by year recedes before us. It eluded us then, but that's no matter—tomorrow we will run faster, stretch out our arms farther... And one fine morning—

So we beat on, boats against the current, borne back ceaselessly into the past.

Notes

1. East Egg 东卵村/东卵居住区，黛西住在东卵，盖茨比住在西卵，他们之间隔着长长的海湾。东卵象征世袭富贵，西卵象征新兴阶层。
2. Dutch sailors 美国早期移民有不少来自荷兰。1615 年即有荷兰探险者抵达如今的纽约州，1624 年荷兰人在现在的曼哈顿岛定居下来。富有经商头脑的荷兰人与其他拖家带口逃难来的很多族裔不同，他们是来美洲寻找新生活的冒险者，很快在北美站稳了脚跟，荷兰人像其他民族一样，用家乡的名字命名新的居住地，建立了“新阿姆斯特丹”这个城市。而这个“新阿姆斯特丹”则是后来赫赫有名的美国经济中心——纽约。

Vocabulary

gleaming *adj.* 闪耀的；明亮的
dazzling *adj.* 耀眼的；辉煌的
incessant *adj.* 不停的；持续不断的
obscene *adj.* 淫秽的；下流的
raspingly *adv.* 刺耳地
inessential *adj.* 非必需的；无关紧要的
pander *v.* 迎合
aesthetic *adj.* 审美的；美学的
contemplation *n.* 深思；沉思
commensurate *adj.* 相称的
brood *v.* 忧思
obscurity *n.* 昏暗；黑暗
orgastic *adj.* 极度兴奋的
recede *v.* 退后
elude *v.* 躲避
ceaselessly *adv.* 不停地

Reading comprehension exercises

I. Choose the best answer to the following questions.

1. Why did Nick think of the Dutch sailors?

   A) Gatsby was also a Dutch immigrant.

   B) The green light had been significant for Dutch sailors.

   C) The immigrants cherished the same dream.

   D) The Dutch sailors developed this fresh, green breast of the new world.

2. What does the green light stand for?

   A) The hazy future

   B) Gatsby's desires to reunite with Daisy

   C) The start of new life

   D) The unreachable dream that lives inside all people

3. The last line of *The Great Gatsby* is a metaphor of trying to row against the flow of current. We can take this metaphor to be：

   A) Depressing and fatalistic, that the past is an anchor and that life only an illusion of forward progress.

   B) Uplifting, that we battle against fate with our will and our strength.

   C) Objectively describing the human condition, that we can't help but repeat our own history.

   D) All of the above.

II. Comprehension questions

1. Is Gatsby great?
2. What makes *The Great Gatsby* great?

第三节 延伸阅读

——《富兰克林自传》节选

一、文本导读

1771—1790 年，步入晚年的本杰明·富兰克林回顾自己的一生，为自己的子女写下《富兰克林自传》，旨在传授自己的人生经验。如自传开篇所言：“我出身于社会最底层，生于贫寒长于贫寒，后来居然改变了人生改变了命运，过上了富裕的生活，在世人眼里，我有很好的名声，而且受人尊敬。”①富兰克林是白手起家的典范，靠自学与自我奋斗，成长为美国杰出的政治家、外交家、科学家和发明家。美国在线曾于 2005 年举办了“最伟大的美国人”票选活动，富兰克林高票当选为美国最伟大人物的第五位。

在 1916 年版《富兰克林自传》的前言中，编辑派恩将富兰克林赞誉为“美国最伟大的白手起家者”(the greatest of our self-made men)，其自传中的故事提供了“美国白手起家的非凡历史中最杰出的记载”(the most remarkable of all the remarkable histories of our self-made men)。《富兰克林自传》被公认为是改变了无数人命运的美国精神读本，两百多年来激励了无数美国人奋发向上，追求梦想。

《富兰克林自传》共分四部分：

① [美]本杰明·富兰克林. 富兰克林自传[M]. 王正林，王权，译. 北京：中国青年出版社，2013：10.

1771 年，65 岁的富兰克林在英国完成了自传的第一部分。他为时任新泽西州长的儿子威廉描述了家族史及自己青少年时期的经历。富兰克林出身贫寒，在十七个兄弟姐妹中排行第十五，仅上过两年学就被迫回家帮父亲干活。12 岁富兰克林开始给从事印刷出版业的哥哥詹姆斯做学徒，一边自学一边开始写作办报。17 岁富兰克林到费城自谋生计，逐步创办了自己的印刷所、报纸和共读社(Junto)，成长为有影响的作家和企业家。

自传的第二部分缘起于两封读者来信。1784 年，富兰克林于巴黎郊区续写自传，以飨读者。他详述了自己的公共图书馆规划，并介绍了自己的道德修养计划。富兰克林一共列出了十三条美德，并制订了严格的计划不断修炼，以期达成道德上的圆满。这也是《富兰克林自传》最广为人知的内容。

1788 年，富兰克林回到费城开始自传第三部分的写作。这一部分阐述了富兰克林的政治观和宗教观，记叙了他的学习、写作、经商和从政经历，也介绍了一些他在自然科学方面的成就，比如发明富兰克林壁炉、从云端收集电火花等。

《本杰明 · 富兰克林取电于天》，本杰明 · 韦斯特绘于 1816 年

1789—1790年，富兰克林动笔写作自传的第四部分，介绍1757年父子俩出使英国的经历。居留英国的五年间，富兰克林向英国人民及政府官员阐述了北美殖民地的状况和意见，力求维护殖民地人民利益。因富兰克林去世，此部分内容未完结且最为简短。

本书原文节选自《富兰克林自传》的第二部分，通常被称作“十三美德”。作者详细介绍了他的修身立德计划，说明了选取节制、缄默、秩序、决心、节俭、勤奋、真诚、正义、中庸、整洁、冷静、节欲和谦逊这十三项美德的原因及其轻重缓急，并对如何培养这些美德做出了规划。

二、原文节选

It was about this time I conceiv'd the bold and arduous project of arriving at moral perfection. I wish'd to live without committing any fault at any time; I would conquer all that either natural inclination, custom, or company might lead me into. As I knew, or thought I knew, what was right and wrong, I did not see why I might not always do the one and avoid the other. But I soon found I had undertaken a task of more difficulty than I had imagined. While my care was employ'd in guarding against one fault, I was often surprised by another; habit took the advantage of inattention; inclination was sometimes too strong for reason. I concluded, at length, that the mere speculative conviction that it was our interest to be completely virtuous, was not sufficient to prevent our slipping; and that the contrary habits must be broken, and good ones acquired and established, before we can have any dependence on a steady, uniform rectitude of conduct. For this purpose I therefore contrived the following method.

In the various enumerations of the moral virtues I had met with in my reading, I found the catalogue more or less numerous, as different writers included more or fewer ideas under the same name. Temperance, for example, was by some confined to eating and drinking, while by others it was extended to mean the moderating every other pleasure, appetite, inclination, or passion, bodily or mental, even to our avarice and ambition. I propos'd to myself, for the sake of clearness, to use rather more names, with fewer ideas annex'd to each, than a few names with more ideas; and I included under thirteen names of virtues all that at that time occurr'd to me as necessary or desirable, and annexed to each a short precept, which fully express'd the extent I gave to its meaning.

These names of virtues, with their precepts, were:

1. TEMPERANCE. Eat not to dullness; drink not to elevation.

2. SILENCE. Speak not but what may benefit others or yourself; avoid trifling conversation.

3. ORDER. Let all your things have their places; let each part of your business have its time.

4. RESOLUTION. Resolve to perform what you ought; perform without fail what you resolve.

5. FRUGALITY. Make no expense but to do good to others or yourself; i. e., waste nothing.

6. INDUSTRY. Lose no time; be always employ'd in something useful; cut off all unnecessary actions.

7. SINCERITY. Use no hurtful deceit; think innocently and justly, and, if you speak, speak accordingly.

8. JUSTICE. Wrong none by doing injuries, or omitting the benefits that are your duty.

9. MODERATION. Avoid extremes; forbear resenting injuries so much as you think they deserve.

10. CLEANLINESS. Tolerate no uncleanliness in body, cloaths, or habitation.

11. TRANQUILLITY. Be not disturbed at trifles, or at accidents common or unavoidable.

12. CHASTITY. Rarely use venery but for health or offspring, never to dullness, weakness, or the injury of your own or another's peace or reputation.

13. HUMILITY. Imitate Jesus and Socrates.

My intention being to acquire the habitude of all these virtues, I judg'd it would be well not to distract my attention by attempting the whole at once, but to fix it on one of them at a time; and, when I should be master of that, then to proceed to another, and so on, till I should have gone thro'the thirteen; and, as the previous acquisition of some might facilitate the acquisition of certain others, I arrang'd them with that view, as they stand above. Temperance first, as it tends to procure that coolness and clearness of head, which is so necessary where constant vigilance was to be kept up, and guard maintained against the unremitting attraction of ancient habits, and the force of perpetual temptations. This being acquir'd and establish'd, Silence would be more easy; and my desire being to gain knowledge at the same time that I improv'd in virtue, and considering that in conversation it was obtain'd rather by the use of the ears than of the tongue, and therefore wishing to break a habit I was getting into of prattling, punning, and joking, which only made me acceptable to trifling company, I gave Silence the second place. This and the next, Order, I expected would allow me more time for attending to my project and my studies. Resolution, once become habitual, would keep me firm in my endeavors to obtain all the subsequent virtues; Frugality and Industry freeing me from my remaining debt, and producing affluence and independence, would make more easy the practice of Sincerity and Justice, etc., etc. Conceiving then, that, agreeably to the advice of Pythagoras in his *Golden Verses*, daily examination would be necessary, I contrived the following method for conducting that examination.

I made a little book, in which I allotted a page for each of the virtues. I rul'd each page with red ink, so as to have seven columns, one for each day of the week, marking each column with a letter for the day. I cross'd these columns with thirteen red lines, marking the beginning of each line with the first letter of one of the virtues, on which line, and in its proper column, I might mark, by a little black spot, every fault I found upon examination to have been committed respecting that virtue upon that day.

I determined to give a week's strict attention to each of the virtues successively. Thus, in the first week, my great guard was to avoid every the least offence against Temperance, leaving the other virtues to their ordinary chance, only marking every evening the faults of the day. Thus, if in the first week I could keep my first line, marked T, clear of spots, I suppos'd the habit of that virtue so much strengthen'd and its opposite weaken'd, that I might venture extending my attention to include the next, and for the following week keep both lines clear of spots. Proceeding thus to the last, I could go thro'a course complete in thirteen weeks, and four courses in a year. And like him who, having a garden to weed, does not attempt to eradicate all the bad herbs at once, which would exceed his reach and his strength, but works on one of the beds at a time, and, having accomplish'd the first, proceeds to a second, so I should have, I hoped, the encouraging pleasure of seeing on my pages the progress I made in virtue, by clearing successively my lines of their spots, till in the end, by a number of courses, I should be happy in viewing a clean book, after a thirteen weeks'daily examination.

FORM OF THE PAGES

EAT NOT TO DULINESS;

DRINK NOT TO ELEVATION.

	S	M	T	W	T	F	S
T							
S	*	*		*		*	
O	* *	*	*		*	*	*
R			*			*	
F		*			*		
I			*				
S							
J							
M							
C							
T							
C							
H							

This my little book had for its motto these lines from Addison's Cato:

> "Here will I hold. If there's a power above us
> (And that there is all nature cries aloud
> Thro'all her works), He must delight in virtue;
> And that which he delights in must be happy."

Another from Cicero,

"*O vitae Philosophia dux! O virtutum indagatrix expultrixque vitiorum! Unus dies, bene et ex praeceptis tuis actus, peccanti immortalitati est anteponendus.*"

Another from the Proverbs of Solomon, speaking of wisdom or virtue:

"Length of days is in her right hand, and in her left hand riches and honour. Her ways are ways of pleasantness, and all her paths are peace." iii. 16, 17.

And conceiving God to be the fountain of wisdom, I thought it right and necessary to solicit his assistance for obtaining it; to this end I formed the following little prayer, which was prefix'd to my tables of examination, for daily use.

"O powerful Goodness! bountiful Father! merciful Guide! increase in me that wisdom which discovers my truest interest. Strengthen my resolutions to perform what that wisdom dictates. Accept my kind offices to thy other children as the only return in my power for thy continual favors to me."

I used also sometimes a little prayer which I took from Thomson's Poems, viz.:
"Father of light and life, thou Good Supreme!
O teach me what is good; teach me Thyself!
Save me from folly, vanity, and vice,
From every low pursuit; and fill my soul
With knowledge, conscious peace, and virtue pure;
Sacred, substantial, never-fading bliss!"

The precept of Order requiring that every part of my business should have its allotted time, one page in my little book contain'd the following scheme of employment for the twenty-four hours of a natural day:

The Morning. *Question.* What good shall I do this day?	5 6 7	Rise, wash, and address *Powerful Goodness!* Contrive day's business and take the resolution of the day; prosecute the present study, and breakfast.
	8 9 10 11	Work.
Noon.	12 1	Read, or overlook my accounts, and dine.
	2 3 4 5	Work.
Evening. *Question.* What good have I done today?	6 7 8 9	Put things in their places. Supper. Music or diversion, or conversation. Examination of the day.
Night.	10 11 12 1 2 3 4	Sleep.

I enter'd upon the execution of this plan for self-examination, and continu'd it with occasional intermissions for some time. I was surpris'd to find myself so much fuller of faults than I had imagined; but I had the satisfaction of seeing them diminish. To avoid the trouble of renewing now and then my little book, which, by scraping out the marks on the paper of old faults to make room for new ones in a new course, became full of holes, I transferr'd my tables and precepts to the ivory leaves of a memorandum book, on which the lines were drawn with red ink, that made a durable stain, and on those lines I mark'd my faults with a blacklead pencil, which marks I could easily wipe out with a wet sponge. After a while I went thro' one course only in a year, and afterward only one in several years, till at length I omitted them entirely, being employ'd in voyages and business abroad, with a multiplicity of affairs that interfered; but I always carried my little book with me.

Comprehension questions

1. What are virtues? Are virtues old-fashioned? Do we need them to thrive in today's society?
2. Is it worthwhile to live a life of virtues?
3. Why did Franklin feel he needed to achieve moral perfection?
4. Franklin attributes his success in life to the virtues he has practiced. To which virtues does he attribute the following—long life and good health? His wealth? The confidence of his countrymen?
5. Do you think that his goal was realistic? Explain why or why not.

第八章
多 元 文 化

第一节　时 代 背 景

作为一个移民国家，美国文化非常多元，多元化是美国文化的基础。在美国许多城市都可见到由移民发展起来的充满族裔风情色彩的街区，几乎每年的每个月都有特定的时间来纪念不同文化为美国社会所作出的贡献，一代代移民在适应美国多元文化中表现出极大的适应能力和创造能力，美国也在移民手中被一次又一次地建造，不断地发生改变。

美国的人口构成很复杂，白种美国人占大部分(约2/3)，而其余1/3的少数人种多集中在沿海或都会区，拉丁美洲裔为少数民族中的最多数。美国人口约3.33亿(截至2021年2月)，非拉美裔白人占60.1%，拉美裔占18.5%，非洲裔占13.4%，亚裔占5.9%，混血占2.8%，印第安人和阿拉斯加原住民占1.3%，夏威夷原住民或其他太平洋岛民占0.2%(少部分人在其他族群内被重复统计)。人口中约46.5%信仰基督教，20.8%信仰天主教，1.9%信仰犹太教，0.9%信仰伊斯兰教，0.7%信仰佛教，0.5%信仰东正教，1.2%信仰其他宗教，22.8%无宗教信仰(少部分人群属于多宗教信仰被重复统计)。根据美国2020年人口普查数据，过去10年，白人人口数量在美国历史上首次出现下降。而跨族裔、西班牙裔和亚裔人口显著增长，成为2010年至2020年美国人口增长的主要动力，其中人口增长最快的是西班牙语系的拉美人。

国家文化和历史是紧密相连的，要了解美国的多元文化，还需要了解美国的移民历史。美国是一个传统移民大国，有着悠久的移民历史。不同于其他国家，美国是由世界各地移民组成的，外来移民占了美国人口的绝大多数，拥有多元人种和文化。众所周知，美国历史很短，在建国之前，美国及其所在的北美大陆还是一片不毛之地。美国原为印第安人的聚居地，但在此之前，印第安人的祖先，最早的美洲人可能在4万年前经由西伯利亚踏着白令海峡到达北美洲，这也说明印第安人也是移民过来的，堪称北美大陆最早的移民。1620年，“五月花”号来到美洲大陆，一批英国人登陆美国，带来了当时先进的技术，奠定了美国的立国基础和文化；自1607年到1733年，英国殖民者先后在北美建立了13个殖民地，成为美国建国初期13个州的基础。1775年北美独立战争爆发，1776年7月4日在费城召开第二次大陆会议，由乔治·华盛顿任大陆军总司令，通过了托马斯·杰斐逊等人起草的《独立宣言》，宣布美国正式成立。在美国建国之初，曾制定过一些限制移民的政策。1796—1815年，到美国的欧洲移民平均每年只有3000人左右。拿破仑战争结束后，欧洲重获和平，随着大批军人的复员，欧洲各国失业现象十分严重，移民美国的人数不断增加。另一方面，美国也因国内建设需要，放松了移民政策，从1820—1920的100年间，美国一共接纳了约3350万移民，形成了美国持续百年的移民潮。在美国历史上，三次大型的移民潮吸引了众多的欧裔、非裔、亚裔和拉丁裔移民。作为一个多民族国家，不同文化之间相互影响，形成了文化多元的局面。

1. 第一次移民潮

第一次移民潮发生在19世纪20年代到60年代，移民总数高达500万，主要来自西欧和北欧，其中爱尔兰人大约200万，从19世纪40年代到南北战争(Civil War)，逃离饥荒的爱尔兰天主教移民促进了城市的发展，为建造运河和修筑铁路提供了大量劳动力。德国人大约170万，还有大量非洲“黑奴”被贩卖到美国，填补当时紧缺的劳动力人口。同时，移民中也有少数来自亚洲，主要是来美国淘金的中国人。

2. 第二次移民潮

第二次移民潮是从1861年到1880年，约有500万移民来到美国。南北战争结束后，美国迎来工业化浪潮，对劳动力需求旺盛。林肯总统为了吸引技术人才，尤其是欧洲移民来美国，在1864年颁布了《鼓励外来移民法》，将引进熟练工人和技术人才作为一项重要的外交任务。

3. 第三次移民潮

第三次移民潮从1881年到1920年，移民人数猛增至2350万。在这一阶段，美国开始对移民群体采取限制措施。美国曾多次立法，希望通过政治手段挑选有利于美国发展的移民群体。限制低技术移民，排斥非法移民，限制欧洲移民，排斥亚洲移民。来自英国、德国、瑞典等西北欧国家的“老移民”增长有限，但来自意大利、俄国等东南欧国家的“新移民”却增长迅速。由于就业、宗教和民族问题上的矛盾，在这一时期，美国的排外主义也愈演愈烈。

经过这三次移民高潮，1920年美国的人口总数首次超过1亿，在1820年到1920年的100年间，移民数量占美国人口年增长的20%以上。美国历史上的这三次移民潮不但对美利坚民族性格的形成产生了深刻影响，而且使得美国在短短一百多年里能够迅速崛起，取代英国成为世界头号经济大国，并为以后成为超级大国打下基础。可以说移民潮铸就了美国的强大。

“二战”结束后，随着美国民众对移民态度的理性化，移民对美国的贡献逐渐被大多数美国人所承认。1965年《哈特-塞勒移民法》(*Hart-Celler Immigration Act*) 的通过成为一个转折点。该法取消了对亚洲、非洲、南欧和东欧移民的限制性配额，建立了一个以家庭团聚和职业优先为主的移民框架。这使美国向世界各地敞开大门，移民的来源国从欧洲转移到拉丁美洲和亚洲，这一具有里程碑意义的法案，改变了美国的人口结构，产生了深远的历史影响。

美国在过去有一段时间被主流认为是大熔炉(Melting Pot)，把与之相异的文化都熔化在以WASP(信奉新教的盎格鲁-撒克逊白人)为主料的“大锅”里，但是随着全球化的不断发展，美国作为一片充满机遇的土地和对种族及文化多元开放的社会继续吸引着新移民。一波又一波的新移民来到美国，移民的来源国也变得更加多元化，美国人口的结构比以往任何时候更加多样化，“美国化”(大熔炉)成为一个争议很大的问题，要想使那些来自与美国文化传统完全不同的国家的移民完全“美国化”是不现实的，更是不可能的。文化多元主义应运而生。随着美国多元文化现实的加剧，多元文化者更倾向于将其描绘成沙拉碗

(Salad Bowl)(其中各种食材皆维持原样，因酱料沙拉酱的不同而改变些许味道)、镶嵌画(Mosaic)或织锦绣(Tapestry)。多元文化主义坚持要求给予所有社会文化群体以平等的政治、社会和文化地位，特别强调少数民族等社会弱势群体的平等权利。由于这些人处于弱势地位，他们要求政府和社会机构采取法律和行政措施来确保他们公民的平等权利得到保障。

由于多元文化主义强调多元、多样、差异与平等，这一理念一定程度上冲击了主流社会所代表的价值体系，加之政府针对少数族裔采取一些优惠政策，从而对主流群体造成伤害，这自然激起保守主义者的反对。差异在美国是事实，更是一种常态，差异适度是社会前进的动力，但差异过度往往会加剧分裂和冲突，带来各种社会问题。不管怎样，多元化已成为不可阻挡的潮流，这个国家需要不断面对社会日趋多样化的挑战，多元化是一个充满活力的过程，表达的不仅是差异，还有沟通、对话和交流。现今的美国已成为一个文化多元与基督教传统并存的国家，创造着既不同于美国主流文化，又不同于家乡文化的新文化现象。

第二节　文本阅读

——《美国英语的特点》

一、文本导读

语言与社会密不可分。语言产生于社会，也同时反映社会生活。美国移民组成的多元文化，是美国语言变化的主要原因。自英国 1607 年在北美建立第一个殖民地，1620 年“五月花号"横渡大西洋，把一批英国清教徒带到美洲大陆之后，英国人面对新大陆从未见过的种种新事物，无时无刻不在用他们原有的语言创造新的词汇和语言。

1776年获得独立的年轻的美国，积极扩张领土，经济发展迅猛，不断吸纳移民，人口快速成长，仅仅用了百多年的时间，到20世纪初就成为了一个政治、经济上的强国，与此同时，美国人在词语上也进行了大规模的发展创造，从各国移民中获得了许多外来语，新闻记者、文学评论家H. L. 门肯(Henry Louis Mencken，1880—1956)敏锐地观察到这一现象，在1919年撰写出版了他的经典之作《美国语言》，此书自1919年出版，多次再版，并在1945年和1948年两次出版增订本，至今仍然是研究美国英语的权威著作。

英语是全球通用的语言，是学习者最多的外语，是全世界近六十个国家的官方语言，也是联合国、欧盟等国际组织使用的沟通语言。不同国家和地区的人们所讲的英语，或多或少会带有一些本土的风格和特点，美国英语也是如此。美国英语是英语受美国多元文化影响以及不断创新而形成的一种变体。美国英语较英国英语来说更为口语化，美国语言的丰富与活力体现了美国社会的多元文化特征。

此文中，门肯指出美国英语的特点："所谓的特点主要是指大家所谈论的美国英语。首先是它全国通用，差别不大。其次是它不注重语法、句法和音韵规则及过去的成例。再次，它大量地(明显的大于当下英语的数量)采用外来的新词和短语，并且把它们变成自己的语言。"①门肯认为美国英语的第一个特点是其"普遍的统一性"（general uniformity），美国不同地区说的英语差别不大，能够相互沟通，正如文中所说："在发音和语调方面，有些地区存在着自己的特点，但就他们日常的用法和方式而言，全美国人都一样，甚至不用什么解释，也没有交流的问题。"而英国却是方言众多，以致一个兰开夏郡的矿工和一位林肯郡的农民都很难彼此明白对方说话的意思。美国英语的这种统一性是如何形成的呢？我们在文章中也可以找到原因：英国人一直生活在一种相对稳定的社会中，他们尊重习俗，拒绝变化，包括他们的语言。比起英国人，美国人热情，不保守，认同好奇和勇敢的品质，"处处都存在着有助于简约的强烈精神"。因此，美国英语经常随心所欲，喜欢简单生动的表达方式，新的语言能够在全国范围内迅速得到接受和传播，形成自成一统的美国英语。不同于英国英语的保守传统，循规蹈矩，美国英语的第二个特点是它经常无视甚至抛弃传统的语言规则，"从一开始，美国英语就一直热衷于已有的修辞。其政治活动充满了尖刻的称呼；其整个历史都被夸张的言辞而粉饰，体系更倾向于美妙的措辞，而非逻辑思维。以小见大，不断地练就了一种无与伦比的能力，使隐含之意和通常的妙语进入引人注目的言语之中"②。美国英语的第三个特点是广泛地吸收外来语。"在不同的词类中，新造

①② The Hall-Marks of American-百度文库. https://wenku.baidu.com/view/109ed3c1b14e852458fb5767.html.

词汇的界限实际上很模糊。畜圈一词，源自西班牙语，很快就变成了一个动词以及一个形容词之父。破产这个词，由破裂演化而来，进而又可用作名词。乞讨，出自德语，由最早的懒汉一词转化而成，可用作名词、形容、动词和副词。"①

本文指出了美国英语的特点和语言魅力，"语言之精华乃为活跃"②。门肯认为，美国英语比英国英语更加丰富多彩、生动和富有创造性。美国英语的这些特点有其历史和社会的原因，使得美国英语富于朝气和活力。阅读此文，对我们了解、欣赏和学习英语大有裨益。语言是不断变化和发展的，可以肯定的是美国人还会随着时代和社会的发展，进一步发展他们的语言，正如作者所说："语言拒绝昨天，它接受的是今天。"③

二、原文

The Hall-Marks of American

By H. L. Mencken

1. The characters chiefly noted in American English by all who have discussed it are, first, its general uniformity throughout the country; second, its impatient disregard for grammatical, syntactical, and phonological rule and precedent; and third, its large capacity (distinctly greater than that of the English of present-day England) for taking in new words and phrases from outside sources, and for manufacturing them of its own material.

2. The first of these characters has struck every observer, native and foreign. In place of the discordant local dialects of all the other major countries, including England, we have a general Volkssprache for the whole nation, and if it is conditioned at all it is only by minor differences in pronunciation and vocabulary, and by the linguistic struggles of various groups of newcomers. No other country can show such linguistic solidarity, nor any approach to it—not even Canada, for there a large minority of the population resists speaking English altogether. The Little Russian of the Ukraine is unintelligible to the citizen of Moscow; the northern Italian can scarcely follow a conversation in Sicilian; the Low German from Hamburg is a foreigner in Munich; the Breton flounders in Gascony. Even in the United Kingdom there are wide divergences. "When we remember", says the *New International Encyclopedia*, "that the

①②③ The Hall-Marks of American－百度文库. https://wenku.baidu.com/view/109ed3c1b14e852458fb5767.html.

dialects of the counties in England have marked differences—so marked, indeed, that it may be doubted whether a Lancashire miner and a Lincolnshire farmer could understand each other—we may well be proud that our vast country has, strictly speaking, only one language." There are some regional peculiarities in pronunciation and intonation, but when it comes to the words they habitually use and the way they use them all Americans, even the less tutored, follow pretty much the same line. A Boston taxi-driver could go to work in Chicago or San Francisco without running any risk of misunderstanding his new fares. Once he had flattened his a's a bit and picked up a few dozen localisms, he would be, to all linguistic intents and purposes, fully naturalized.

3. Of the intrinsic differences that separate American from English the chief have their roots in the obvious disparity between the environment and traditions of the American people since the seventeenth century and those of the English. The latter have lived under a relatively stable social order, and it has impressed upon their souls their characteristic respect for what is customary and of good report. Until the World War brought chaos to most of their institutions, their whole lives were regulated, perhaps more than those of any other people save the Spaniards, by a regard for precedent. The Americans, though partly of the same blood, have felt no such restraint, and acquired no such habit of conformity. On the contrary, they have plunged to the other extreme, for the conditions of life in their country have put a high value upon the precisely opposite qualities of curiosity and daring, and so they have acquired that character of restlessness, that impatience of forms, that disdain of the dead hand, which now broadly marks them. From the first, says a literary historian, they have been "less phlegmatic, less conservative than the English. There were climatic influences, it may bethere was surely a spirit of intensity everywhere that made for short effort." Thus, in the arts, and thus in business, in politics, in daily intercourse, in habits of mind and speech. The American is not, of course, lacking in a capacity for discipline; he has it highly developed; he submits to leadership readily, and even to tyranny. But, by a curious twist, it is not the leadership that is old and decorous that commonly fetches him, but the leadership that is new and extravagant. He will resist dictation out of the past, but he will follow a new messiah with almost Russian willingness, and into the wildest vagaries of economics, religion, morals, and speech. A new fallacy in politics spreads faster in the United States than anywhere else on earth, and so does a new fashion in hats or a new revelation of God, or a new means of killing time, or a new shibboleth, or metaphor, or piece of slang. Thus the American, on his linguistic side, likes to make his

language as he goes along, and not all the hard work of the schoolmarm can hold the business back. A novelty loses nothing by the fact that it is a novelty; it rather gains something, and particularly if it meets the national fancy for the terse, the vivid, and, above all, the bold and imaginative. The characteristic American habit of reducing complex concepts to the starkest abbreviations was already noticeable in colonial times, and such highly typical Americanisms as O. K., N. G., and P. D. Q., have been traced back to the early days of the Republic. Nor are the influences that shaped these tendencies invisible today, for institution-making is yet going on, and so is language-making.

4. But of more importance than the sheer inventions, if only because much more numerous, are the extensions of the vocabulary, both absolutely and in ready workableness, by the devices of rhetoric. The American, from the beginning, has been the most ardent of recorded rhetoricians. His politics bristles with pungent epithets; his whole history has been bedizened with tall talk; his fundamental institutions rest far more upon brilliant phrases than upon logical ideas. And in small things as in large he exercises continually an imcomparable capacity for projecting hidden and often fantastic relationships into arresting parts of speech. Such a term as rubberneck is almost a complete treatise on American psychology; it reveals the national habit of mind more clearly than any laboured inquiry could ever reveal it. It has in it precisely the boldness and contempt for ordered forms that are so characteristically American, and it has too the grotesque humour of the country, and the delight in devastating opprobriums, and the acute feeling for the succinct and savoury. The same qualities are in rough-house, water-wagon, has-been, lame-duck, speed-cop, and a thousand other such racy substantives, and in all the great stock of native verbs and adjectives. There is, indeed, but a shadowy boundary in these new coinages between the various parts of speech. Corral, borrowed from the Spanish, immediately becomes a verb and the father of an adjective. Bust, carved out of burst, erects itself into a noun. Bum, coming by way of an earlier bummer from the German, becomes noun, adjective, verb, and adverb. Verbs are fashioned out of substantives by the simple process of prefixing the preposition: to engineer, to stump, to hog, to style, to author. Others grow out of an intermediate adjective, as to boom. Others are made by torturing nouns with harsh affixes, as to burglarize and to itemize, or by groping for the root, as to resurrect and to jell. Yet others are changed from intransitive; a sleeping-car sleeps thirty passengers. So with the adjectives. They are made of substantives unchanged; codfish, jitney. Or by bold combinations; down-and-out, up-state, flat-footed. Or by shading down suffixes to barbaric simplicity; scary, classy, tasty.

Or by working over adverbs until they tremble on the brink between adverb and adjective; right, sure, and near are examples.

5. All these processes, of course, are also to be observed in the history of the English of England; at the time of its sturdiest growth they were in the most active possible being. They are indeed, common to all tongues; "the essence of language", says Dr. Jespersen, is "is activity." But if you will put the English of today beside the American of today you will see at once how much more forcibly they are in operation in the latter than in the former. The standard southern dialect of English has been arrested in its growth by its purists and grammarians, and burdened with irrational affectations by fashionable pretension. It shows no living change since the reign of Samuel Johnson. Its tendency is to combat all that expansive gusto which made for its pliancy and resilience in the days of Shakespeare. In place of the old loose-footedness there is set up a preciosity which, in one direction, takes the form of clumsy artificialities in the spoken language, and in another shows itself in the even clumsier Johnsonese of so much current English writing—the Jargon denounced by Sir Arthur Quiller-Couch in his Cambridge lectures. This "infirmity of speech" Quiller-Couch finds "in parliamentary debates and in the newspapers;... it has become the medium through which Boards of Government, County Councils, Syndicates, Committees, Commercial Firms, express the processes as well as the conclusions of their thought, and so voice the reason of their being". Distinct from journalese, the two yet overlap, "and have a knack of assimilating each other's vices."

6. American, despite the gallant efforts of the pedagogues, has so far escaped any such suffocating formalization. We, too, of course, have our occasional practitioners of the authentic English Jargon, but in the main our faults lie in precisely the opposite direction. That is to say, we incline toward a directness of statement which, at its greatest, lacks restraint and urbanity altogether, and toward a hospitality which often admits novelties for the mere sake of their novelty, and is quite uncritical of the difference between a genuine improvement in succinctness and clarity, and mere extravagant raciness. "The tendency", says one English observer, "is... to consider the speech of any man, as any man himself, as good as any other." The Americans, adds a Scots professor, "are determined to hack their way through the language, as their ancestors through forests, regardless of the valuable growths that may be sacrificed in blazing the trail". But this Scot dismisses the English neologisms of the day, when ranged beside the American stock, as "downy, feeble stuff"; "it is to America", he admits, "that we must

chiefly look in future for the replenishment and freshening of our language." I quote one more Briton, this time an Englishman steeped in the public school tradition:

The English of the United States is not merely different from ours; it has a restless inventiveness which may well be founded in a sense of racial discomfort, a lack of full accord between the temperament of the people and the constitution of their speech. The English are uncommunicative; the Americans are not. In its coolness and quiet withdrawal, in its prevailing sobriety, our language reflects the cautious economies and leisurely assurance of the average speaker. We say so little that we do not need to enliven our vocabulary and underline our sentences, or cry "Wolf!" when we wish to be heard. The more stimulating climate of the United States has produced a more eager, a more expansive, a more decisive people. The Americans apprehend their world in sharper outlines and aspire after a more salient rendering of it.

7. This revolt against conventional bonds and restraints is most noticeable, of course, on the lower levels of American speech; in the regions above there still linger some vestiges of eighteenth-century tightness. But even in those upper regions there are rebels a-plenty, and some of them are of such authority that it is impossible to dismiss them. I glance through the speeches of the late Dr. Woodrow Wilson, surely a conscientious purist, an Anglomaniac if we have ever had one, and find, in a few moments, half a dozen locutions that an Englishman in like position would certainly hesitate to use, among them we must get a move on, to hog, to gum-shoe, ornery in place of ordinary, and that is going some. I turn to the letters of that most passionate of Anglomaniacs, Walter Hines Page, and find to eat out of my hand, to lick to a frazzle, to cut no figure, to go gunning for, nothin doin, for keeps, and so on. I proceed to Dr. John Dewey, probably the country's most respectable metaphysician, and find him using dope for opium. In recent years certain English magnificoes have shown signs of going the same route, but whenever they yield the corrective bastinado is laid on, and nine times out of ten they are accused, and rightly, of succumbing to American influence.

8. Let American confront a novel problem alongside English, and immediately its superior imaginativeness and resourcefulness become obvious. Movie is better than cinema; and the English begin to admit the fact by adopting the word; it is not only better American, it is better English. Bill-board is better than hoarding. Office-holder is more honest, more picturesque,

more thoroughly Anglo-Saxon than public servant, Stem-winder somehow has more life in it, more fancy and vividness, than the literal keyless watch. Turn to the terminology of railroading (itself, by the way, an Americanism); its creation fell upon the two peoples equally, but they tackled the job independently. The English, seeking a figure to denominate the wedge-shaped fender in front of a locomotive, called it a plough the Americans, characteristically, gave it the far more pungent name of cow-catcher. So with the casting which guides the wheels from one rail to another. The English called it a crossing-plate; the Americans, more responsive to the suggestion in its shape, called it a frog. American is full of what Bret Harte called the "saber-cuts of Saxon", it meets Montaigne's ideal of "a succulent and nervous speech, short and compact, not as much delicate and combed out as vehement and brusque, rather arbitrary than monotonous, not pedantic put soldierly, as Suetonius called Caesar's Latin". One pictures the common materials of English dumped into a pot, exotic flavorings added, and the bubbling assiduously and expectantly skimmed. What is old and respected is already in decay the moment it comes into contact with what is new and vivid. "When we Americans are through with the English language", says Mr. Dooley, "it will look as if it had been run over by a musical comedy."

9. All this boldness of conceit, of course, makes for vulgarity. Unrestrained by any critical sense-and the crritical sense of the pedagogues counts for little, for they cry wolf too often—it flowers in such barbaric inventions as tasty, alright, go-getter, he-man, goaheadtiveness, tony, goof, semi-occasional, and to doxologize. But vulgarity, after all, means no more than a yielding to natural impulses in the face of conventional inhibitions, and that yielding to natural impulses is at the heart of all healthy language-making. The history of English, like the history of American and of every other living tongue, is a history of vulgarisms that, by their accurate meeting of real needs, have forced their way into sound usage, and even into the lifeless catalogues of the grammarians., The purist performs a useful office in enforcing a certain logical regularity upon the process, and in our own case the omnipresent example of the greater conservatism of the English restrains, to some extent, our native tendency to go too fast, but the process itself is as inexorable in its workings as the precession of the equinoxes, and if we yield in to it more eagerly than the English, it is only a proof, perhaps, that the future of what was once the Anglo-Saxon tongue lies on this side of the water. Standard English now has the brakes on, but American continues to leap in the dark, and the prodigality of its movement is all the indication that is needed of its intrinsic health, its capacity to meet the ever-changing needs of a

restless and emotional people, inordinately mongrel, and disdainful of tradition. Language, says A. H. Sayce,

> *is not artificial product, contained in books and dictionaries and governed by the strict rules of impersonal grammarians. It is the living expression of the mind and spirit of a people, every changing and sifting, whose sole standard of correctness in custom and the common usage of the community...The first lesson to be learned is that there is no intrinsic right or wrong in the use of language, no fixed rules such as are the delight of the teacher of Latin prose. What is right now will be wrong hereafter what language rejected yesterday she accepts today.*

Vocabulary

locution *n.* 词语，惯用语；语言风格
disdain *v.* 鄙视，轻视，蔑视
phlegmatic *adj.* 冷静的；镇定的；迟钝的；冷漠的
decorous *adj.* 有礼貌的，高雅的；端正的
Messiah *n.* 弥赛亚(犹太人所期待的救世主)；救星
shibboleth *n.* (正式)陈旧思想，陈规陋习
pungent *adj.* 辛辣的，刺激性的；苦痛的；尖刻的
epithet *n.* (表示性质、特征等的)词语；绰号，诨名
bedizen *v.* 华丽而俗气地打扮(装扮)
opprobrium *n.* (正式)耻辱，羞辱
pliancy *n.* 柔软；柔韧
preciosity *n.* (语言)过分讲究；(尤指文笔)矫揉造作
denounce *v.* 谴责，指责，斥责
syndicate *n.* 辛迪加，商业财团，企业联合组织
pedagogue *n.* 教师，教员；卖弄学问
succinct *adj.* 简明的；简洁的
neologism *n.* 新词；新义；新词的使用
replenishment *n.* 补给，补充
sobriety *n.* 清醒；未醉；严肃；节制
salient *adj.* 显著的；突出的；跳跃的
magnifico *n.* 显要人物；权贵；贵族

bastinado *n.* 打脚掌的刑罚
vulgarity *n.* 粗俗；粗俗语
inexorable *adj.* 不可阻挡的；无法改变的
equinox *n.* 昼夜平分时（指春分或秋分）
prodigality *n.* 浪费，挥霍
mongrel *n.* 杂种；混血儿；杂种动物

Reading comprehension exercises

I. Choose the best answer to the following questions.

1. What is the main idea of this passage?
   A. The comparison of American and English language.
   B. General features of American English.
   C. National characters of American people.
   D. American way of thinking and culture.
2. Which of the following statement is true?
   A. American English varies greatly from place to place.
   B. A Lancashire miner and Lincolnshire farmer in England can understand each other very well.
   C. The term as rubberneck reveals that Americans have the habit of exploring the reasons and evidences.
   D. The obvious disparity between environment and traditions of American people and those of English since the Seventeenth Century accounts for the intrinsic difference between them.
3. Which of the following is not a reason for the uniformity of American English?
   A. The immigrant spirit.
   B. The mobility of the American.
   C. American capitalism.
   D. The restlessness of the American.
4. What is the author's attitude toward American English?
   A. Positive. B. Pessimistic. C. Indifferent. D. Ironic.
5. The Little Russian of the Ukraine is unintelligible to the citizen of Moscow; the northern Italian can scarcely follow a conversation in Sicilian; the Low German from Hamburg is a foreigner in Munich; the Breton flounders in Gascony. (Paragraphy 2) The word

"unintelligible" most probably means ________.

A. unabated B. incomprehensible C. inaccurate D. unalienable

II. Comprehension questions

1. Do you agree that "language in a sense defines a culture"? Does English have words from Chinese? Could you explain the relationship between language and culture based on Mencken's ideas?
2. Language changes all the time. What are the reasons for language change? What do you think is the relationship between these changes and the functions of language?
3. Is the Internet changing language and making us vulgar? Do you think that our definition of "vulgarity" is the same as Mencken's?

第三节 延伸阅读

——《一位美国农夫的来信》节选

一、文本导读

格里夫各(J. Hector St. John de Crevecoeur)所著《一位美国农夫的来信》(*Letters from an American Farmer*)之第三封信《何为美国人?》("What Is an American?")是美国众所皆知的篇章。格里夫各出身欧洲贵族家庭，儿时在法国受教育，成年后移居英国，曾在法国军队进入北美殖民地时担任测量以及地图制作员，此工作使他十分熟悉北美的荒野以及印地安人，虽一生多次重返北美，最后他仍在欧洲度过余生。

《一位美国农夫的来信》一共有十二篇文章，1782 年，作者把这些散文改为书信在英国出版，从而一举成名，并吸引了很多人从法国移民到美国。在第三封信中，美国农夫詹姆斯自豪地向一名英国绅士 F. B. 介绍了美国人的特点以及美国各地的不同生活面貌，包括沿海、中部、森林等，对照出与欧洲迥异的文化。作者在此文中这样写道："这里的社会组织与欧洲不同，不像那里那样，一方面是拥有着一切的豪门贵族，另一方面是一大群一无所有的赤贫。这里没有巨室阀阅，没有宫廷，没有帝王，没有主教，没有教会势力，没有少数人享有的那种似乎无形然而有形的特权，没有雇用着成千上万人手的工厂厂主，没有穷奢极侈的高级享受。这里贫与富之间的距离远远没有欧洲那么悬殊。"①此文反映了

① 美国文明读本：缔造美利坚的40篇经典文献-钱满素-Google 图书.

美国人崇尚个人自由的文化传统，个人自由是美国移民们的共同追求。为了逃避宗教和政治迫害及阶级压迫，第一批清教徒在1620年秋天乘坐"五月花号"到达北美，在甲板上就签署了一份《五月花号公约》，以自治的方式来管理自己的生活，通过公约来建立社会秩序，希望在"新大陆"上开创一片属于自己的自由天地，可以说，这一追求在此文中得到了充分的表达，通过这十二封信，作者充满热情地描绘了北美新大陆的风土人情以及平等自由的社会环境："我们乃是一个务农的国家，它横亘绵延于一片广域之上，道路四通八达，广有舟楫之利；在政治维系方面，则若断若连，温和宽容，人人皆知遵纪守法，而无所惮惧于其苛暴，因为在这里人人都能平等相待。"①

《一位美国农夫的来信》体现了美国文化大镕炉的特色，作者认为美国人是一种新人，是英格兰人、苏格兰人、爱尔兰人、法国人、荷兰人、德国人和瑞典人等的混合体，世界各地的人们在这里被熔铸成一个新的民族。在文中作者写道："那么这种美利坚人，又是怎样一种情形呢？他们一般是欧洲人，至少是欧洲人的后裔，因而在血统方面已无所谓纯，这点与有些国家很不相同。姑举一个我知道的家庭为例，在这个家中，祖父自己为英国人，其妻荷兰人，其子娶法国人为妻，妻生四子，四子的妻室又娶自不同国家。现在一个美利坚人即是这种情形，他的许多古旧偏见习惯既已抛置脑后，新的种种遂从他目前投入的生活方式，所拥戴的政府以及所居处的地位而产生出来。他已经在我们伟大母亲恩泽深厚的宽广怀抱里被接受为美利坚人。"②

文中这些描述比较理想化，具有一定的蒙蔽性，毕竟作者事实上并不是一位美国农夫，而是出身上层的欧洲贵族。此文也体现了一个跨多元文化个体尝试以写作界定文化身份认同的历程，作者尝试吸纳北美文化来建立并巩固自己的美国身份认同，此文中对北美有大量的赞颂之词，但也不乏负面描绘，比如：第三封信中他对中部居民性好诉讼的批判态度，反映出作者在文化认同上的冲突，虽然对18世纪的美国农业社会进行了理想化的描述，但他对旧世界的灿烂文明也难以忘怀，在一个急剧变化的年代无所适从，这时写作成了个人纪录生命历程，对自我生命进行定位的一个方式。

作为美国集体记忆的早期文学作品，该文在美国文学史上有着重要的地位，开启了至今仍在讨论的"美国性"或"美国本质"的问题。欧洲移民如何成为美国人？如何看待自己的文化身份？人生的巨变下，如何协调新旧世界的文化竞争和思想冲突？通过阅读此文，我们可以对美国特质和美国多元文化传统的形成和原因有进一步的认识。

①② 美国文明读本：缔造美利坚的40篇经典文献-钱满素-Google图书.

二、原文节选

Letters from an American Farmer: Letter Ⅲ—What Is an American

I wish I could be acquainted with the feelings and thoughts which must agitate the heart and present themselves to the mind of an enlightened Englishman, when he first lands on this continent. He must greatly rejoice that he lived at a time to see this fair country discovered and settled; he must necessarily feel a share of national pride, when he views the chain of settlements which embellishes these extended shores. When he says to himself, this is the work of my countrymen, who, when convulsed by factions, afflicted by a variety of miseries and wants, restless and impatient, took refuge here. They brought along with them their national genius, to which they principally owe what liberty they enjoy, and what substance they possess. Here he sees the industry of his native country displayed in a new manner, and traces in their works the embryos of all the arts, sciences, and ingenuity which nourish in Europe. Here he beholds fair cities, substantial villages, extensive fields, an immense country filled with decent houses, good roads, orchards, meadows, and bridges, where an hundred years ago all was wild, woody, and uncultivated! What a train of pleasing ideas this fair spectacle must suggest; it is a prospect which must inspire a good citizen with the most heartfelt pleasure. The difficulty consists in the manner of viewing so extensive a scene. He is arrived on a new continent; a modern society offers itself to his contemplation, different from what he had hitherto seen. It is not composed, as in Europe, of great lords who possess everything, and of a herd of people who have nothing. Here are no aristocratical families, no courts, no kings, no bishops, no ecclesiastical dominion, no invisible power giving to a few a very visible one; no great manufacturers employing thousands, no great refinements of luxury. The rich and the poor are not so far removed from each other as they are in Europe. Some few towns excepted, we are all tillers of the earth, from Nova Scotia to West Florida. We are a people of cultivators, scattered over an immense territory, communicating with each other by means of good roads and navigable rivers, united by the silken bands of mild government, all respecting the laws, without dreading their power, because they are equitable. We are all animated with the spirit of an industry which is unfettered and unrestrained, because each person works for himself. If he travels through our rural districts he views not the hostile castle, and the haughty mansion, contrasted with the clay- built hut and miserable cabin, where cattle and men help to keep each other warm, and dwell in meanness, smoke, and indigence. A pleasing uniformity of decent competence appears throughout our habitations. The meanest of our log-houses is a dry and comfortable habitation. Lawyer or merchant are the fairest titles our towns afford; that of a farmer is the only appellation of the rural inhabitants of our country. It must take some time ere he can reconcile himself to our dictionary, which is but short in words of dignity, and names of honour. There, on a Sunday, he sees a congregation of respectable farmers and their wives, all clad in neat homespun, well mounted, or riding in their own humble waggons. There is not among them an esquire, saving the unlettered magistrate. There he sees a parson as simple as his flock, a farmer who does not riot on the labour of others. We have no princes, for whom we toil, starve, and bleed: we are the most perfect society now existing in the world. Here man is free as he ought to be; nor is this pleasing equality so transitory as many others are. Many ages will not see the shores of our great lakes replenished with inland nations, nor the unknown bounds of North America entirely peopled. Who can tell how far it extends? Who can tell the millions of men whom it will feed and contain? for no European foot has as yet travelled half the extent of this mighty continent!

The next wish of this traveller will be to know whence came all these people? they are a mixture of English, Scotch, Irish, French, Dutch, Germans, and Swedes. From this promiscuous breed, that race now called Americans have arisen. The eastern provinces must indeed be excepted, as being the unmixed descendants of Englishmen. I have heard many wish that they had been more intermixed also: for my part, I am no wisher, and think it much better as it has happened. They exhibit a most conspicuous figure in this great and variegated picture; they too enter for a great share in the pleasing perspective displayed in these thirteen provinces. I know it is fashionable to reflect on them, but I respect them for what they have done; for the accuracy and wisdom with which they have settled their territory; for the decency of their manners; for their early love of letters; their ancient college, the first in this hemisphere; for their industry; which to me who am but a farmer, is the criterion of everything. There never was a people, situated as they are, who with so ungrateful a soil have done more in so short a time. Do you think that the monarchical ingredients which are more prevalent in other governments, have purged them from all foul stains? Their histories assert the contrary.

In this great American asylum, the poor of Europe have by some means met together, and in consequence of various causes; to what purpose should they ask one another what countrymen they are? Alas, two thirds of them had no country. Can a wretch who wanders about, who works and starves, whose life is a continual scene of sore affliction or pinching penury; can that man call England or any other kingdom his country? A country that had no bread for him, whose fields procured him no harvest, who met with nothing but the frowns of the rich, the severity of the laws, with jails and punishments; who owned not a single foot of the extensive surface of this planet? No! urged by a variety of motives, here they came. Every thing has tended to regenerate them; new laws, a new mode of living, a new social system; here they are become men: in Europe they were as so many useless plants, wanting vegetative mould, and refreshing showers; they withered, and were mowed down by want, hunger, and war; but now by the power of transplantation, like all other plants they have taken root and flourished! Formerly they were not numbered in any civil lists of their country, except in those of the poor; here they rank as citizens. By what invisible power has this surprising metamorphosis been performed? By that of the laws and that of their industry. The laws, the indulgent laws, protect them as they arrive, stamping on them the symbol of adoption; they receive ample rewards for their labours; these accumulated rewards procure them lands; those lands confer on them the title of freemen, and to that title every benefit is affixed which men can possibly require. This is the great operation daily performed by our laws. From whence proceed these laws? From our government. Whence the government? It is derived from the original genius and strong desire of the people ratified and confirmed by the crown. This is the great chain which links us all, this is the picture which every province exhibits, Nova Scotia excepted.

There the crown has done all; either there were no people who had genius, or it was not much attended to: the consequence is, that the province is very thinly inhabited indeed; the power of the crown in conjunction with the musketos has prevented men from settling there. Yet some parts of it flourished once, and it contained a mild harmless set of people. But for the fault of a few leaders, the whole were banished. The greatest political error the crown ever committed in America, was to cut off men from a country which wanted nothing but men!

What attachment can a poor European emigrant have for a country where he had nothing? The knowledge of the language, the love of a few kindred as poor as himself, were the only cords that tied him: his country is now that which gives him land, bread, protection, and consequence: Ubi panis ibi patria, is the motto of all emigrants. What then is the American, this new man? He is either an European, or the descendant of an European, hence that strange mixture of blood, which you will find in no other country. I could point out to you a family whose grandfather was an Englishman, whose wife was Dutch, whose son married a French woman, and whose present four sons have now four wives of different nations. He is an American, who, leaving behind him all his ancient prejudices and manners, receives new ones from the new mode of life he has embraced, the new government he obeys, and the new rank he holds. He becomes an American by being received in the broad lap of our great Alma Mater. Here individuals of all nations are melted into a new race of men, whose labours and posterity will one day cause great changes in the world. Americans are the western pilgrims, who are carrying along with them that great mass of arts, sciences, vigour, and industry which began long since in the east; they will finish the great circle. The Americans were once scattered all over Europe; here they are incorporated into one of the finest systems of population which has ever appeared, and which will hereafter become distinct by the power of the different climates they inhabit. The American ought therefore to love this country much better than that wherein either he or his forefathers were born. Here the rewards of his industry follow with equal steps the progress of his labour; his labour is founded on the basis of nature, SELF-INTEREST: can it want a stronger allurement? Wives and children, who before in vain demanded of him a morsel of bread, now, fat and frolicsome, gladly help their father to clear those fields whence exuberant crops are to arise to feed and to clothe them all; without any part being claimed, either by a despotic prince, a rich abbot, or a mighty lord. Here religion demands but little of him; a small voluntary salary to the minister, and gratitude to God; can he refuse these? The American is a new man, who acts upon new principles; he must therefore entertain new ideas, and form new opinions. From involuntary idleness, servile dependence, penury, and useless labour, he has passed to toils of a very different nature, rewarded by ample subsistence. —This is an American.

British America is divided into many provinces, forming a large association, scattered along a coast 1, 500 miles extent and about 200 wide. This society I would fain examine, at least such as it appears in the middle provinces; if it does not afford that variety of tinges and gradations which may be observed in Europe, we have colours peculiar to ourselves. For instance, it is natural to conceive that those who live near the sea, must be very different from those who live in the woods; the intermediate space will afford a separate and distinct class.

Men are like plants; the goodness and flavour of the fruit proceeds from the peculiar soil and exposition in which they grow. We are nothing but what we derive from the air we breathe, the climate we inhabit, the government we obey, the system of religion we profess, and the nature of our employment. Here you will find but few crimes; these have acquired as yet no root among us. I wish I was able to trace all my ideas; if my ignorance prevents me from describing them properly, I hope I shall be able to delineate a few of the outlines, which are all I propose.

Those who live near the sea, feed more on fish than on flesh, and often encounter that boisterous element. This renders them more bold and enterprising; this leads them to neglect the confined occupations of the land. They see and converse with a variety of people, their intercourse with mankind becomes extensive. The sea inspires them with a love of traffic, a desire of transporting produce from one place to another; and leads them to a variety of resources which supply the place of labour. Those who inhabit the middle settlements, by far the most numerous, must be very different; the simple cultivation of the earth purifies them, but the indulgences of the government, the soft remonstrances of religion, the rank of independent freeholders, must necessarily inspire them with sentiments, very little known in Europe among people of the same class. What do I say? Europe has no such class of men; the early knowledge they acquire, the early bargains they make, give them a great degree of sagacity. As freemen they will be litigious; pride and obstinacy are often the cause of law suits; the nature of our laws and governments may be another. As citizens it is easy to imagine, that they will carefully read the newspapers, enter into every political disquisition, freely blame or censure governors and others. As farmers they will be careful and anxious to get as much as they can, because what they get is their own. As northern men they will love the cheerful cup. As Christians, religion curbs them not in their opinions; the general indulgence leaves every one to think for themselves in spiritual matters; the laws inspect our actions, our thoughts are left to God. Industry, good living, selfishness, litigiousness, country politics, the pride of freemen, religious indifference, are their characteristics. If you recede still farther from the sea, you will come into more modern settlements; they exhibit the same strong lineaments, in a ruder appearance. Religion seems to have still less influence, and their manners are less improved.

Now we arrive near the great woods, near the last inhabited districts; there men seem to be placed still farther beyond the reach of government, which in some measure leaves them to themselves. How can it pervade every corner; as they were driven there by misfortunes, necessity of beginnings, desire of acquiring large tracts of land, idleness, frequent want of economy, ancient debts; the re-union of such people does not afford a very pleasing spectacle. When discord, want of unity and friendship; when either drunkenness or idleness prevail in such remote districts; contention, inactivity, and wretchedness must ensue. There are not the same remedies to these evils as in a long established community. The few magistrates they have, are in general little better than the rest; they are often in a perfect state of war; that of man against man, sometimes decided by blows, sometimes by means of the law; that of man against every wild inhabitant of these venerable woods, of which they are come to dispossess them. There men appear to be no better than carnivorous animals of a superior rank, living on the flesh of wild animals when they can catch them, and when they are not able, they subsist on grain. He who would wish to see America in its proper light, and have a true idea of its feeble beginnings and barbarous rudiments, must visit our extended line of frontiers where the last settlers dwell, and where he may see the first labours of settlement, the mode of clearing the earth, in all their different appearances; where men are wholly left dependent on their native tempers, and on the spur of uncertain industry, which often fails when not sanctified by the efficacy of a few moral rules. There, remote from the power of example and check of shame, many families exhibit the most hideous parts of our society. They are a kind of forlorn hope, preceding by ten or twelve years the most respectable army of veterans which come after them. In that space, prosperity will polish some, vice and the law will drive off the rest, who uniting again with others like themselves will recede still farther; making room for more industrious people, who will finish their improvements, convert the loghouse into a convenient habitation, and rejoicing that the first heavy labours are finished, will change in a few years that hitherto barbarous country into a fine fertile, well regulated district. Such is our progress, such is the march of the Europeans toward the interior parts of this continent. In all societies there are off-casts; this impure part serves as our precursors or pioneers; my father himself was one of that class, but he came upon honest principles, and was therefore one of the few who held fast; by good conduct and temperance, he transmitted to me his fair inheritance, when not above one in fourteen of his contemporaries had the same good fortune.

Forty years ago this smiling country was thus inhabited; it is now purged, a general decency of manners prevails throughout, and such has been the fate of our best countries.

Comprehension questions

1. How did Crevecoeur describe America? What are the major differences between Americans

and Europeans? How do these characteristics make him a "new man"?

2. The author claims "Men are like plants; the goodness and flavour of the fruit proceeds from the peculiar soil and exposition in which they grow." And then describes different lives in different parts of America. How do you understand this simile? Do you agree? How do Americans differ from place to place?
3. The author says "The American is a new man." If you lived in a multicultural environment, would you rather choose to be melted into a new man, living in a country that is described as a "melting pot" (a place where people from many different countries blend together and lose their original cultural identity) or a "salad bowl" (a place where people from many different countries mix together but still retain their original cultural identity)? Why?
4. What aspects do you think have become outdated and what are still applicable to the current America?

参 考 答 案

第一章

Ⅰ.

1. D　2. D　3. C　4. C

Ⅱ.

略

第二章

Ⅰ.

1) 13 colonies

2) unalienable

3) fails

4) new government

5) light and transient

6) King George III

7) futile

8) separation

9) the United States of America

10) alliances

Ⅱ.

1. 1) self-evident　2) created　3) Creator

4) Life　5) Liberty　6) the pursuit of Happiness

2. 1）Free 2）Independent 3）levy 4）conclude

Ⅲ.

略

Ⅳ.

略

第三章

Ⅰ.

1. F 2. F 3. T 4. T 5. F 6. F 7. T 8. T

Ⅱ.

略

第四章

《解放黑人奴隶宣言》

Ⅰ.

1. T 2. F 3. T 4. F 5. T

Ⅱ.

略

《葛底斯堡演讲》

Ⅰ.

1. F（devotion）
2. E，C（we cannot…；dedicate，consecrate，hallow）
3. B，A（living and dead，add or detract；poor power）
4. D，A（our fathers，conceive；new nation）
5. E，C（of the people，by the people，for the people）
6. A（score，seven）

Ⅱ.

1. score，conceived，all men are created equal
2. dedicated，devotion，devotion，freedom，of，by，for，perish

Ⅲ.

略

第五章

Ⅰ.

1. C　2. D　3. A　4. B　5. C

Ⅱ.

略

第六章

Ⅰ.

1. D　2. A　3. A　4. D

Ⅱ.

略

第七章

Ⅰ.

1. C　2. D　3. D

Ⅱ.

略

第八章

Ⅰ.

1. B　2. D　3. C　4. A　5. B

Ⅱ.

略

参考文献

钱满素. 自由的刻度：缔造美国文明的40篇经典文献[M]. 北京：东方出版社，2016.

钱满素，张瑞华. 美国通史[M]. 上海：上海社会科学院出版社，2020.

王金虎，侯学华. 美国历史[M]. 开封：河南大学出版社，2009.

周毅. 美国历史与文化[M]. 北京：首都经济贸易大学出版社，2020.

闫怡恂. 英语演讲名篇修辞与文化赏析[M]. 沈阳：辽宁人民出版社，2019.

[美]罗伯特·瑞米尼. 美国简史：从殖民时代到21世纪[M]. 朱玲，译. 杭州：浙江人民出版社，2019.

[美]查尔斯·艾略特. 人生必读的美国经典历史文献[M]刘庆国，宿哲骞，译. 北京：中华工商联合出版社，2018.

[美]斯陀夫人. 汤姆叔叔的小屋[M]. 王家湘，译. 北京：人民文学出版社，1998.

[美]托马斯·潘恩. 常识[M]. 计毅，译. 哈尔滨：北方文艺出版社，2017.

[美]詹姆斯·费尼莫尔·库柏. 最后的莫西干人[M]. 张顺生，译. 武汉：长江文艺出版社，2007.

[美]查尔斯·W. 爱略特. 美国历史文献精选集[M]. 北京：中华工商联合出版社，2020.

伊丽莎白·惠特克. 解析贝蒂·弗里丹《女性的奥秘》[M]. 周伟，王坤，译. 上海：上海外语教育出版社，2020.

[美]蕾切尔·卡森. 寂静的春天[M]. 吕瑞兰，李长生，译. 上海：上海译文出版社，2014.

[美]马丁·路德·金. 我有一个梦想：马丁·路德·金告诉我们[M]. 王婷，戴登云，等，译. 北京：中央编译出版社，2001.

[美]本杰明·富兰克林. 富兰克林自传[M]. 王正林，王权，译. 北京：中国青年出版社，2013.

[美]戴安娜·拉维奇. 美国读本：感动过一个国家的文字[M]. 林本椿，等，译. 北京：三联书店，1995.

Carson, R. Silent Spring[M]. New York: Crest Books, 1964.

Friedan, B. The Feminine Mystique[M]. New York: W. W. Norton & Company, 2001.

Martin Luther King, Jr. I Have a Dream. https://www.usconstitution.net/dream.html.

Roosevelt, T. Excerpts from The Conservation of Natural Resources (1907) [EB/OL]. Retrieved from https://millercenter.org/the-presidency/presidential-speeches/december-3-1907-seventh-annual-message https://cdn. britannica. com/w: 690, h: 388, c: crop/73/200573-050-194DB760/Mahatma-Gandhi-1931.jpg.

https://cdn. britannica. com/w: 690, h: 388, c: crop/67/148867-050-72C2D082/Selma-March-Alabama-March-1965.jpg.

https://www. nps. gov/common/uploads/people/nri/20160323/people/68BA8E45-1DD8-B71B-0B518D5539CCC257/68BA8E45-1DD8-B71B-0B518D5539CCC257.jpg.

https://tse1-mm. cn. bing. net/th/id/R-C. b35a622b9faef5d6d15cfaf7c2ed6b9a? rik = J6Vz7NYaTPN2QA&riu=http%3a%2f%2fwww.history.com%2fs3static%2fvideo-thumbnails%2fAETN-History_VMS%2f1017%2f447%2fHistory_Rosa_Parks_Montgomery_Bus_Boycott_179889_SF_HD. jpg&ehk = CdVuiDUluM0LJgGQHuOMYT9aW75yL93KFA%2bqToVi3eM%3d&risl=&pid=ImgRaw&r=0.

https://cdn. britannica. com/46/7546-050-1DB8A70E/Martin-Luther-King-Jr-civil-rights-supporters-August-1963.jpg.

https://www.worldatlas.com/r/w960-q80/upload/85/5a/90/shutterstock-1024044865.jpg.

https://beinecke.library.yale.edu/collections/highlights/rachel-carson-papers.

袁一平. 门肯论“美国英语特点”浅释[J]. 江苏外语教学研究，1995(2).

姜飞. 美国文化寓言：从“大熔炉”“沙拉碗”到“织锦”[N]. 中国社会科学报，2011-11-17.

[美]里德·上田(Reed Ueda). 一个永未完成的国家——爱问共享资料[EB/OL]. https://is hare.iask.sina.com.cn/f/1Ye Paln jag zp.html.

韩家炳. 美国的人口移民潮与多元文化主义的兴起[J]. 科学社会主义，2014(5).

张剑. 从大熔炉到“沙拉碗”[N]. 光明日报，2015-09-19.

徐丁娟，游长松. 新型研究生综合英语教程[M]. 武汉：武汉大学出版社，2021.

美国2020最新人口普查数据：过去10年，白人人口自建国以来首次下降. https://

baijiahao.baidu.com/s? id=1707936643121170895&wfr=spider&for=pc 2021.

美国人口_百度百科. https://baike.baidu.com/item/%E7%BE%8E%E5%9B%BD%E4%BA%BA%E5%8F%A3/3198477

多元文化主义-搜狗百科. https://baike.sogou.com/v404288.htm.

多元文化的美国-百度文库. https://wenku.baidu.com/view/3df07714240c844768eaee58.html.

钟淑华. Identity in St. John de Crevecoeur's Letters from an American Farmer[J]. 英语文暨口笔译学集刊，2012(8).

周淑娟. 文化跨界中主体的建立/崩解：《来自北美农夫的信》中美洲自我与欧洲他者的交错"[C]. 2010第二届翻译与文化国际学术研讨会会议论文.

刘畅.《一位美国农夫的来信》：美国重农主义的典范之作[EB/OL]. https://www.docin.com/p-1334155736.html.

凌乐祥. 美国文学中探寻其文化传统的成因[EB/OL]. https://www.21ks.net/lunwen/ctwxfzlw/25479.html.

吴新华，赵菊珊，Bob Eckhart，Minru Li. 文化交流英语——学生实用手册[M]. 武汉：武汉大学出版社，2012.

美国文明读本：缔造美利坚的40篇经典文献-钱满素-Google图书. https://books.google.com.hk/books?id=jATGCQAAQBAJ&pg=PT92&lpg=PT92&dq=%E4%B8%80%E4%BD%8D%E7%BE%8E%E5%9B%BD%E5%86%9C%E5%A4%AB%E7%9A%84%E6%9D%A5%E4%BF%A1&source=bl&ots=hoHceC_8xa&sig=ACfU3U0X9dze5qgtdlKhT1-g5n0AwDxTew&hl=zh-CN&sa=X&ved=2ahUKEwjg4tK664r4AhVHTmwGHWnLAQUQ6AF6BAgSEAM#v=onepage&q=%E4%B8%80%E4%BD%8D%E7%BE%8E%E5%9B%BD%E5%86%9C%E5%A4%AB%E7%9A%84%E6%9D%A5%E4%BF%A1&f=false.

贾荟. 美国英语的特点[J]. 散文百家·学术百家，2011(8).

https://wenku.baidu.com/view/300643c1561810a6f524ccbff121dd36a32dc462.html.

The Hall-Marks of American-百度文库. https://wenku.baidu.com/view/109ed3c1b14e852458fb5767.html.

https://graph.baidu.com/api/proxy? mroute=redirect&sec=1654572817455&seckey=725987e78b&u=http%3A%2F%2Fwww.51yuansu.com%2Fsc%2Frrcxkqdwob.html.

Fitzgerald, F. S. The Great Gatsby[M]. London: Wordsworth Editions Limited, 1993.

Franklin, B. Autobiography of Benjamin Franklin[M]. New York: Henry Holt and Company, 1916.

https://www.jing.fm/clipimg/full/175-1758834_new-england-png-new-england-colonies-outline.png.

https://upload.wikimedia.org/wikipedia/commons/3/38/Map_of_territorial_growth_1775.svg.

https://commons.wikimedia.org/wiki/File:California_Clipper_500.jpg.

https://commons.wikimedia.org/wiki/File:TheMeltingpot1.jpg.

https://commons.wikimedia.org/wiki/File:1925_Ford_Model_T_touring.jpg.

https://upload.wikimedia.org/wikipedia/commons/5/5f/Benjamin_West%2C_English_%28born_America%29_-_Benjamin_Franklin_Drawing_Electricity_from_the_Sky_-_Google_Art_Project.jpg.

独立宣言(美国立国文书之一)_百度百科(baidu.com).

https://en.wikipedia.org/wiki/Mayflower_Compact.

https://www.gutenberg.org/files/147/147-h/147-h.htm.

http://mayflowerhistory.com/mayflower-passenger-list/Declaration of Independence.

https://www.archives.gov/founding-docs/declaration-transcript.

https://www.archives.gov/founding-docs/constitution.

https://teachingamericanhistory.org/document/the-significance-of-the-frontier-in-american-history.

https://www.gutenberg.org/files/940/940-h/940-h.htm.

https://www.archives.gov/milestone-documents/emancipation-proclamation.

https://www.britannica.com/event/Gettysburg-Address.

https://www.gutenberg.org/files/203/203-h/203-h.htm.

https://sydneyrising.files.wordpress.com/2013/04/native-tribes-2.jpg.

https://www.alamy.com/stock-photo-world-map-before-columbus-1490s-135097668.html.

http://www.luminarium.org/renlit/ditchleyportrait.jpg.

http://www.virginiaplaces.org/graphics/image008.jpg.

https://en.wikipedia.org/wiki/Mayflower_Compact_signatories#/media/File:The_Mayflower_Compact_1620_cph.3g07155.jpg.

https://i.pinimg.com/originals/6b/a3/b2/6ba3b2b8e2ec6b655e750ab04503522c.jpg.

https://www.edmaps.com/thirteen_colonies_1775.png.

https://www.worldatlas.com/geography/thirteen-colonies.html.

https://npg.si.edu/object/npg_NPG.2008.5.

https://upload.wikimedia.org/wikipedia/commons/5/54/Of_Plimoth_Plantation_First_1900.jpg.

https://www.britannica.com/event/Boston-Tea-Party.

https://en.wikipedia.org/wiki/Declaration_of_Independence_(painting)#/media/File:Declaration_of_Independence_(1819),_by_John_Trumbull.jpg.

https://www.gettyimages.co.uk/detail/news-photo/the-american-star-circa-1803-artist-frederick-kemmelmeyer-news-photo/1206218424.

https://th.bing.com/th/id/R.1e40b67051dd63044c4a35705568efbf?rik=vP5BVBC6P8ztoQ&riu=http%3a%2f%2fapushcanvas.pbworks.com%2ff%2f1350563302%2fBEFAT.JPG&ehk=ck84RiLD%2fwFXQUcGHc3JiNtbNGxRLfK0RfHNwiK3LhM%3d&risl=&pid=ImgRaw&r=0.

https://www.archives.gov/founding-docs/declaration.

https://www.themagazineantiques.com/article/new-world-wonder-how-a-geological-oddity-became-an-enduring-symbol-of-the-nation-in-american-art/.

https://www.timetoast.com/timelines/american-history-w-jqa-1607-1861.

https://www.fasttrackteaching.com/ffap/Unit_2_Westward/U2_Maps_Westward_Expansion.html.

https://en.wikipedia.org/wiki/Treaty_of_1818#/media/File:U.S._Territorial_Acquisitions.png.

https://thatdevilhistory.com/wp-content/uploads/2016/04/Trail-of-Tears-Map.jpg.

https://en.wikipedia.org/wiki/Hannibal_Bridge#/media/File:Kansas_city_mo_1869.gif.

https://en.wikipedia.org/wiki/Hannibal_Bridge#/media/File:Hannibal-bridge.jpg.

https://www.pinterest.ca/pin/458452437048902130/.

https://en.wikipedia.org/wiki/Geography_of_the_United_States#/media/File:Map_of_USA_with_state_and_territory_names_2.png

http://haygenealogy.com/hay/1893fair/1893fair-29court.jpg.

https://www.penguin.com.au/books/the-last-of-the-mohicans-9780553213294.

https://www.worldatlas.com/articles/which-states-are-considered-the-deep-south.html.

https://pixels.com/featured/a-ride-for-libertythe-fugitive-slaves-digital-remastered-edition-eastman-johnson.html.

http://torreshistory.weebly.com/recursos-de-claseclassroom-resources.html.

https://hamiltonhistoricalrecords.com/2019/03/31/the-great-fire-of-richmond-virginia/.

https://rememberinglincoln.fords.org/node/1114.

https://upload.wikimedia.org/wikipedia/commons/thumb/a/ab/Abraham_Lincoln_O-77_matte_collodion_print.jpg.

https://upload.wikimedia.org/wikipedia/commons/3/31/UncleTomsCabinCover.jpg.

新时代外国文学与文化系列教材

（丛书主编：王爱菊）

《识读美国》

《莎士比亚戏剧与西方社会》

《莎士比亚戏剧导读》

《英语诗歌欣赏》

《日本文化漫谈》

《电影中的俄罗斯文学》

《近现代日本社会与文化》

《俄罗斯社会与文化十讲》

《中西民俗文化对比赏析》

《中日文化交流史话》

《英国历史文化》

《跨文化交际礼仪》

《国外新闻业与新闻英语导读》

《英文小说名篇导读：从文字到光影的嬗变》